Lillie Devereux Blake

Lillie Devereux Blake

Retracing a Life Erased

Grace Farrell

University of Massachusetts Press

Amherst and Boston

Copyright © 2002 by University of Massachusetts Press
All rights reserved
Printed in the United States of America
LC 2002024570 ISBN 1-55849-349-2
Designed by Mary Mendell
Set in Adobe Minion by Graphic Composition, Inc.
Printed and bound by The Maple-Vail Book Manufacturing Group

Library of Congress Cataloging-in-Publication Data

Farrell, Grace, 1947–
    Lillie Devereux Blake : retracing a life erased / Grace Farrell.
        p. cm.
    Includes bibliographical references and index.
    ISBN 1-55849-349-2 (alk. paper)
    1. Blake, Lillie Devereux, 1835–1913. 2. Women and literature—
United States—History—19th century. 3. Authors, American—
19th century—Biography. 4. Suffragists—United States—Biography.
5. Journalists—United States—Biography. 6. Feminists—United States—
Biography. I. Title.

PS1102.B86 Z66 2002
813'.4—dc21
[B]
2002024570

British Library Cataloguing in Publication data are available

For
Lois A. Cuddy
An expert witness
and extraordinary friend

Contents

Illustrations follow page 120

ERASURES

1. An Ordinary Day in New Haven

Real and unreal are two in one: New Haven
Before and after one arrives
—Wallace Stevens, "An Ordinary Evening in New Haven"

I

IT WAS WHISPERED TO ME in the archives of the New Haven Colony Historical Society that Lillie Devereux Blake was a lady of the night. "A lady of the night?" I whispered back. "You mean . . . ?" Yes, the whisperer nodded firmly, "a lady of the night." The Lillie Devereux Blake I thought I knew had grown up in New Haven and had been a well known and highly respected figure in nineteenth-century America. She was a Washington-based Civil War journalist, a successful lecturer and political organizer for the suffrage movement, and a popular speaker for the labor movement. Blake attained such prominence in the woman suffrage movement that in 1900 Elizabeth Cady Stanton supported her to succeed Susan B. Anthony as president of the National American Woman Suffrage Association. When Blake was dying, the *New York Times* kept a vigil, reporting on her condition each day. During her lifetime, she published at least seven novels, two collections of stories and essays, and hundreds of uncollected pieces of short fiction. Blake had even been an invited speaker at the Yale Divinity School in 1878 for "a Sunday course of lectures."

But a lady of the night? So insistent was the authority in that whispering voice that my years of recovering Blake's work and researching her life began to vanish; my knowledge of how full and how public that life had been began erasing itself until only enough of a trace remained for me to marvel: where had she found the time?

I had come to the Historical Society on an ordinary day, anticipating some tedious fieldwork looking for traces of Blake's childhood. What I found were echoes of Wallace Stevens's long poem "An Ordinary Evening in New Haven," a poem about the intertextuality of the real and the imaginary. From that first whisper, which threw into question all that I thought I knew about Lillie Devereux Blake, to the proclamation in which a consultant paid by Yale University reasserted the rumors two weeks later, I was whirled back and forth between the real and the imaginary, the past and the present, until I finally understood how these categories construct one another out of "intricate evasions of as, / In things seen and unseen, created from nothingness."[1] And I understood, in a visceral way, how authoritative proclamations, however softly whispered, can erase a woman from history.

I had two research goals in New Haven: I wanted to check out Blake's 1854 involvement with a Yale student and, as a bit of a sideline, I wanted to know if her beloved Maple Cottage, the house in which she had grown from girlhood to womanhood, still existed. What I would find was a New Haven which, in the 1840s and 1850s, had nurtured Blake's intellectual and social development but had also abruptly, and brutally, reined in her spirit. Then it had attempted to erase her from its memory.

I had located two of Blake's mother's houses in Stratford, Connecticut, fifteen miles away. Edged by both the Housatonic River and Long Island Sound, Stratford in the nineteenth century boasted broad streets under gracefully arched elms that formed leafy domes down the length of its Main Street.[2] Here still sits the massive Johnson family residence, a grand colonial which had been Blake's mother's childhood home. Here Lillie had lived when she was five and six; here she had celebrated family holidays and summer reunions with her cousins. It contained the 10,000-volume library of her great-grandfather, William Samuel Johnson, president of what is now Columbia University, and his father before him, Samuel William Johnson, the founder and president of Kings College, Columbia's name prior to the Revolutionary War. Here in the octagonal drawing room hung a portrait of Jonathan Edwards, Puritan poet and divine, who was Lillie's great-great-grandfather on both sides of her family.[3]

As I walked to the massive front door of the Johnson home, I thought about the little girl, nurtured in such privileged surroundings, who would grow to write *Fettered for Life*, in which she would worry over the plight of a prostitute and a seamstress and a pretty rich girl with an unrequited dream of becoming a lawyer and practicing with her father—a father who could respond only with shock and disgust at the very idea. It was Sunday and the home, now housing offices, was closed. I walked away, heading down the street, when a woman carrying a briefcase came up from the side of the house and around to the front door. I called out and introduced myself, and she let me in and showed me around her first-floor offices. Then she told me that she was a lawyer—in practice with her father! "Everything," Wallace Stevens wrote, "as unreal as real can be."[4] In 1874, Blake had imagined what seemed unimaginable, and here, in the very house where she had spent much of her childhood, it had become a reality. I told the attorney about Blake's novel and about its leading feminist, a woman doctor, one of the new professional women who created such debate in the 1870s and '80s. Down the hall, she pointed out, were the offices of a female physician. I felt double-visioned, mingling with what Stevens called the "residuum"—the "imaginative transcripts ... [the] shedding shapes ... the nameless, flitting characters ... [who] still walk in a twilight muttering lines," on the "street or about the corners" of this place.[5]

Down the road from the Johnson mansion is a smaller house that Lillie's mother built on a portion of the Johnson estate in 1856 and named Elm Cottage. It sits across from the Episcopal church in which Lillie Devereux was confirmed just before her marriage in 1855 to Frank Umsted. Here, in a second-story bedroom overlooking the elms along Main Street, Lillie began her first novel, Southwold: "Among the many beautiful villages that lie along the Sound coast of New England there is none more beautiful than Stratford. It rests among green meadows, on the shore of the peaceful Housatonic, where it pours its calm waters into the sea. It has wide streets, full of glorious old elms, and quaint houses looking out over neat white palings."[6] I had found Lillie's quaint house with the help of Joyce Bradbury of the Stratford Historical Society, who arranged for me to have a tour of its first floor.[7] Now known as the Golden Rooster, in honor of the weathervane on Christ Episcopal Church which it faces, Elm Cottage houses the church's consignment shop on the first floor and an attorney's office on the second but still retains some original elements. I stopped to take a picture of Joyce and me in Lillie's mirror—more hallucinations from her future. I walked up Lillie's curling staircase, smoothing my hand over the silky wornness of the banister, introduced myself to the attorney, and was given a tour of the rooms where Lillie had walked, written, mothered her infants, and grieved for her dead young husband. Lost in a conflation of memories, hers mingling with mine, I looked out Lillie's bedroom window. "It is the window that makes it difficult," says Stevens, "To say good-by to the past."[8]

Lillie Devereux's past began here in Stratford, where her parents both grew up. They were second cousins and childhood sweethearts, Sarah Elizabeth Johnson (1798–1867) and George Pollok Devereux (1795–1837). George Devereux's parents, John and Frances Pollok Devereux, owned large plantations in North Carolina, but they lived in Stratford every summer until their sons graduated from Yale University. George graduated in 1815, studied law in Litchfield, Connecticut, and was admitted to the bar in 1818.⁹ He then returned to North Carolina to live with his bachelor uncle, for whom he was named and who intended to make him his heir. On June 12, 1827, after a five-year grand tour of Europe with his uncle, George Devereux married Sarah Johnson in the octagonal parlor of the Johnson home. Upon his marriage, George's father gave him a plantation, Runeroi, lying along the Roanoke River in North Carolina, and there Lillie's parents went to live.

Lillie was born Elizabeth Johnson Devereux in Raleigh, North Carolina, on August 12, 1833. Her birth, preceded by those of two sisters who died in infancy, was followed by that of another girl who died shortly after birth. In the midst of all these losses, her mother was pregnant again in the spring of 1837, when, on their yearly journey from North Carolina to Connecticut, George Devereux became seriously ill in Suffolk, Virginia, and died there of a stomach hemorrhage at the age of forty-two. His widow continued the long journey home to Stratford and gave birth in August to yet another girl, named Georgina after her father.

Because George Devereux was a second son, with no male heirs, property that had been intended for him upon the death of his uncle was not forthcoming. Half of that $1.6 million estate went to Blake's paternal grandmother, who settled between $50,000 and $100,000 upon each of her two granddaughters. When her grandmother died, Blake's uncle absorbed the estate, offering $200 each to his brother's daughters. Sarah Devereux had, however, inherited Runeroi, which she sold several years after her husband's death to a neighbor who she felt certain would treat the plantation slaves with care and not break up their families. During Blake's childhood, Mrs. Devereux had an income large enough that she did not have to consider remarrying for support.

Sarah Devereux never returned to live in the South. Both she and her husband had lived in North Carolina in large part as a family obligation, but each year they had spent many months in Stratford. Although they profited from it, they considered slavery an intolerable institution and a corrupting influence on both master and servant. "My mother has told me," Lillie wrote in her autobiography, "that after his afternoon's ride over the plantation, my father would come in utterly discouraged by some evidence of degradation of the poor creatures. 'Wife,' he would say, 'what can we do? It is a dreadful property to hold!'"[10] On his deathbed, George Devereux told his wife to settle in the North, and Mrs. Devereux had no intention of doing otherwise. In 1839, she made the decision to move to New Haven, where her husband had been educated and where her mother, Jonathan Edwards's granddaughter Susan, had been raised. It was there she wanted to raise her daughters.

Briefly, she made her home on St. John Street, moving in May 1840 to a gable-fronted Federal style colonial at 117 Church Street on the southeast corner of Church and Wall Streets, across from the house of the president of Yale and now the site of a multistoried office building.[11] A block and a half away, in the Church Street jail, were forty-nine African men from the Spanish schooner *Amistad,* held on charges of murder and mutiny. They had been captured and sold into slavery from the Sierra Leone area of western Africa. After surviving the passage across the Atlantic, crammed into four-foot-high holds, they arrived in Cuba, where they were kept in open-air pens until sold again and loaded onto the *Amistad.* Led by a rice farmer named Singbe Pieh but known as Joseph Cinque, the Africans revolted. Captured, they were sent to New Haven to await trial. During the seventeen months they were kept in New Haven, the Africans drew large crowds, some of whom paid a New York shilling (12 1/2 cents) to view them in jail, while others mobbed the New Haven Green, across the street, where the Africans exercised, delighting the crowds with flips and somersaults.[12]

It is unlikely that the inquisitive seven-year-old Lillie did not join the throng on the Green to catch a glimpse of the Africans. Very likely her mother viewed the painting of Joseph Cinque by New Haven engraver Nathaniel Jocelyn (1796–1881), which, because it depicts him in heroic classical garments, was a source of much controversy.[13] The painting, which hangs in the New Haven Colony Historical Society, around the corner from the most important of Blake's childhood homes, portrays a commanding presence—handsome, head upright, without chains. In 1841 the Artist Fund Society of Philadelphia refused to exhibit the piece for fear that it might offend some of its patrons. Jocelyn resigned from the Society, and the portrait's owner, Robert Purvis, charged it with racism. Mrs. Devereux was a noted New Haven hostess, and in all probability Lillie would have overheard discussions among the New Haven elite concerning both portrait and trial. Indeed, the controversy surrounding the portrait echoed the substance of the trials of the Africans: their defense, argued by New Haven attorney Roger Sherman Baldwin, who was funded by abolitionists, was that they were not slaves who had revolted and murdered, but free persons who had been seized and brought illegally to Spanish soil and who killed in self-defense. Public sympathy for the *Amistad* Africans factored into the growth of antislavery sentiment "then forming in the public mind," as one chronicler of New Haven put it.[14] More than twenty years later, in a short story called "The Rescued Fugitives," Blake would let stereotypes of the dangerous and the noble savage clash until, out of their unresolved juxtaposition, emerges a heroic figure, a leader of men, a man we can recognize in the portrait of Cinque painted by Nathaniel Jocelyn.

Throughout Lillie's childhood, the New Haven Green was the site of demonstrations and debates, church services, country fairs, and riots. It was both the marketplace and the Yale football field. During the 1840 presidential campaign, parades originated from the Green, snaking their way throughout the city with cries of "Tippecanoe and Tyler too" and "Van, Van, a used-up man." The 1844 elections brought orations on the Green by Henry Clay, whom Mrs. Devereux ardently supported. "Then followed," writes New Haven historian Henry Taylor Blake, "the Mexican war and next the prolonged and exciting agitation over slavery in the territories, the Fugitive Slave law, the compromise measures, the repeal of the Missouri compromise, and finally the struggle between freedom and slavery for the possession of Kansas. Through this eventful period there was no place where the fires of political discussion blazed more frequently or more fiercely than on the Green."[15]

Here in the early 1840s the newly formed temperance reform societies held demonstrations. "There were music and banners and vehicles bearing awful examples of the drink habit, in striking contrast with beautiful young ladies who wore badges inscribed with the blood-curdling motto, 'Tee total or no husband.'"[16] In 1854 the "Maine Law" was passed which outlawed private sales of alcohol; after August 1, only municipalities could sell liquor for medicinal, chemical, or sacramental purposes. "As the dreaded day approached every vehicle in town, from wheelbarrows to hackney coaches, seemed to be engaged in the transportation of liquid refreshment in every form of receptacle, and even the most reputable temperance advocates were sometimes seen with lumps in their garments which they were careful to protect from contact with stone posts."[17] A diarist writes that on the night before the Maine Law went into effect, "from dark till 12 at night the town was made hideous by the shouts of the drunken rabble, but at midnight they ceased as by magic." The next day, he writes, "I should have supposed it the Sabbath."[18]

With or without drink, the students at Yale were often a rowdy bunch, cited on many a blue "Courts of Discipline" slip for riotous behavior.[19] "Our streets were always full of students who formed a band of somewhat lawless fellows, ever ready to discuss any young lady of the least prominence," wrote Blake.[20] Two notable riots broke out on the Green while Lillie lived in New Haven. On October 30, 1841, a series of skirmishes boiled over between students playing football and firemen preparing the Green for their first annual review. The fight, in which the students were outmastered, led to their breaking up the firemen's banquet and vandalizing the engine house. Thereafter the battle between the students and the firemen became something of an annual event. In a much more serious incident, on March 17, 1854, Yale students and New Haven townies fought it out on the Green as an ever-enlarging mob gathered, threatening the students as they attempted to retreat to the campus. When one of the town boys grabbed a Yalie, he was stabbed to death; the mob went out of control, bringing out a cannon and aiming it at the college. Peace was finally restored by the arrival of the mayor and his troops, but the student who had stabbed the town boy was never brought to justice. Four days later, a Yale student noted in his diary that "the Townies had a meeting at Ball Springs house yesterday afternoon and decided upon—no one knows what—." He writes that President Woolsey met with students the next day and said, "'Act merely on the defensive, but if they set foot inside the College grounds send them to————.'"[21]

Mrs. Devereux, meanwhile, had moved from Church Street three blocks north and a block west to settle into Maple Cottage. In the spring of 1843, Eli Whitney, Jr., son of the inventor of the cotton gin and first cousin to Sarah Devereux, had helped her find the five-bedroom house which stood in the center of an acre of land running the length of Trumbull Street between Hillhouse and Whitney Avenues.[22] The lower floor had two parlors, a drawing room, a boudoir, and a dining room, all of which connected and could be "thrown open" for parties. Called Maple Cottage for the maple trees that surrounded it, the house was part of a planned community designed by Alexander Jackson Davis and Ithiel Town. The centerpiece of the plan was Hillhouse Avenue, lined with lavish, elm-shaded mansions and crossed by streets lined with maples and smaller, but still stately, homes. Davis, a preeminent nineteenth-century architect and a founder of the architectural profession in America, designed the house in 1836. Maple Cottage is the first of an innovative American form known as the picturesque cottage, which Davis would popularize two years later in his book *Rural Residences*.[23] Davis's planning for Maple Cottage, writes architectural historian Jane B. Davies, "had a crucial effect on house design, for along with its emphasis on irregularity came freedom and flexibility. It brought a release from the rigidity and limitations of the traditional box shape, which was opened in all directions, both upward and outward."[24]

Before Mrs. Devereux bought it, Maple Cottage had housed a School for Young Ladies, teaching English, classics, and vocal and instrumental music. "What," ask historians Eric Robert Papenfuse and Catherine Ann Lawrence, "must next-door-neighbor Benjamin Silliman [the internationally renowned scientist] have thought of the 'special attention' paid to 'training the voice for accompanying Piano or Organ'? The chemistry professor's many illustrious visitors, from President John Quincy Adams to the great Swiss naturalist Louis Agassiz (on his first visit to the United States), must have gazed admiringly upon the 'pretty' Cottage, even if the acre of 'grounds around it were in a most wretched state.' How relieved must Silliman have been when" the Devereuxs moved in.[25] Mrs. Devereux immediately laid out a lawn, as Lillie remembered, "in shrubbery with winding walks and fancy arbors. The garden . . . was full of beautiful flowers while a fine green house kept up the supply in winter as well as in summer." And she threw open those connecting doors of her parlors and drawing rooms to host "more parties than anyone else."[26] Besides a ball in summer and one in winter, there were receptions and parties. The Hillhouse/Trumbull neighborhood's Revolver Club held its first open house at Maple Cottage, followed by receptions at neighboring homes until a ball at Lillie's climaxed the social season just before Lent. Besides dancing, there were mock trials, charades, and tableaux, in which party-goers would dress themselves and pose as figures in great paintings. The house would fill with Yale faculty, esteemed guests visiting New Haven from home and abroad, and Yale students bringing letters of introduction to Mrs. Devereux. One notable visitor to New Haven whom Mrs. Devereux did not entertain was Charles Dickens. When asked to host him during his first U.S. lecture tour, she refused because he failed to bring the prerequisite letters of introduction.[27]

From the windows of Maple Cottage, the Farmington Canal can be seen. Here, in 1839, a boat had carried the *Amistad* Africans from New Haven on their way to trial in Hartford. Here, too, a group of neighborhood householders protested to the mayor that naked men and boys cavorted, bathing in the waters. When the famous Professor Silliman hurried across the frozen canal to the college one day, it was here that the ice gave way and in he went. He survived, his dignity in check.[28] Before 1849, when the canal was drained and turned into a railroad bed, Lillie Devereux learned to iceskate here. She and her friends played on the bridge at the foot of Hillhouse Avenue, fished in the canal, and spied on Mr. Skinner as he came up Lovers' Lane.[29]

Aaron Skinner, who ran a school for boys in the rear of his Hillhouse Avenue mansion, served as a state senator in the 1840s and as mayor of New Haven in 1850–1854. He and his wife were frequent guests at Mrs. Devereux's. He describes her "Ash Wednesday party": "fiddling and dancing in the east room, a crowd in the hall and west room. . . . 'on went the dance' and away went the squire with Eli Whitney through the kitchen escaping to our north parlor where we had an hour of quiet all to ourselves—We did not confine ourselves entirely to the 'feast of reason' but added some earthly comforts and went back to see the party disperse at twelve."[30]

The neighborhood was a most convivial one, interconnected by old family relationships and intellectual partnerships. Adjacent to Yale's first medical school, and home to many of its scientists, Hillhouse Avenue and Trumbull Street housed the social and intellectual elite of New Haven. Abolitionist and United States Senator James Hillhouse had laid out the neighborhood as an experiment in urban planning; "his intellectual energy and vision for Hillhouse Avenue as a place of architectural beauty and distinction attracted many brilliant people to the neighborhood."[31] While Lillie Devereux was growing up, her neighbors included not only the renowned Professor Silliman, but Professor Noah Porter, Clark Professor of Mental and Moral Philosophy, and later president of Yale, who would provide Lillie with introductions in Washington when she served there as a Civil War correspondent; the poet James A. Hillhouse, son of the developer of the neighborhood; the educators Aaron Skinner and Elizabeth Apthorp; the geologist and mineralogist James Dwight Dana, who held the Silliman Professorship in Natural History and whose textbooks remain current even today; and professor of agricultural chemistry John Pitkin Norton. The Skinners, the Danas, the Winthrops and Whitneys, the Prichards, Jessups, Hewitts, Devereuxs, and Hillhouses were in and out of one another's homes. Mr. Skinner once took a jug of hot port sangaree across the street to Mrs. Prichard's saying, "'Now Miss Sally, get out the glasses.'"[32] Even after Sarah Devereux sold Maple Cottage in 1856 and moved back to Stratford, she would return for long visits with her friends in New Haven, as would Lillie, who often stayed with the novelist John DeForest and his family. A voluminous letter-writer, Aaron Skinner wrote to Mrs. Prichard of a meeting of the Female Education Society, the exclusive Hillhouse neighborhood group known as "Our Society," which, having nothing to do with the education of females, was dedicated to the care of struggling male theological students. "Our Society" was meeting in Maple Cottage, now owned by Professor Colin Ingersoll, Connecticut's antislavery congressman and adjutant general who served as the United States envoy to the Russian court.[33] Mrs. Devereux was there, a guest in her former home. Mr. Skinner writes that he and Mr. Ingersoll were "shockingly abused" while having a quiet glass of wine: "the ladies opened the door upon us, pointed their pretty fingers at us—gathered around us—offered the pledge—proposed to send for Father Matthews, etc. Mrs. Devereux, Mary Hillhouse, Miss Hewitt and Mrs. Skinner kept up the farce all the way home—trying to get a laugh out of poor old me."[34]

Lillie attended the Apthorp School for Young Ladies on Hillhouse Avenue, which "long had a well-deserved reputation."[35] Mrs. Elizabeth Apthorp and two of her five daughters taught a variety of traditional subjects including Latin, mathematics, and composition. After school, Lillie had lessons in French, piano, drawing, and dancing. Mrs. Apthorp retired and her school closed when Lillie was fifteen; thereafter she was tutored by a Yale theological student, following the Yale undergraduate curriculum, the only way a woman could obtain some measure of a Yale education.

Lillie also incorporated, as part of her general education, the wisdom of the day concerning "woman." She would have known Lydia Sigourney's *Letters to Young Ladies,* which was reproduced in new editions during each decade from the 1830s through the 1870s. Sigourney, Connecticut's leading female poet of sentimental verses, was, as a colleague of poet James Hillhouse, a frequent visitor to Lillie's neighborhood. In her 1874 novel, *Fettered for Life,* Blake would mention Sigourney and her home in Hartford.[36] *Letters to Young Ladies* promoted sentimental stereotypes of woman as the nurturing agent of Nature who is best equipped to teach the young and who, subduing self, influences all those within her sphere—that "domestic sphere . . . [a woman's] own native province." While Sigourney stressed the value of self-abnegation ("she should govern herself, that she may be better able to obey"), she also called for reform in dress, which was becoming an issue with women activists, and she articulated an admonition that informed Blake's long life—although "woman is deficient in physical strength, it does not follow that she need be so in moral courage."[37] Sigourney, along with other advisers to young ladies, preached the value for women of independent learning, and Blake developed a lifelong habit of study, incorporating systematic reading programs and language study into her days as an adult. As a girl, Lillie also frequently attended public lectures at the college, and she would have heard her cousin, Yale's President Theodore Dwight Woolsey, speak on the "woman question." His historical survey of cultural differences in the treatment of women is echoed in her first novel, *Southwold*. She agreed with him that women should be the companions, not the subordinates, of men, and that women's obligations in the home must have concomitant duties in the world. But she would struggle against his feelings of "disgust" at proponents of woman's rights; "such persons," Woolsey wrote, "undermine that fair fabric of culture . . . they are one-sided persons . . . [who] would spoil women by making them half-men."[38]

Because it opened her to the spirit of inquiry and debate, the Hillhouse/Trumbull neighborhood was the spiritual source of Blake's lifetime work. It formed her intellectual background and played an important role in the development of her personality. Here we find the high seriousness of academic endeavor cut with regular doses of social gaiety that marked her own life. Her scholarly neighbors, engaged in both the academic preservation of knowledge and the questioning of it, were leaders of invention. It was a neighborhood where tradition and revolution converged, and here grew a woman who would disguise, beneath a highly conventional demeanor, a well-articulated, radical ideology.

But long before she developed positions on social issues, it was in the Hillhouse/Trumbull neighborhood that, with her favorite cousin, Sarah Winthrop, Lillie would lie "in the long grass on a summer day and [wait] with intense longing to see a fairy."[39] Here she sledded in winter, once spinning out of control and knocking herself unconscious. Here she was thrown from her horse and broke her collar bone. Here a neighbor across the street would reminisce about "Miss Devereux's adorers," who could be seen approaching Maple Cottage with nervous high hopes and retreating in agonies of rejection.

I, too, approached Maple Cottage with nervous high hopes. I had found Lillie's house. It was just around the corner from the Historical Society, at 85 Trumbull Street. Once the property had stretched from one end of the block to the other; now the house was crammed into a little city plot. Mrs. Devereux's beautiful gardens had turned into parking lots. But there it was, a modified Italianate villa, now overhung with fire escapes instead of balconies. Maple Cottage, once filled with life and laughter, where Lillie Devereux began to write and to experiment with her ideas about women and their rights, looked a bit detached from the traffic and tar of New Haven.

Blake's name had literally, and most graciously, opened doors for me in Stratford, so it was with great anticipation that I walked up the front steps of Maple Cottage, shading my eyes from the sun reflected off the window panes. But the door was locked, and as I peered through the filthy glass of the sidelight, I saw that the house was empty. Then I read the demolition notice.

II

Of all the cities I have visited in conjunction with my research on Lillie Devereux Blake, only New Haven seemed oblivious of her significance. Interest in Blake ran high just down the Post Road in Stratford; Public School no. 6 on Madison Avenue in New York City is named in her honor; her portrait hangs in Columbia University's Low Library;[40] her journals, papers, and letters are carefully preserved at the Missouri Historical Society in St. Louis. Why in her hometown, which houses a great research university, would her work be not only forgotten, but erased almost beyond all retracing by rumors like the one whispered to me in the Historical Society?

There the only reference to Lillie is captioned "The House and Escapades of Lily [sic] Devereaux [sic]. Notes As To 1852 [sic] and Later of Mrs. F. B. Dexter in 1915." The accompanying photograph of Lillie is misnamed and misspelled "Mrs. Lillian Devereaux Blake." The reference reads: "The Devereux house was associated with one of the rare scandals in modern New Haven life, as Lily Devereux was a great students' belle, and her career was marked by a disgraceful affair—the young man concerned in it being expelled from the College. She was twice married afterwards and has been well known as Mrs. Lily Devereux Blake as an ardent woman's rights woman, dying only a short time since."[41]

The three details Mrs. F. B. Dexter selects from Blake's long and useful life are ones chosen to accentuate, in 1915, a portrait of a disreputable woman: she was involved in an affair so disgraceful that her partner in it was expelled from Yale; she was "twice married," in this context implying divorce; and she was a "woman's rights woman," one of those "persons who undermine the fabric of culture." All three items imply promiscuous female desire, independent of patriarchal control. And all three items are the sum total of what was known about Blake in New Haven on the day I arrived. As the *New Haven Register* put it in its report of efforts to save Maple Cottage from demolition, "the plot thickened" with the discovery that the cottage had been the home of writer and suffragist Lillie Devereux Blake.[42] And indeed it did. The Friends of Hillhouse Avenue, preservationists valiantly fighting to save the cottage on the basis of its architectural significance, understood, via Mrs. Dexter,[43] that the Devereuxs were, as it was discreetly put to me, "perhaps not as conventional as others in the neighborhood." Perhaps, they were, it was added gently—so as not, I think, to insult me by insulting the subject of my research—"somewhat disreputable." I detected that whispered rumor behind these mild remarks.

I knew of Lillie's "disgraceful affair." It happened in 1854, not 1852, and did indeed result in the expulsion of a Yale student. As a measure of the embarrassment the incident caused, it goes unmentioned in her daughter's biography of her mother. Blake relates it in her autobiography twenty years after the fact, saying that she would be "glad to pass the matter over in silence" and carefully omitting names: During the winter of 1853–54, Blake says, she had an admirer—a Yale undergraduate, handsome, agreeable, slightly younger, with a "ready wit and pleasant manner." But because she was in danger of "an entanglement" which she did not want, in the spring of 1854 she traveled, chaperoned by an old friend of her mother's, to her relatives in the South. She remembers receiving a letter from the young man to which she responded with a firm refusal. Apparently teased about being another of "Miss Devereux's victims," he contended that she, rather than he, was the victim. "From this the story grew to a shocking scandal which assumed I know not how many improbable and ridiculous forms. President Woolsey . . . took up the matter with well meant but injudicious zeal," Blake writes, with compassion for the youth who showed none for her, "and the young man was expelled from college." She characterizes this time as "most wretched. . . . I had enemies and defenders and was the subject of many a violent dispute and of much unpleasant notoriety. . . . To prove how little real belief attached to the stories to my disadvantage, I may mention that within two months I had five offers of marriage."[44] The importance of male approval of female innocence is signaled by that final count in her favor.

In Blake's diary of August 12, 1853–August 12, 1854, the only diary that remains of the 1849–60 period, she twice mentions the name of W. H. L. Barnes. On November 5, 1853, she went to New York, where she stayed overnight at the home of her uncle, Edwards Johnson, went to a concert in the evening, and returned to Maple Cottage the next day. Travel to New York had become an almost casual occurrence after the New York–New Haven railroad was completed in 1850. A trip that had taken fifteen hours by stage coach or slightly less (but unreliably so) by sloop now took only three to four hours at the very low cost of $1.50.[45] And the passenger depot was right around the corner, at the foot of Hillhouse Avenue. Lillie, her mother, and her sister, Georgie, often took advantage of the train to make quick trips into New York. However, the November 5 diary does not mention her mother or sister, but it does mention "W. H. L. Barnes Esq." It is unclear whether she traveled to New York with him or whether she saw him there. Subsequently, Lillie makes reference to "her fiancée" [sic], and it seems more than probable, with no other name or important incident intervening, that the fiancé is William Barnes.[46] On March 16, 1854, Lillie began a trip to New York, Philadelphia, and Raleigh, where, as she notes in her diary on April 20, she broke off her engagement. After arriving home at the beginning of June—"I woke up so happy to be home"—Lillie walked with her sister to a class. They were joined by as many as fifteen "ladies" and several young men. They saw "a great many students," she writes, "but not Barnes."[47] Lillie had a record of staying on friendly terms with her disappointed beaux, but in this case such an ending was not to be. In her autobiography she writes that she "accomplish[ed] as much mischief among men as I could. Foolish child, I did not know that I was amusing myself with fire, and that the most dangerous. I was absolutely innocent of the sin or wickedness of this world and I played with men's hearts as a baby might with torpid snakes, never realizing the danger I ran from the passions I might arouse."[48]

The remainder of her diary, which ends on her birthday, August 12, 1854, is oblivious of Barnes and of any impending problem. It is filled with notations of parties, picnics, and regattas; crews of Yale students row Lillie and her friends out into New Haven harbor; a flower is pressed and labeled "from Georges Lampsen"; and an exuberant "Reflection" is written as the last entry, August 12, 1854, on her twenty-first birthday: "A glorious life has been mine from the time I first drew breath . . . a happy childhood, a joyous school life, a glorious and triumphant young lady career." Her triumphs—and her naiveté—ended with William Barnes's revenge.

In the Yale Archives, searching through an uncataloged box of index cards labeled Nineteenth-Century Student Disciplinary Cases and through faculty records of the period, I came across a reference to a petition to the faculty made by W. H. L. Barnes, who was accused of "impeaching the character of a young lady of the town." Thanks to the help of Archivist Diane E. Kaplan, who persisted, over a number of weeks, in searching for the petition itself, the mystery of Lillie's "disgraceful affair" finally can be disclosed. While Lillie is never mentioned by name, her own mention of Barnes in her diary along with her account of the scandal and a letter I found in the personal papers of Yale's President Woolsey, makes it clear that it is she whose character Barnes was accused of "impeaching."

It was Georges Lampsen's attentions that precipitated Barnes's rumors. In the fall of 1854, when, according to Barnes, Lampsen was on the verge of proposing to Lillie, Barnes felt it "his duty" to apprise Lampsen of her true character, to save him "from a fate worse than death."[49] On December 13, when Barnes pleaded his case before the faculty which accused him of "impeaching the character of a young lady of the city,"[50] he stated that he had proposed marriage to the woman only after succumbing to her artful temptations, which "no man could have resisted." Marriage was a way "to wipe away the stain." But he ended their engagement when he learned that during the course of it (when, it should be noted, Blake was on an extended visit to her southern relatives), "intimacies inconsistent with the character of a virtuous female" existed between her and a very large number of Yale students. Maintaining that he had told the story only to some of his "very intimate friends" when they demanded to know the facts and after they pledged secrecy, Barnes reverses the issue by complaining that *he* is the victim of rumor: "the story that I had traduced the character of a virtuous woman was freely circulated, and I was, and am, excluded from Society." While Barnes demands *"direct proof"* (emphasis his) that he intended to spread scandal, his defense, rife with rumor, offers no direct proof of his accusations and deals only in innuendo, leaving the specifics to the reader's imagination: "I have not undertaken to show the circumstances which made me sin and brought all this distress upon me. But they were such as no man could have resisted. . . . These circumstances, and many others which need not here be named . . . facts still more atrocious in their nature reached me."

William Barnes was caught in a bit of a dilemma. He was the source of the rumor about his "sinful intimacy" with Lillie; Georges Lampsen went to the family and told them. If Barnes denied the crime of that intimacy, he would have no defense against the charge that he had impugned Lillie's character and he would be expelled. His strategy was to stand by his statement no matter what, in order to threaten far-reaching public exposure if the faculty took action against him. Repeatedly Barnes threatens that if he is expelled, "widespread publicity" will "inevitably" result: "It can only render it disgracefully public; it can only bring utter and lasting shame on those who are undeserving such disgrace. It can only brand an indelible impress of guilt where now an undefined rumor rests. . . . If, at this time, I am expelled, the facts will be notorious, and I can take no means which will prevent their become [*sic*] public." His is the rhetoric of fiction, accompanied by melodramatic flourishes: "Your verdict condemns not only me—it utterly ruins every prospect of mine and drives me out in the world an outcast and wanderer, but it condemns another, with a condemnation which no length of time, no future act can wipe away." He concludes with a plea, wrapped around another threat, that if he must be expelled, let the action be postponed, so that he can graduate and leave New Haven: "If I am not here, it will be unnecessary to make a public exposure, and to spread abroad this wretched story of misery and sin."

Notwithstanding his repeated threats, on December 14, 1854, Barnes was expelled midway in his senior year, accused, in his own words, of robbing "a defenseless girl of the priceless treasure of an unsullied reputation:" "Resolved in a meeting of the Faculty of Yale College that whereas W. H. L. Barnes has impeached the character of a young lady in this city by telling a story about her and himself which even if true could only require his expulsion, he be and hereby is expelled."[51]

Whether or not anything sexual occurred between Lillie Devereux and William Barnes, she certainly led him on and then dropped him, just as she had done many times to many others, a practice warranted by a culture in which young women were supposed to tally marriage offers as measures of their homebound marketability. Lillie had always been an outrageous flirt, her vanity flattered by the attention given to her as the reigning belle of New Haven. She delighted in telling how she and her friend Annie Wetmore were once indicted for "disturbing the peace of the college." A mock trial was held: "We were solemnly tried, found guilty and condemned 'to wear thick blue veils for the rest of our natural lives."[52] During Yale commencement exercises, to the annoyance of her cousin President Woolsey (who, however, kept inviting her back), Lillie, seated prominently to the right of the stage, threw bouquets at her favorite speakers and flirted with students whom a bewildered usher attempted to order away. Graduates wore her rose-colored ribbons in their buttonholes.

Just as Barnes had threatened it would, his expulsion inflamed the scandal. On December 22, 1854, Theodore Winthrop, Lillie's cousin who had often dropped in at Maple Cottage, wrote to his uncle, President Woolsey, that "apparently matters have gone so far that now nothing can be done to check or crush the story."[53] Winthrop became a poet and novelist whose career was cut short when he died on June 10, 1861, on the battlefield at Big Bethel. Lillie was deeply saddened by his death:

> after my marriage and especially during my residence at St. Louis, he was a frequent visitor at my house. Somewhat haughty in manner and singularly reserved in disposition, he did not win many friends among his ordinary associates, but his cultured mind, his refined tastes and a certain dry, ready wit made him to me a delightful companion. During his early youth he had been blamed for not faithfully adhering to the duties of his desk in a counting house. I was among the few who knew how he longed for opportunity to indulge his literary tastes and I have often sighed to think how tardily reputation came to him, how the fame he so longed for was only able to twine a laurel wreath for his tomb![54]

But in 1854, on December 22, Winthrop wrote on behalf of the "men of the family," requesting that President Woolsey communicate to Mrs. Devereux "that Lilly [sic] *should not come* to NYork [sic] as she intends to do next week. . . . she is liable, not merely to be remarked upon and stared at but to be insulted in the street or in society. *She can hardly escape insult* and must keep quiet and out of sight as much as possible. . . . Why—Lilly could hardly walk down Broadway without a body guard—with the increasing publicity of the story she might almost be mobbed" (emphasis his). Winthrop concludes, "We of course will all continue to protect the lady and her family and to speak with the deserved detestation of the man's conduct."[55]

For a young woman of Lillie Devereux's time and place, even talk of impropriety was punishable. The faculty declared that William Barnes had "impeached" her character, but her cousin makes clear that the "truth or falsity of the tale" is beside the point: it is Lillie who "must keep quiet and out of sight. . . . If Mrs. Devereux could be persuaded to go away, leave the country, and remove her daughter, in Europe perhaps, for a few years, it would be the best thing."[56]

Blake's maternal great-grandfather, Jonathan Edwards's son Pierrepont, did much more than flirt a bit too enthusiastically. Blake writes that one of the "most respectable families in New Haven [owes] its origin to his intimacy with a near relation of his wife's." Among the family, the story went that as Susan Ogden Edwards lay dying, she "murmured her rival's name saying 'She has killed me!'"[57] The eminent Judge Edwards, however, was not advised to get out of town. By all accounts he was honored by his colleagues. He died in 1826, two years before a woman was forced to stand for an hour with a noose around her neck upon a platform erected on the New Haven Green. She had given birth to a stillborn illegitimate child and had attempted to hide the baby.[58] What are the differences between her behavior and that of Judge Edwards? He was married, so his offense was adultery. But she was of a different sex and a different class, and her child was "illegitimate" because, of course, it had no legally recognized father and no legitimate patriarchal status. It was female sexuality that needed controlling; Pierrepont Edwards's reputation for "living high and loving often" could be acknowledged with a gentlemanly, perhaps even a congratulatory, wink.[59] And what was the difference between the offenses of Lillie and of her esteemed ancestor? He fathered at least one child out of wedlock; she was the victim of a malicious rumor. He is remembered as a leader of the New Haven judiciary system. But New Haven is where I was told that Lillie Devereux Blake was a "lady of the night."

Mrs. F. B. Dexter's innuendoes in the Dana Collection of the Historical Society ignore the fact that the "disgraceful affair" was, as the faculty of Yale College made clear, the impugning of Lillie Devereux's character. Mrs. Dexter does not tell us that "modern New Haven life," of which Lillie's "disgraceful affair" was a "rare scandal," included the imprisonment of the *Amistad* Africans, and, in the same year as William Barnes's disappointment, the stabbing death of a town boy by a Yale student. Also, that summer was marked by the embezzlement of $1,000,000 by the president of the New Haven–New York Railroad.[60] In Blake's hometown, all the accomplishments of her life have been reduced to rehearsals of William Barnes's vengeful rumor. Indeed, at least in New Haven, for a hundred and forty-five years, her character has been "impeached."

III

On November 3, 1998, the misinformation supplied by Mrs. F. B. Dexter was cited in a successful argument made before the Connecticut Historical Commission to discredit Lillie Devereux once again and thus to further justify the destruction of Maple Cottage. Only days before the commission hearing, I had brought evidence of the importance of Lillie Devereux Blake to the attention of Richard Levin, president of Yale University, which owned Maple Cottage. The Friends of Hillhouse Avenue, in a statement to the Connecticut Historical Commission, wrote that the new information "convinces us that Lillie Devereux Blake's home should be a national landmark."[61] But Yale, instead of reconsidering its demolition plans in light of the new evidence of the value of the house, especially for women's history, allowed its paid consultant to allude to Mrs. Dexter's innuendoes—particularly those regarding Blake's supposed sexual life—in order to dismiss her significance out of hand. She was important to New Haven only for an affair she had had with a Yale student.

Three days later, on a Sunday, Yale planned to quietly demolish Maple Cottage. Only because members of the Friends of Hillhouse Avenue noticed workmen removing asbestos (always preliminary to demolition) did they investigate and discover Yale's intentions. By posing as a Yale representative, one of the Friends convinced workers to disclose the demolition date. Racing through New Haven to the home of a judge, the Friends were able to obtain a last-minute injunction that forced a work stoppage pending a court appearance on January 12, 1999. Later, they learned that Yale had notified the New Haven City Building Department of its intent to destroy the cottage just minutes before closing time on Friday, November 6, 1998, thus effectively eliminating public notice.

Instead of the wrecking ball, there was a candle-light vigil on the Sunday on which Yale had planned to quietly and quickly demolish Maple Cottage. "According to Yale, a woman's history isn't enough of a history," read a placard at the vigil. But a woman's sexual history, it seems, was of interest to Yale, if it could be used to manipulate her standing in her rightful community.

The Friends of Hillhouse Avenue, understanding the significance of the evidence concerning Lillie Devereux Blake, brought suit against the university. I wrote again to President Levin on November 4, 1998, informing him that his paid consultant had presented false information concerning Blake, information at odds with the conclusions Yale itself had drawn in 1854. I requested that he take corrective action on the matter and repudiate the misstatements made before the Connecticut Historical Commission. Instead, during the January 1999 trial, Yale attorneys themselves repeated the Dana Collection's rumors and even attempted to introduce the material into evidence. Furthermore, in an attempt to preempt the contention that the information brought forth on Blake in October was new evidence in light of which Yale should have reconsidered its demolition plans, the Yale attorneys allowed Yale's consultant to testify that he himself was the person responsible for rediscovering Lillie Devereux Blake—he had known all about her all along and "with very little effort."[62] Under cross-examination, he admitted that he had not consulted her archives in Missouri. But he stated that he had discussed Blake with the student from the University of Missouri. This last remark was in reference to me—a professor for decades, never at the University of Missouri. I should be flattered, it was suggested, that I could be mistaken for a graduate student, and while my vanity permits such fun, I know full well the sexism which leads to the dismissal of women, however old or accomplished, as young and novice until, of course, they become so undeniably old that they can be dismissed as "little old ladies." I should also point out that, although Yale's consultant and I had been introduced on October 20, 1998, by Anstress Farwell, architectural historian with the Friends of Hillhouse Avenue, and she had apprised him of my information, we never, although he stated so under oath, had a discussion about Lillie Devereux Blake.[63]

In letting references to the malicious rumors enter the public record, Yale contradicted the decision of its own faculty, which had punished with expulsion in the senior year the student with whom the rumors had originated. Documentary evidence affirms the continuing high status of Mrs. Devereux and her daughter in the elite Hillhouse/Trumbull neighborhood and their involvement there even after Lillie had been married from Maple Cottage and moved away and Mrs. Devereux subsequently returned to her own childhood home of Stratford. But, in willful ignorance of the facts, Yale's representatives, both in the November commission hearing and in the January trial, stated that Lillie Devereux Blake was known in New Haven only for a scandal involving a Yale student and that she and her mother had to leave town because of her sexual behavior.[64] In his report, the consultant to a major research institution referenced none of Blake's significant contributions to American culture. And although the president of that institution was presented with documented evidence of the truth, he chose not to act upon it and not to correct the false testimony presented in the name of Yale University.

In her autobiography, Blake recognized that what delighted her about flirting was the "sense of power" that it gave her.[65] Here is perhaps a clue as to her real offense. She had a certain power over men, and she delighted in it. Her power and her delight were all too reminiscent of the specter of unleashed female desire, so dangerous and forbidden in the 1850s, and in the 1990s still so useful in the course of discrediting a woman. If we wonder how women like Blake could have been dismissed from history, we need only look at these actions in New Haven to see how the process continues to play itself out.

On Monday, May 7, 1999, at the very moment that an appeals court was preparing a restraining order to stop demolition and while workmen removing asbestos were still visible on the roof of Maple Cottage, Yale administrators and campus police rushed to cordon off Trumbull Street and direct a Yale-hired mechanical claw to begin demolition. First the campus police had to haul away and arrest three sitting protestors, including a former New Haven alderwoman. The claw consumed two large chunks of Blake's home before the arrival of the court order. The "Maple Cottage Three" were released after promising not to sue the university. Yale then disingenuously declared that because the house was rendered unstable by the claw's destruction, in the interests of public safety it should immediately be razed.

On May 13, 1999, an appeal was filed with the Connecticut Superior Court on behalf of the Friends of Hillhouse Avenue citing fifteen points of possible error or misjudgment in the decision of the court regarding the January trial. In addition, they offered to buy the house from Yale and refurbish it themselves. But on the morning of July 7, 1999, Yale University demolished Maple Cottage, the centerpiece of Trumbull Street and the home of its most illustrious nineteenth-century woman. "It doesn't redound to the reputation of the University to do what they did," said the eminent art historian Vincent Scully. "They've been ruthless. It's just a great mistake."[66] The site is now a parking lot.

IV

New Haven is a neoclassical town filled with Federal and Greek Revival buildings, a retrospective architecture that earned the city a name it proudly held—the "Athens of Connecticut." The architecture of Yale also makes a backward glance, mixing "Gothic and Georgian ensembles" as one architectural historian puts it which "contrive a metaphor of history."[67] The colleges and quadrangles of the university have a centuries-old look, but are actually the product of the 1920s and '30s, a period that produced "The Waste Land," *Ulysses,* and Pound's *Cantos.* These modernist works would seem at first glance to be the antithesis of the neoclassical buildings of Yale, but when George Steiner writes of the "deliberate assemblages . . . the long sequence of imitations, translations, masked quotations, and explicit historical painting"[68] which typifies the work of Eliot, Joyce, and Pound, he could be describing Yale's architecture with its "historical vignettes" and irregularities which seek to create in the course of a decade the illusion of an accumulated production spanning centuries.[69] The neoclassical façade of the university, like modernist poetry, even at its most revolutionary, locates itself within a background that bespeaks its investment in the renewal of traditions that have been paradigmatically male-oriented.[70] The single-mindedness with which Yale moved to demolish Maple Cottage, especially in light of revelations concerning its connections with women's history, has the feel of urgency shared by the modernist poets, whose aesthetic is characterized by "ingatherings of a cultural past felt to be in danger of dissolution."[71]

Yale University condemned the Trumbull Street home of Lillie Blake while another woman stood enshrined at the other edge of the campus, in the center of the Yale Art Gallery's Trumbull Room. Hiram Powers's *The Greek Slave* (1841–43) is a neoclassical sculpture of a nude woman in chains. This "explosive subject," in the words of Joy S. Kasson, "shocking, titillating, potentially even pornographic,"[72] is the image of nineteenth-century womanhood which Yale chooses to remember. While Nathaniel Jocelyn's rendition of Joseph Cinque, with its classical images of the free and the heroic, had the effect of elevating an enslaved man, the neoclassical treatment of an enslaved woman had the counter effect. The sculpture's submissively bowed head with, as Powers himself put it, "an expression of modesty and Christian resignation"[73] not only made the act of gazing at an erotically beautiful nude woman socially acceptable, but it invested female sexuality with a dramatically emotional quotient of subservience. Chains cover the female genitals, enabling the sculptor to dispense with drapery and present a fully nude woman while still maintaining a modicum of decorum. But because the chains are the thematic focal point of the sculpture, the eye is drawn to them, and thence to the genitals. *The Greek Slave*'s sexuality is at the heart of the sculptural narrative as, indeed, chains over female genitals are at the heart of the nineteenth century's patriarchal narrative. Controlling female behavior was easy when all colluded in a system that made a woman valuable in proportion to her sexual innocence and when words alone, uttered, for instance, by a disappointed man, had the power to expose her sexuality to public discussion as much as *The Greek Slave*'s genitals were exposed to public view.

The figure of a chained woman had long been the icon of female activists in the antislavery movement. When it appeared in the work of white males produced for an elite culture, the significance of the iconography was reversed from a call to activism to a response of resignation.[74] Through appropriation and recodification of the antislavery icon, *The Greek Slave,* as Jean Fagin Yellin points out, "pressed that powerful iconography into the service of patriarchal discourse."[75] The woman of Trumbull Street, educated in the Yale curriculum, imbued with the spirit of inquiry and independent thought of Hillhouse society, resisted such discourse. Knowing her innocence of the rumors spread about her, Lillie Blake, with her mother by her side, "brazened out" (as her cousin put it) the hostility and refused to hide indoors or to leave town. Lillie Blake, as vulnerable to sexual exploitation as *The Greek Slave,* is the antithesis of that portrayal of woman. Her life was devoted to action rather than resignation, equality rather than subservience, independence rather than helplessness. But even at the cusp of the Third Millennium, Yale's choice has been to preserve its chained, rather than its revolutionary woman.

Museums are sanctuaries within which time is frozen.[76] Yale's impulse has been to transfer the frozen time of the Trumbull Room to the historical time of Trumbull Street; century-old innuendoes have frozen Lillie Blake's reputation against history's vindication of her achievements. In New Haven, the frozen marble of *The Greek Slave* finds its feminist counterpart chained in time to the ghostlike whispers of 1854 which still surround Trumbull Street.

But outside of New Haven, Lillie Devereux did not remain immured by rumor. After the 1854 attempt to rein in her spirit, she would never again be quite as heedlessly fearless as she had once been. The scandal was her first real awakening to the precariousness of her position as a woman. But she did not choose resignation. Instead, she went undercover, becoming adept at articulating her most radical messages in disguised forms. After the New Haven scandal, Lillie became deeply aware of a disjunction between convention and her sense of her own self; she began to grapple with a dual consciousness of who she was and who she was supposed to be, of what she desired and what she was taught to desire.[77] Her life and work would begin to encode similar struggles in other women to free themselves not only from legislative inequities but from the even more powerful cultural dictates that shaped their identities and would try to keep them chained to the patriarchy's retrogressive version of the feminine past.

V

The *Yale Daily News* on November 6, 1998, reported students' acquiescence in moving Spring Fling in order to protect $3 million worth of new sod and landscaping which "students said they liked," and declared in its editorial that Yale had the right to demolish Maple Cottage because it could not afford the $670,000 it would take to preserve this "collection of boards and nails."[78] Wallace Stevens, whose imagination went well beyond Spring Flings and likable sod, wrote:

> These houses, these difficult objects, dilapidate
> Appearances of what appearances,
>
> .   .   .
>
> Suppose these houses are composed of ourselves,
> So that they become an impalpable town, full of
> Impalpable bells, transparencies of sound,
> Sounding in transparent dwellings of the self . . .
>
> (i, 7–8; ii, 1–4)

Like her beloved Maple Cottage, once derelict and decaying, a "difficult object," Lillie Devereux Blake stands neglected and maligned in New Haven. Yet New Haven, Maple Cottage, and Blake are compositions made out of one another. She is a transparency, moved and formed by the assumptions of her culture. When she struggles against certain of those assumptions—those transparencies of sound—her struggle is not just against the world without, but also against that world as it is mirrored within. And her struggle explains not only herself and others like her, transparent dwellings of the self, but it sounds out her culture, illuminating her place—that impalpable town of whispers and innuendoes which would choose to forget her, as well as a wider world which could not but listen.

2. Figuring The Self

. . . the whole universe . . . make[s] common cause
against the woman who swerves
one hair's breadth out of the beaten track.
—Nathaniel Hawthorne, *The Blithedale Romance*

I

WHEN, IN 1854, Lillie Devereux's high spirits and flirtatious behavior slammed against mid-nineteenth-century social mores, she had a taste of the price a woman might pay for swerving one hair's breadth out of the beaten track. That beaten track was very well defined by a profusion of etiquette manuals, tracts, and popular forms of literature that identified core beliefs about women, especially their passivity, their vulnerability, and their nurturing nature. "Shouldn't I like to make a bon-fire of all the 'Hints to Young Wives,' 'Married Woman's Friend,' etc., and throw in the authors after them?" commented journalist Fanny Fern at the beginning of her own etiquette tract, entitled, like so many of the others, "Hints to Young Wives."[1] President Woolsey of Yale lectured that "I take it for granted that the female sex has a destination which men perceive though they may not reflect upon; that there is an idea, more or less brought out in the mind, and in the opinion of society, of the sphere, the rights, and the duties of woman."[2] The prevalent use of the singular "woman" in the discussions of women's nature and role in society connoted a univalent view that all women were of a singular character with well-defined attributes. Of course, the very fact that the young women toward whom the tracts and etiquette manuals were directed must be trained in dependency belies its intrinsic quality and points not only to the constructed nature of what was defined as woman's essence but to a generalized cultural anxiety over the proper role and place of women in the rapidly changing era of industrialization.

Middle-class women's acceptable tasks in life were consistently linked to home and hearth and had to do with their caring for others. President Woolsey enumerated the types of worldly activities in which woman can participate: "She can visit the homes of the destitute and forsaken, penetrating where man is excluded, into the miseries of her own sex, and soothing the sorrows of children by the voice of gentleness. She can act as the servant of the Church in many of its plans of benevolence. She can with peculiar success instruct the young. She can compete with man in authorship wherever refined taste and sentiment form the staple of the work and wherever knowledge is to be adapted to the mind of the earlier years of childhood."[3] Despite the rhetoric of Woolsey and others who called upon women to move out of the domestic sphere, their prescriptions for so doing served only to keep women in their proper place by circumscribing and idealizing it. The action of women in the world was to be limited to their moral influence upon others. Any ambition, any yearning for achievement, any strong definition of self was judged to be unfeminine. Dr. John Gregory, in *A Father's Legacy to His Daughters,* widely printed throughout the first half of the nineteenth century, advised "modest reserve" and "retiring delicacy" for women and warned against displaying any quickness of mind, superior knowledge, or even common sense: "Wit is the most dangerous talent you can possess. It must be guarded with great discretion and good nature, otherwise it will create you many enemies. . . . Be even cautious in displaying your good sense. It will be thought you assume a superiority over the rest of the company. But if you happen to have any learning, keep it a profound secret."[4] Not only were women encouraged to be quiet, passive, and languid, but adolescent girls were prescribed frequent periods of bed rest and no excitable activities so that their bodies could begin to accommodate the growth of their reproductive organs, in which, as Harvard Professor of Medicine Edward H. Clarke put it in 1872, "humanity has so large an interest."[5]

The icon of the passive lady of leisure flourished at a time when the middle classes were disassociating themselves from the lower classes and linking the wealthiest among them with their idea of a leisured aristocracy. This was the moment when the ideology of the Revolutionary War collided with the economic facts of the newly industrialized world; ideals of equality easily gave way to a value system based on wealth, which in turn reemphasized class in the classless society. An industrialized nation had replaced the eighteenth-century conglomeration of cottage industries in which women had played important economic roles as producers of goods. But while production moved out of the house into factories, women in the rising middle class remained homebound, their very idleness a mark of their family's status. Gender roles were affirmed and narrowed at a moment in time when they were simply ignored by droves of women in the lower classes who were crucial to the commercial success of the burgeoning textile industries. Thus, while vast numbers of poor women went out to work in mills, for women in the middle and upper classes work outside the home was prohibited. Woman's sphere, modeled upon the prescribed life of the privileged female, was isolated from the world of work. As the historian Gerda Lerner points out in her seminal essay "The Lady and the Mill Girl," by the 1840s American women of the middle classes, having previously enjoyed wide-ranging freedom in occupation and social status, found that active life outside the home was condemned and their proper sphere was "narrower and more confined than ever."[6]

One of the best-selling novels in the United States and England during the nineteenth century was Susan Warner's *The Wide, Wide World*, which, although it bears an 1851 publication date, was out for Christmas in 1850, the year of Lillie Devereux's "coming out" party. *The Wide, Wide World* is filled with lap-sitting. Little Ellen, our heroine, is welcomed into the laps of kindly males frequently enough to disturb many early twenty-first century readers attuned more to issues of pedophilia than to the childlikeness of grown women. The disturbance is justified, for there is a deeply erotic connection in this novel between the innocence of the heroine and her dependence upon men. The energy of the eighteenth-century sentimental novel, which involved the seduction of a confined woman, arose from charged issues of gender and power converging in the eroticism of the trapped female. Nineteenth-century domestic novelists discarded many elements of seduction from the tradition, but they retained the eroticizing of female dependence and submission. In *The Wide, Wide World*, the heroine must learn not only to be submissive, but to desire submission—to find it sexy.

Ellen's education into adulthood is a process of suppressing selfhood for the infantile pleasures of dependency. Bending her will to the demands of male authority is as erotically charged as if she were swept away by one of the mysterious dark strangers of the Gothic tradition. Her submissive posture throughout the novel is indistinguishable from the shy bowing of her head when, stirred, she blushfully listens to the righteous orations of her future husband.

We enter the novel to find Ellen's face "pressed against the window-frame," gazing out at the wide, wide world.[7] Her framed position is one prescribed for every nineteenth-century middle-class woman—confined within the home, powerless. Her one heroic foray out into that wide world—astride a galloping horse, racing for a doctor—is abruptly cut short when she is accosted by an unsavory male. She learns how dangerous the world is for a woman alone. Thereafter, Ellen submits to the protective confinement of her rescuer and husband-to-be, a familiar paradigm which, in our own time, has been termed "the protection racket we sometimes call the 'patriarchy.'"[8]

When we leave the novel, Ellen enters a room of her own, but one not of her own making.[9] Provided for her by her husband, it has access—and egress—only through his private study. Once framed within the windowpane which at least provided a view of the world, Ellen's life is now framed by that of her husband, through whose eyes only she will be allowed to form impressions of the world without. Her private space within her husband's home is a domestic dead end, a second-story cul-de-sac, but one that she finds completely satisfactory. Her rebellious spirit has been subdued, her drive toward independence quelled, her sexuality contained: "'I am satisfied,' said Ellen softly, nestling again to his side;—'that is enough. I want no more.'" She wants no more. Has she been given all that she wants, or has she learned to want no more than what may be given to her? Or perhaps she no longer has the capacity to want at all, her ability to desire having been extinguished. She wants no more; she is ready to hop upon her caretaker's lap and cozily remain there forever.

Who among us has not found it difficult to resist the domestic seduction of that nestling comfort, the lovely carefree ease of it? It is the seduction of every fairytale romance, and it persists whenever women are trained to find dependence sexy. Its regressive nature resonates in the first word of *The Wide, Wide World*—Ellen's cry of "Mama." Lap-sitting transfers the comfort of mother onto that of lover. The nineteenth-century sentimental ethos presumed upon the natural dependence of women and arranged the parameters of middle-class women's lives to meet that presumption. It was into this world that Lillie Devereux Blake was born. More often seen careening around New Haven on her pony than sitting on someone's lap, she still had to struggle against the seductive power of middle-class mores in order to shape a life of her own.

The sexual implications of women astride galloping horses were, for the culture that created both Ellen Montgomery and Lillie Devereux, troubling ones; unleashed female sexuality, projected as dangerous for women, was actually a threat to the well-regulated world of the nineteenth-century middle class. The maturation of girls was a matter of reining in the unrestrained spirit and independent desires of the female. Ellen in *The Wide, Wide World* submits herself to the framing perspective of her husband and the social order for which he stands; Blake, her freedom checked by her own assimilation of the cultural prescriptions of what it meant to be a woman, was still able to "brazen out" New Haven's attempt to render her invisible. However, Blake was not a rebel who could jauntily discard social prescriptions. Hers was the dilemma of a woman struggling to form an individual identity within a culture that had already defined her in carefully prescribed, categorical terms: hers the complicatedly earnest path of self-doubt and struggle.

In contrast to the persistent calls for female passivity, inaction, and subordination that deeply permeated the character and life of countless women, a large body of sensational stories poured off the presses in penny newspapers and cheap pamphlets offering a variety of female figures—not only gentle do-gooders, but spunky adventurers, sensuous sirens, abused wives, exploited seamstresses, con artists, murderers, and more. As David Reynolds points out, the pious, domestic best-sellers like *The Wide, Wide World* "were rhetorical constructs in which the troubled social and philosophical climate of antebellum America was determinedly meliorated and an alternative world of village pastoralism and victorious moral exemplars was offered as mythic correctives for thorny realities such as crime, urbanization, tangled reform movements, and savage frontier life."[10] The cult of domesticity promoted by sentimental novels was in some part a reaction against an urban underworld reflected in seamy adventure stories filled with sex and violence.

By the end of the century, Mary Putnam Jacobi, noted physician and president of the Association for the Advancement of the Medical Education of Women, wrote that women have served as society's "crystal vases," maintaining a "fixed and immovable" standard of behavior, a still point around which the social order may whirl without fear. Because of that, she made clear, "any symptom of change in the status of women seems . . . always to have excited a certain terror."[11] Throughout the period of industrialization, that terror was most often manifested in a need to control female desire; indeed, female sexuality was brought to bear on class differences and was crucial to the development of the idea of the middle class. The sexually contained middle-class woman was seen as essential to the stability and continuity not only of the middle-class family but of the middle class itself.[12]

These were the forces which impinged on the development of Lillie Devereux. Inculcated with the notion that "for a woman there could be only social success, for her there was no arena but that of the drawing room,"[13] Lillie's world was confined to that small space, her ambition channeled into the maintenance of personal beauty, the manipulation of men, and the preservation of reputation. The only failure for a woman in this drawing-room world was rejection by a man; a mark of her brilliance was the accumulation of admirers and offers of marriage. Although Blake lived to grow beyond these narrow signifiers of a woman's worth, they were deeply etched upon her personality, and she often described women in terms of their acceptance by men. Early in her autobiography she would enumerate all the important men who had proposed to her mother, and, of course, after the New Haven scandal, she carefully tallied her own offers of marriage. After her first widowhood, when she was determined not to remarry, she caused friction between herself and other women because of her need to have men fall in love with her. And, later in life, she at least once took delight in having a man half her age fall under her spell.[14]

A year after the 1848 woman's rights convention at Seneca Falls, at which Elizabeth Cady Stanton's *Declaration of Sentiments* was presented, sixteen-year-old Lillie Devereux wrote a propitiously titled document: "I live to redress the wrongs of my sex." However, the text illustrates how Blake's impulse toward rebellion was already circumscribed by the narrow confines of her drawing-room world, for it is merely a sixteen-year-old coquette's oratory:

> Women have been from time immemorial duped and deserted by men, their feelings trifled with, their hearts broken. This shameful injustice I have determined to redress. I will devote to it youth, beauty, life; I will forget myself and my own feelings in avenging on men their faithlessness. For this their hearts must be interested and then trifled with; therefore I give myself heart and soul to making men miserable. If they love me, I will refuse them, no matter how much I may be interested. I will live but to redress these terrible wrongs.[15]

Lillie's sense of wrongs needing redress is crimped into courtship games, "the only mode of redress which seemed open to me," she wrote in her autobiography. "If I had been shown any goal which I should win, how I would have toiled for it! but no, I was warned that for a woman there could be only social success. . . . What wonder then that I resolved to reign queen in the only realm open to me."[16] Only after she extracted herself from the circumscribed orbit the world had prescribed for her, would she live up to the self asserted in that early title, "I live to redress the wrongs of my sex."

On February 22, 1847, when Lillie was thirteen, a visitor to Maple Cottage gave her a journal, the first of many which she would keep for the rest of her life. In that first diary, she records her music and French lessons, her games of chess, her reading of Washington Irving's *Columbus* and Merle d'Aubigné's just published *History of the Great Reformation*, along with sledding, flying kites, hiding in closets with her friends, and the "good snowballing" she gives classmates.[17] She pursued everything she loved with a fierce eagerness; she loved learning and was a fine student; she loved riding her pony and would race around New Haven on Jenny's back; she loved storytelling and would induce nightmares in her cousins with extravagant tales. From her boy cousins, who would converge at Christmas and during the summers, she learned to play cards, fire a pistol, and sneak cigarettes: "A good deal of horse and dog lore I obtained from them, also, and I even went so far sometimes, when the air about us was thick with tobacco smoke, as to venture on a cigarette to keep them company."[18]

This last detail was shocking enough for Blake's daughter, Katherine Devereux Blake, to single it out from her mother's list of escapades and to omit it from her biography of Blake, published in 1943. The omission points to ways in which we might reconstruct the values of a person and of an era through the documents we fall heir to. Along with her fiction and essays, we have four texts which give Blake's, or her family's, perspective on her life: her extant diaries; a typescript of many of the diaries, some extant, but some now lost, compiled by her daughter; an autobiography in draft form which she began in 1873; and her daughter's biography of 1943.

Each text implies motives and establishes a self in relation to a readership, and each is subject to the revisions of a subsequent text. My approach has been to unravel differences in these representations by comparing the texts for gaps, silences, and instances of censorship in order to reconstruct values underlying the life. Katherine Blake's simple omission of incidents of smoking indicates both the degree of perceived impropriety in a lady's smoking and her determination to present her mother in the best possible light to a readership which presumably shares her perception of that impropriety. The omission reveals that Katherine valued the social mores of the status quo more than a rebellion against them. It would seem that Blake taught her daughter well the hard lesson she herself had learned in New Haven. While less careful than Katherine in censoring all mention of unacceptable behavior, Blake, too, is careful to locate herself within the parameters of appropriate conduct. She qualifies her admission of smoking with a reassertion of social approbation: "These dissipations were not, however, of very frequent occurrence as I only saw my cousins at Christmas or for a few weeks in summer."[19] Blake's impulse was to pull back from the appearance of defiant behavior and recenter herself within the status quo. She displays a need to be acceptable—a need she would struggle with her entire life, and a need that was formed in the city which, as late as the end of the twentieth century, knew her as a lady of the night.

Instead of suppressing any mention of presumably offensive behavior, both Blake and her daughter might have reveled in it. That certainly was the attitude taken by Blake's predecessor, the satiric columnist Fanny Fern, born almost a generation earlier. Her childhood pranks were relished, at least in retrospect, as part of the persona of the outspokenly independent Sara Willis, who used her waywardness for comic effect throughout her career. Fern saved letters containing reminiscences of her rebelliousness; one from Harriet Beecher Stowe, for instance, recalled their school days filled with "the many scrapes which occasioned for you secret confabulations with [headmistress] sister Katie up in her room."[20] Fern's brother, N. P. Willis, published a poem in the *Galaxy* titled "To My Wild Sis," and in his memoir of Fern, her third husband, the biographer James Parton, provided numerous examples of her girlhood insubordination. But, however much Fern's youthful escapades were celebrated, she was not supported by her family in her unconventional decision to divorce her abusive second husband, whom her family had pushed her to marry after her first husband had died. Her brother, probably, as a later biographer suggests, unwilling "to tarnish his social standing by becoming associated with her," ruthlessly refused to help launch her writing career when she was in dire financial need.[21] She responded by throwing "To My Wild Sis" into the fire, but then, on second thought, snatched it out. It remains with her papers in the Sophia Smith Collection at Smith College, a charred token of how much she valued her own wildness. Throughout her journalistic career, Fanny Fern countered custom and framed herself as a rebel, although she often expressed conventional views on women and upheld sentimental ideology.[22] Lillie Blake, on the other hand, who would go on to develop radical views on gender issues, always presented herself as a nice, middle-class lady.

From the vantage point of middle age, Blake reminisced how as an adolescent she would race her horse

madly through the streets, urging him until men would rush out to stop what they thought was a runaway steed. I would dance later and longer than anyone else. My laugh rang loudest in any scene of gayety and I would outswim and outwalk any girl of my acquaintance, but I shrank with absolute horror from anything that could be called "fast," and I held my womanhood sacred. Whatever of wrong there was in me arose I now know from the false system of repression under which I was brought up. The warm vitality which urged me into folly might have found a safer vent in work. I was ambitious, but like a barrier across my path stood the words, "You are only a woman!"[23]

Blake had energy, ambition, and an independent streak as well as a strongly developed sense of social decorum. One way her society restricted women's behavior was to blur the lines between female assertion, which was discouraged, and sexual freedom, which was forbidden. For instance, for asserting herself and divorcing her second husband, Fanny Fern was hounded for the rest of her life by innuendoes about her sexual activities. From childhood on, Blake resisted the passivity prescribed for her, but, as we see in this passage, she felt the need to qualify her list of high-spirited activities with a profession of her sexual innocence—she was not "fast"; she held "her womanhood" sacred. The notion of the sanctity of womanhood was an effective tool to control behavior; few women wanted to endure the persistent social marginalization that Fanny Fern had endured or even the months of anguish which Lillie Devereux suffered in 1854. But the emptiness of woman's canonization is made clear with the paired expression, "You are only a woman." If the threat of being perceived as "fast" curtailed a young woman's vitality, the admonition "You are only a woman" made sure that her spirit would find no other release.

The conflicts between Blake's carefree, tomboyish behavior and the social restrictions placed on middle-class women began when she reached adolescence. The winter that saw the publication of *The Wide, Wide World* was the winter of Lillie's "coming out" party, and thereafter this girl, who with her male pals had built dams across streams in the woods and hiked over the crackling ice of half-frozen ponds, could not, unchaperoned, even take a walk with a boy. Her exuberant first diary, teeming with details of daily life and full of feeling even over small incidents, as when the cow escaped its barn and, to

Lillie's extreme mortification, Mayor Skinner had to drive it back in, becomes, in her second extant diary, a mere series of notations, unelaborated even for events of magnitude: "Jan. 7. My fiancée [*sic*] arrived. . . . April 2. I broke my engagement."

What happened to that passionate little girl, so full of self-expression? The exuberant, independent Lillie Devereux seems to have grown into a silence concomitant with the lessons learned from nineteenth-century domestic novels and etiquette manuals and later underscored by her own brush with scandal. In her autobiography, among the accounts of her social activities in New Haven, Newport, Saratoga Springs, and other social spots, Blake presents two anecdotes that contour her girlhood and give us a glimpse of the personality which could both absorb and resist the restrictive attitudes of the times. They speak of her daring and her endurance, attributes which she saw and valued in herself and which would become keynotes of her character, freeing her finally from the restrictive grasp of small-town gossip and the confines of woman's space. Doubling their importance, elements of both stories were incorporated into her first published work. Blake tells us that once she was out riding with friends on Hillhouse Avenue when her pony stumbled and rolled over:

> We were racing our horses and I was thrown with great violence, striking on my right shoulder. I got up at once and though I was in great pain, said I would remount my horse and ride home, but when I tried to mount, my right arm fell powerless at my side. . . . The young gentleman immediately rode back to get a conveyance for me, and Mattie and I sat on a big stone by the wayside waiting. . . . I was lifted into the chaise . . . and driven home. Poor Mother ran out to meet me in great alarm. Dr. Knight was summoned and found that my collar bone was broken. I suffered a good deal but I uttered no cry nor did I faint when the bone was set.[24]

Blake swerves from the anticipated behavior of a mid-nineteenth-century lady for whom fainting fits were part of the standard flirting repertoire. How better to convince a young man of one's submissive nature than to be not just passively languid, but quite out cold? How better to inspire rescue than to be totally helpless? As the Reverend James Fordyce put it in *Sermons to Young Women,* which was widely read in the early nineteenth century, a woman "was to be delicately sickly so as to arouse a man's protective nature."[25] What

Sandra Gilbert and Susan Gubar have called the nineteenth-century "aesthetic cult of ladylike fragility" was often induced by "tight-lacing, fasting, vinegar-drinking."[26] With all these artificial inducements to fainting, what a missed opportunity not to swoon when one's collarbone is being set.

But Blake's survival instincts did not depend upon manipulative cries for rescue. Although considerations of beauty and attractiveness to men are of clear value to her in her second anecdote, she demonstrates her resourcefulness and her ability to save herself:

> During my visit to Raleigh two years before my marriage, I was, one evening, dressing for a party when the lace ruffle around my shoulders caught fire from a candle which stood on the toilette table. My neck and arms were bare and the pain of the burns was at once intense. It was a warm June evening, my dress was of pink organdie and the window and door of my room were both wide open. I did not lose my presence of mind as so many unhappy ones had done under similar circumstances. Realizing that if I stepped into the draft between the window and the door, my fate would inevitably be sealed, I neither ran nor screamed. My first attempt to extinguish the fire was by pressing over it a thick handkerchief which lay on the table. It was useless, the flame curled up all around my hand. That was one of the most agonizing moments of my life, and I own that the cruelest pang I suffered was the dread of possible disfigurement. I thought, in another moment my curls would catch fire and all the beauty that has been so admired would be lost to me. I gave one despairing glance around the room. I could not even reach the bed without stepping into the draft and the bed had only a white cotton spread over it. Beside me a heavy table stood on a bit of carpet before the fire-place. I dropped on my knees, upsetting the table, pulled out the rug and wrapped it around me, extinguishing the flame. Then for the first time I called for help.[27]

Lillie Devereux so loved her own bravery that she has her first fictional hero fall in love with a woman because she saves herself in just this way. While her heroine tries to "suppress the cries which I feared the agony I endured might wring from me," it is her hero who responds in a stereotypically female way: with "a deep groan," he clasps his hands and turns "pale as marble."[28]

At first glance, "My Last Conquest," published in *Harper's Weekly* in November 1857, seems like so many stories of the period in which a woman sets a strategy for letting a man win her in marriage. But with a very self-conscious look at the social demands placed on women's behavior, Blake's tale combines the conventions of courtship narratives with a twist on gender stereotypes. The story reveals much about both the expectations for middle-class women in mid-nineteenth-century America and Lillie Blake's struggle with those expectations. In most courtship narratives, the vulnerability of a woman wins her the love of a courageous man. A woman's timidity, frailty, and helplessness supposedly attracted the opposing traits in a man; but in Blake's version, the man is conquered by the woman's courage.[29] Laura Duncan, who shares her author's initials, is introduced, like many of Blake's brave and intelligent heroines, as bored and restless, listlessly reading novels after the distractions of the social season. Well aware of the expectation that she marry, Laura finds the idea of accepting any of her many avid suitors "horrid!" But, while visiting her old friend Ella Ringwood, Laura meets Ella's rather disdainful, and therefore challenging, cousin, Henry.

Laura Duncan acts out with perfection the roles assigned to women. Blake uses not only military metaphors to turn the drawing room into a battleground between the sexes[30] but also stage metaphors to imply that prescribed feminine behavior is all an act. Blake was as bored as Laura with the limited roles available to her and looks to the male arena, signified by the battleground, as a space large enough to accommodate her. Laura's goal is to conquer, not to be conquered, and her strategy is a matter of shifting roles and donning new disguises. She decides to discover what Henry "*does* admire in a woman" and recast herself. Because flirting holds no appeal for him, she "laid aside all of the 'dashing belle,' and took up so much of the timid woman as almost to make me seem as simple a country-girl as Ella herself."[31] When a train approaches their carriage, Ella, sick with fright that their horse may bolt, bolts herself, leaping out of the carriage and running away in abject terror. The horse, on the other hand, "stood quite unmoved." Blake's autobiographical anecdote about her own bravery when thrown from her horse stands in contrast here to the behavior presumed typical of a woman facing the possibility of a dangerous situation. According to the advice books, Henry's "protective male nature" should be aroused by such timidity, but he finds Ella's behavior foolish; it confirms his belief that women lack courage. Laura begins to understand the connection between behavior sanctioned as feminine and the underlying disdain that leads men to see women, as Henry does, "as mere playthings." While Blake works within the confines of conventional assumptions about the value of male approval, she exposes timidity and vulnerability, traits encouraged in women, as leading only to their disparagement.

Unlike Ella, Laura is unafraid of the thought of bolting horses and discovers that it is her innate courage and self-assurance that will finally conquer Henry. By having Laura's fearlessness, rather than any vulnerability, radiate through her role-playing exterior, her author questions sentimental notions of womanhood. Blake swerves from the sentimental ideal of "transparency" whereby the goodness and simple innocence within a "true woman" shines through to her exterior manner.[32] She complicates the ideal of the transparent female, whose personal sincerity is set against deception and calculation, for Laura, who has the intelligence to see through the parameters of the courtship game and is "fully determined on his conquest," must look for ways to make the truth of her real character obvious to Henry. In the very act of devising strategy, even if in the interests of her "true" character, Laura takes on shades of the coldly calculating females of the sentimental tradition, which often pitched angelic, vulnerable, child-women against shrewd, ambitious bitches.

While the sentimental model held up the guileless woman as ideal, Blake reveals guilelessness itself to be a learned role in a patriarchal script that suppresses women by emptying them of their own desires and ambition. Laura Duncan stands in contrast to Ellen Montgomery of *The Wide, Wide World*. Laura asserts her needs and pursues her goals with candid ambition, while Ellen learns to suppress her desires and submit to male authority. Ellen's success in learning her proper role in life is equivalent, as Jane Tompkins has put it, to "the extinction of her personality."[33] However, at the point where Laura's strategy concludes successfully, she becomes just as vulnerable as Ellen to the erasure of her own self: Henry Ringwold "claims" her as his own. Not only is Blake's story, literally, over; so is Laura's. The endpoint of all successful courtship strategy and the conclusion of most nineteenth-century fiction—marriage—was, for even the most ambitious of nineteenth-century heroines, a return to dependency and an erasure of self. Augusta Jane Evans's 1867 novel *St. Elmo* makes this fact clear. Despite the accomplishments, independence, and devotion to her art of its protagonist, an acclaimed novelist named Edna Earl, when Edna marries, her husband declares, "There shall be no more books written! . . . You belong solely to me now."[34] Marriage for nineteenth-century characters and for their authors, for women like Laura Duncan or Lillie Devereux, meant the end of their ability to plot lives of their own.

II

Blake was engaged twice before she married Frank Umsted in 1855. Prior to her brief engagement to William Barnes during the winter of 1853–54, which her mother never officially acknowledged, she was engaged, at seventeen, in 1850, to Henry Lord Page King, a student at Yale whose family owned cotton plantations on the Sea Islands off the coast of Georgia. Her diary, quoted by her daughter but no longer in existence, might have given us insights into her reasons for breaking this early engagement. She reminisces in her autobiography that "I was fond of him and perhaps should have married him but that the engagement was broken by the slanders of a politician who hated his father. Henry blamed me, and with justice, for if the bond had not already irked I should not have listened to stories to his disadvantage."[35] Her daughter speculates that while on a trip with her mother to visit Henry's family, Lillie began to seriously consider the implications of living in the deep South in plantation society, a prospect not at all appealing to a young girl raised amid abolitionists in New Haven's Hillhouse neighborhood.

Henry King remained a close friend and renewed his suit when Lillie was widowed. In November 1860, when he visited to say good-bye before returning home to join the Rebel army, she laughed and said in jest, "'To find a bloody grave?' 'Very likely I shall,' he replied solemnly."[36] She never saw him again. On December 13, 1862, he died on the battlefield at Fredericksburg. Henry is memorialized in Blake's May 1863 story "Shot Through the Heart. A Tragedy of Fredericksburgh." Her title sardonically conflates the injuries of war and love: Henry Carlyon is pierced through the heart first by his unrequited love and then, fatally, in battle.[37] In her diary, Lillie wrote, "Pierced by five bullets that heart that never beat for any woman but me . . . My friend, my lover is gone! . . . I know that my coldness embittered. . . . Now he is gone and what is the wreath of fame worth? Thorns and briars to the touch and ashes under the feet. The smile of one true man, the companionship of one beloved friend is better than all the empty honors of gratified ambition!"[38] It seems that she bore Henry King the same regretful love that her protagonist, Kate, bears Henry Carlyon. In "My Last Conquest," "Shot Through the Heart," and frequently thereafter, Blake's chief male characters are named Henry.

One of the five offers of marriage which were made to Blake in the wake of William Barnes's libelous tale came from Frank Umsted, a Philadelphia lawyer whom she had met the previous March while on her journey to her southern relatives. He traveled to New Haven in January 1855, and after two visits they were engaged. Her mother must have felt that the best ending to the previous fall's scandal was confirmation in the church and a proper marriage. Lillie was confirmed on May 20, 1855, and married on June 20.[39] Later, with a painful honesty, Blake would write that their marriage "had been on my part the result rather of circumstances than of that strong and passionate love which alone should unite two beings, but his devotion to me amounted almost to adoration and I felt for him very sincere and tender affection."[40] It was inevitable that Lillie's attempts to avoid entanglements and reign as queen of the drawing room would end. She was almost twenty-two.

Lillie was married in Maple Cottage, and after a wedding trip she and Frank returned to New Haven for a week and then headed west. Blake's mother and sister accompanied them for part of the journey into New York State. When they parted, Lillie wept her way through Niagara and across Lake Erie. Her tremendous grief over leaving her home and her mother was compounded the following year when her mother sold Maple Cottage. Her childhood had been a period of relative freedom and independence, and she left it with great reluctance. It seems that she had in Frank a kind and thoughtful companion, but the nature of a nineteenth-century marriage forced Blake to suppress those ambitious impulses which she, like her alter ego Laura Duncan in "My Last Conquest," had diverted into courtship games. Beyond the conclusions of women's stories lay a vague and content-less "ever after." And now the game was over; the conquest made; the long and undefined "ever after" had commenced.

The couple's aimlessness as they drifted westward—to Detroit, Chicago, St. Louis—felt like adventure and thus distracted Blake for a time from her yearning for some larger purpose in life. After a brief trip to Kentucky, the Umsteds returned to St. Louis to settle down. For several months they lived in the Planter's Hotel and then the Washington Hotel, before furnishing a house on Pine Street in the spring of 1856. Lillie's mother and sister spent the winter with them, and in the summer she and Frank traveled to see their families in Philadelphia and Connecticut.

By law, when Lillie married, almost all her money, which was the considerable fortune of between $50,000 and $100,000 that had been settled upon her by her paternal grandmother, became the property of her husband, and it was spent most freely during their first two years together. Only after fifteen months, in the fall of 1856, did Frank try to establish himself as a lawyer in

St. Louis, but with their traveling back to the East Coast in the summers and the easy access to Lillie's money to blunt ambition, he achieved limited success. Lillie later learned that a large portion of her estate was lost in the financial panic of 1857, but whenever she asked just how money matters stood, Frank would refuse to discuss the subject with her. It was the only topic over which they quarreled, and it highlighted the restrictions placed upon her as a married woman. Legally a wife had no existence independent of her husband, who, in fact, had ownership not only of her money but of her body, her children, her wages, any gifts that might be given to her, and the proceeds of any books that she might write.[41] When she married, Lillie had lost control over both the aim and the details of her life.

Nothing made Blake's inability to direct her own life more clear to her than her two pregnancies. In good Victorian style she never mentions them overtly, but, by counting back from the births of her children, we find that both are signaled by the words, "I was not well." Distancing herself from the acceptable cant of the day, Blake never idealized maternity. Pregnancy was a physical event that she experienced as illness and confinement. It forced the fact of her biology upon her and underscored the social restraints already existing for her. The winter of 1856–57, she writes, "dragged slowly by. I was not well and the forced inaction of my life was intolerable to me. For hours I would lie on the sofa or bed, reading or thinking, and my heart was often full of fierce rebellion against the fate that had imprisoned a spirit full of restless activity in a woman's form and condemned it to stagnation."[42] Pregnant again the following year, Blake wrote, "In every respect this was a very unhappy winter to me. . . . I was again not well and my old restless craving for something beyond my present life was strong upon me."[43] She rails against a confinement in which her own body is complicit. Both her pregnancies brought home the dissonance between her ambitious nature and the restrictive codes placed on her life. Each pregnancy constituted a crisis in which her need to transform her life struggled against a despair that she might not be able to do so.

Blake's response to the birth of her first child, Elizabeth Johnson Devereux Umsted, in February 1857, reveals the depth of her feelings about what it meant to be born female: "When they told me that it was a girl, I almost felt as if I could not see it. Had I brought into the world another being destined to live always under the curse of her sex? a creature that like me was to eat out its heart with longing that would never be satisfied because it was a woman?"[44] Her response was not uncommon; the mother of suffragist Lucy Stone is recorded as having responded to the birth of her daughter by sighing, "I am sorry it is a girl. A woman's lot is so hard."[45] A little more than a year earlier, however, Elizabeth Cady Stanton had given birth to her daughter Harriot and had written with joy to Susan B. Anthony: "Dear Friend: Well, another female child is born into the world! Last Sunday afternoon, Harriot Eaton Stanton—oh! the little heretic thus to desecrate that holy holiday—opened her soft blue eyes on this mundane sphere."[46] It would be more than ten years before Blake's path would cross that of Elizabeth Cady Stanton. In the context of the woman's movement and in a community of like-thinkers, Blake's radical instincts would finally lead her out of despair to the hope that springs from rebellion. But until then, Blake fully comprehended that she was supposed to be happy and she anguished over the fact that she was not:

> To some women perhaps, my present position would have been such as to satisfy them entirely. I had a devoted and most adoring husband, a lovely baby, a happy home, and hosts of friends. Why could I not employ my leisure time in worsted work and be satisfied. I did try it and I have now complicated embroidered devices with which I endeavored to amuse myself, but it is not enough. Why should it be to a woman anymore than to a man. I was twenty-four years old and yet I was told in the cant of the day that my life was over and I ought to live in my children. Tell any man of my age such folly as this and he would laugh it to scorn. He would say he loved his home and his family as much as anyone but his life instead of being over was but just begun. If you bade him solice [sic] his asperations [sic] with worsted work he would treat the proposition with derision. I cannot see why my feelings should not be identical with his. I too loved my child and my home, but the little duties of a fashionable lady's life were not enough for me. I was restless and often unhappy and I longed for change in the vague hope that in a new place I should find the happiness that had thus far escaped me.[47]

After the summer of 1857, Lillie and Frank decided to move to New York City. Lillie remained with her baby at her mother's new home, Elm Cottage, built on a portion of her family's property in Stratford, where they had spent much of the summer. Frank returned to St. Louis where, in the midst of a national financial panic, he sold their furniture and lease and closed his little-used office there to open another on Wall Street. Late in the year, he rented a large, fully furnished house on Lexington Avenue close to Gramercy Park.

Here, with Bessie less than a year old and pregnant with Katie, Blake wrote "A Tragedy of the Mammoth Cave," a story that would appear anonymously in the *Knickerbocker* in February 1858, and its companion piece, "Despair," a poem also published anonymously there three months later.[48]

"A Tragedy of the Mammoth Cave" was inspired by a trip Lillie and Frank took to Mammoth Cave shortly before they returned west to settle in St. Louis. They traveled by train from St. Louis to Cairo, Illinois, boarded a steamer to Louisville, Kentucky, and then journeyed eighty-five miles by stagecoach to the cave. Later, in the 1870s, this trip would become both easier, because the railroad came within ten miles of the cave, and more dangerous, because the stagecoach became the target of bandits including, most famously, Jesse James. Most probably Blake was guided into the cave by Materson Bransford, known as Mat, a slave leased by his owner to work at Mammoth Cave. Self-taught and knowledgeable about geology, cave formation, and Indian lore, Mat fathered generations of knowledgeable cave guides. The trip within the cave would take at least four hours and involve a descent of over three hundred feet.[49] "Three times," Blake writes, "Frank and I went into the Cave and the impression which its intense shadows, its fantastic rocks, its mysterious black darkness made on me was deep and lasting."[50]

Blake was not the only writer to brave the hardships of the journey both to and within Mammoth Cave and to be struck by its majestic caverns. Emerson used his experience there to introduce his 1860 discussion of illusions in "The Conduct of Life:" "I saw high domes and bottomless pits; heard the voice of unseen waterfalls; paddled three quarters of a mile in the deep Echo River, whose waters are peopled with the blind fish; crossed the streams 'Lethe' and 'Styx.'"[51] Dickens came, too, during his U.S. tour of 1860, grumbling about "how we bounced, and bumped, and tilted, and groaned, as we were dislocated over the deep rutted road . . . I feel as Dante should have felt when he began his gloomy journey. . . . A scramble down the bank and we are under the archway of the cave—a place to dream of—a place for Lazarus to have emerged from into sunshine, his face first paling out through the darkness—a grave for Rembrandt to study in—a den for Michael Angelo's giants—a place whence the Deluge might have risen over the earth."[52]

Blake's narrator in "A Tragedy of the Mammoth Cave" remembers, fifteen years after the action of the story, how she would retreat deep within the underground chambers to meditate on her overwhelming desire for her Yankee tutor: "feverish and excited, under the magnificent domes and low-bending arches . . . I reached the first river; there I climbed to an overhanging rock and seated myself beside that inky stream, whose mysterious source and outlet are alike unknown. . . . I sat there all day long, listening to the low murmur of the waves, and thinking fearfully of the great love that I felt welling up in my heart."[53] Like the subterranean corridors of the Mammoth Cave which run below her father's plantation, covert longings course beneath Melissa's haughty southern exterior. Finally, "the wild tornado of passion swept down every barrier that stood between me and the attainment of his love."

Blake, who complained that "I was twenty-four years old and yet I was told in the cant of the day that my life was over," creates a narrator who cannot be more than thirty when she looks back at her early life but seems much older, "tottering on the brink of the grave," her life over. Not unlike Blake, the Melissa of fifteen years past is "proud, headstrong, and self-willed"—traits the nineteenth century sought to expunge from its females. Acting upon her desire, she is rejected. Her tutor, William Beverleigh, well aware of her courageous nature, prefers a "fair, frail thing." He is reminiscent of Hollingsworth in Hawthorne's *Blithedale Romance,* who prefers Priscilla's "little puny weakness" rather than the "passionate warmth" and "proud, intellectual sympathy" of Zenobia.[54] But while Zenobia turns her anger inward and drowns herself, Blake's Melissa takes revenge. Months after the rejection, her tutor is left on the banks of the underground Echo River when the rest of his party is ferried the three-quarters of a mile back toward the cave entrance. Melissa appears and leads him along a treacherous path called Purgatory, which runs parallel to the river. She abandons him there without light, hoping to terrify him and expose his cowardice. Perhaps Blake's unexpressed rage against the cowardly William Barnes helped to energize Melissa's revenge against William Beverleigh, who never emerges from the Mammoth Cave. For fifteen years, Melissa guiltily hides a crime that she considers to be an act of murder. Now, as a final expiation, she plans to entomb herself in the cave: "The gloom and horror to which, years ago, I doomed my victim, shall be around me when I die . . . perhaps from amid the silent rocks which witnessed my crime, my last prayer for forgiveness will find acceptance."

Blake's poem "Despair" also alludes to a "fierce revenge . . . wrought / Upon my lover." However, its first verse in particular clearly reflects the despair Lillie felt the winter she wrote it, unhappy "in every respect": "Mournfully, silently, falls the snow / Through the still and wintry air, / And in my heart a voice of wo / Ever whispers, Despair, despair!"[55] In both "A Tragedy of the Mammoth Cave" and "Despair," Blake undermines the cultural stereo-types of feminine frailty and purity by insisting that women share in the hu-man capacity for desire and violence and even murderous rage.[56] The emo-tions she treats in these two pieces—intimations of death, desire which has no sanctioned outlet, and frustration turned to revenge—reflect her per-sonal turmoil as she battled to contain her ambition and submit her life to the script prescribed for a married woman. Saturated as Blake was with the so-cial ideology of woman's sphere, her guilt over not fitting into the scenarios prescribed for her life haunted her early works. Unlike Ellen Montgomery in *The Wide, Wide World,* who learned to "want no more," Blake always wanted more; her desires were never extinguished by her restrictive circumstances. Her furious and vengeful women serve her much as the haunted madwomen of other nineteenth-century women authors served them: as Gilbert and Gubar put it, these authors "constructed the emblematic figure of an enraged but tormented madwoman in order simultaneously to repress and express their feelings of anger."[57]

III

The conflicts with which Blake struggled are tellingly revealed in the se-quence of chapter titles of the first part of her autobiography. Following the prescribed bourgeois life cycle, they move from "Ancestral" and "Mother and Father" through "Infancy," "Childhood," "Girlhood," and "Young Lady Life" to "Motherhood," whereupon the predictable order ends. Significantly, Blake positions her marriage not at the beginning of a new chapter in her life, but at the conclusion of "Young Lady Life." Her story, the story of every middle-class young woman prepped for finding a husband, was over the moment she married, when she became the adjunct of another's life, a supporting player in the plot of his story, not hers. As if to signal that her story was no longer her own, immediately after she married and until her first child was born, Blake stopped writing and gave up her journal.

"Motherhood" is one of the most intriguing chapters in Blake's autobiog-raphy because it does not seem to be about becoming a mother at all. While it mentions the births of her two daughters, it is taken up with her traveling, her restlessness, and her melancholia. She tells us that she was obliged to have her babies wet-nursed, and thus was "very free" of their care. Her greatest en-thusiasm is reserved for her first publication. She had sent "My Last Conquest" in secret to *Harpers' Weekly*, vowing that if it were rejected she would give up her dream of being published. Hearing nothing from the editor, she assumed the story had been rejected, until, one day in November 1857, she opened her copy of *Harpers* and found her story printed anonymously. Her amazement and joy at looking down and seeing, not her baby, but her title "staring me in the face" is the galvanizing event of "Motherhood."[58]

Blake attempts to counteract the clear impression of her discontent evident throughout this chapter of her autobiography by assuring her reader that "it must not be supposed that I was during this time a mournful and discontented person going about with pale face and dull eyes. I was on the contrary always of an extremely lively and cheerful disposition, fond of a joke, with a great deal of humor; in short, a laughter-loving woman in the very prime of blooming youth."[59] It seems that she had learned well Lydia Sigourney's lesson that "a cheerful demeanour is particularly expected *young ladies*."[60] Her daughter states, even more insistently than the mother, that Lillie's happiness was complete except that she needed more of an object in life: "Lillie's autobiography for this time gives a clear picture, both of her marital happiness, and of the recurring sense of dissatisfaction and frustration that all her life drove her on to new efforts and new successes."[61] Only when we read the interstices, however, the little cracks and crannies between the expectations set up in the title of "Motherhood" and what is actually delivered, can we truly gauge the upheaval that this chapter represented in Blake's life. Reading between its lines, we can see Blake's struggle to minimize one story and to conceal another. She minimizes the fact that, like the title of the only poem she produced during this period, she is a woman not just needing "more in life," but one who is enraged by the confinement of a woman's life and who is often in despair. In addition, she conceals, perhaps from herself as much as from her reader, the truth about her husband, who, she tells us, is kind and patient and loving. But we can deduce from the details of their life together that, in addition to those fine qualities, he lacks ambition, spends money needlessly by setting up offices in which he does little work, and does not manage his wife's fortune well at all. After moving to the house near Gramercy Park, Blake, aware that their expenses must be very high, reports that she "practiced the strictest economy. Our table was very frugal and my own dress was as simple as possible."[62] Unfortunately, they were forced to give up the house within half a year and take rooms at a hotel. Although the move must have signified a crisis in the Umsted's personal finances, in her autobiography

Lillie passes over it without comment, while in her biography Katherine Blake suppresses all mention of the move by deleting the first part of her mother's account: Blake writes, "On the first day of May we gave up our house and went to room at the Union Place Hotel; there the summer slowly deepened, life passing to me almost like a drowsy dream, and on the tenth of July my second child was born." Her daughter's edited account reads, "'The summer deepened, passing for me almost like a drowsy dream, and on July 10, 1859, my second child was born.'"[63] It was in the hotel that Lillie gave birth to her second daughter and future biographer, Katherine Muhlenbergh Devereux.

While becoming a mother was assumed to be the event that would complete a young woman's surrender of self for a life focused on others, for Blake it was the catalyst for her work to begin. After the birth of Bessie, she had "tried to stifle the cravings of my soul with the mere frivolities of fashionable life," but she was not able to do so.[64] After Katie was born, she was even more resolved to have, as she put it, "an object in life." She was determined to "carve out my destiny; I will make for myself a place in literature; I will write a book."[65] Motherhood enabled Blake to find herself, but not in the way the nineteenth-century patriarchy would have predicted. Through the crises of her pregnancies, Lillie Blake became a mother to herself, giving birth to an independent woman and a writer.

IV

"It seems strange," Blake's daughter remarked in sincere puzzlement and without mention of her own place in her mother's life, "that the theme of the mother and child had so small a place in her narrations, as her love for her mother was a deep and rich emotion throughout her life."[66] The nineteenth century's sentimental ethos was epitomized by self-sacrificing maternal devotion. Venerating motherhood and defining women through it were the most important ways to contain females within a fixed domestic order, erasing independence and self-assertion. Domestic novelists often conveyed the clear cultural message that only motherhood could fulfill a woman; motherhood solved their heroines' ennui and gave purpose to their sacrifice of self. Motherhood was "the fairest success of a woman's life," wrote Louisa May Alcott in her first novel, *Moods*, published in 1864.[67] Fanny Fern, whose stock in trade was the rupturing of cultural rubrics, wrote about mothers with unabashed sentiment: "a mother's reward is in secret and in silence. . . . I am the center [of my child's] little world; its very life depends upon my faithful care."[68] *Godey's Lady's Book,* famous throughout the nineteenth century for its steel-engraved "fashion plates," produced numerous images of secular Madonnas ministering to their children.[69] Sermons were preached on the sanctity of motherhood: when in 1883 the Reverend Morgan Dix, rector of Trinity Church in New York City, declared that womankind redeemed the sin of Eve through the glory of maternity, he voiced the pervasive dogma of the nineteenth century.[70] "By the 1840s," writes historian George B. Forgie, "the domestic 'sphere' (as it was everywhere known) was competing with, and then in the 1850s surpassing, 'nature' as the locus of paradise on earth":

> As early, indeed, as 1839, George Frederic Simmons denied that "any appearances of nature are more exciting to the imagination, or gratifying to the taste than the choice scenes of domestic life." Nature began to lose its paradisiacal image as it gradually lost its association with maternal love. As nature seemed progressively less nurturing and less gentle— "careless of the single life" as [Charles Eliot Norton] put it—its symbolic role of mother was assumed by the home, which, at least ideally, could be counted on always to provide shelter and security as though it were an extension of the embracing presence of the figure who dominated it.[71]

So insistent was the ideology of motherhood that the popular imagination engaged in revisions of any representation that undermined it. For example, even Medea, a mother of mythically demonic proportions, was transformed by mid-century popular culture into a persecuted figure who murdered only to save her children from a worse fate. During her 1866 American tour, the Italian actress Adelaide Ristori played Medea in a performance in which "the demonic implications of the narrative were blunted to the point of unrecognizability. Rather than an unnatural mother . . . [she] is a devoted mother. She kills her children from an *excess* of maternal devotion."[72] Ristori inspired the marble *Medea* produced in 1866 by William Wetmore Story, whom Hawthorne made legendary by describing his *Cleopatra* in *The Marble Faun.* Story had a knack for transforming even the most ominous of women into frail, delicate creatures. Appealing to audiences that repeatedly reinscribed the ideals of "true womanhood" into whatever female image they gazed upon, Story, like other artists of the period, "alluded to female demonism only to domesticate it."[73]

Blake, on the other hand, in 1883 publicly ridiculed the Reverend Morgan Dix's declarations on the redemptive qualities of maternity:

> If from the easy chair of his study he dimly discerns the forms of women madly struggling in the great river of life, striving vainly for bread, for honest living, he says to them, Peace, retirement, these are women's happiness. If he sees a wretched mother shuddering on the brink of the river, and clasping to her breast a miserable baby that is her shame and her disgrace, to her he says, "Maternity is your highest function!" If he hears penetrating even through his curtained windows the voices of women who cry and plead for better opportunities for their sex, he bids them be silent; meekness, forbearance, patience are the virtues which most adorn womanhood.
>
> Ah, he is himself too late, this respectable relic of the middle ages! The chariot of progress is moving on. At its front sits awakened womanhood with the glory of hope in her starry eyes, and not even the Rector of Trinity Church is strong enough to block the wheels of that triumphant car![74]

Aware as she was of the struggles of mothers seeking to raise children in a world that denied women financial independence, Blake never ceased to point out the hypocrisy inherent in such idealized versions of motherhood. And, unlike the domestic novelists, she never suggested that becoming a mother could ease the longing her female characters have for meaning in their lives.

In "Motherhood," Blake refits the maternal icon for a mother who is a working woman; she ends the chapter with an image of herself writing her first novel, *Southwold,* her babies asleep beside her in Stratford's Elm Cottage:

> I shall ever remember those August days when I wrote the first pages. My two babies were sleeping beside me, the window near me stood open and the soft wind came sighing through the lattice while beyond I could catch a glimpse of the road that wound away among the elm trees. From down-stairs I could hear the sound of the light laughter of my sister and her young companions, but I was in a world of my own. With the enthusiasm of youth I dreamed only of success and saw rising there before me the starry crown of fame.[75]

Blake's self-portrait with children shares enough elements of the sentimental topos to disguise her implicit challenge to it. This mother is neither doing needlework nor instructing or attending to her children. They sleep, giving her time to work. Absorbed in a world of her own, she dreams not of them but of her own ambitions. Having broken through the old code, after "Motherhood," Blake's autobiographical chapter titles began to trace not the prescribed progression of a lady's life, but the chronology of a career, a career that would dramatize the struggle of a nineteenth-century woman to reimagine herself in the face of a culture which would persistently attempt to erase all trace of her.

3. Captives of Culture: A Quartet from 1859

Much madness is divinest sense
To a discerning eye;
Much sense the starkest madness.
'Tis the majority
In this, as all, prevails.
Assent, and you are sane;
Demur,—you're straightway dangerous,
And handled with a chain.
—Emily Dickinson

I

ALONG WITH IMAGES OF WOMEN portrayed as devoted mothers tending to their children, the nineteenth century produced myriad engravings and sculptures of victimized females—naked and vulnerable, their sensuality traced on steel plates or blocked in stone. Hundreds of thousands of Americans viewed these art works in public expositions during the middle part of the century and left records of their responses in diaries, pamphlets, and essays. The images provoked stories about woman's powerlessness and submission. The most famous statue of nineteenth-century America, in the tradition referred to as "ideal sculpture," was Hiram Powers's *The Greek Slave*. While it is often read as a narrative of resignation in the face of captivity and imminent rape, Joy Kasson points out that such responses cloaked others that suggested a certain pleasure in viewing "emotional captivity."[1] Lillie Blake would allude to Powers's sculpture in her 1874 novel, *Fettered for Life*, in which she portrays Flora Livingston, hostage to a brutal upper-class marriage market, drawn through elegant salons as if she were "some fair Grecian captive led in chains to adorn the triumph of a victor."[2] Trained to find a sexual component in dependency, women as well as men conflated the nudity and the submissive pose of statues like *The Greek Slave* and responded with pleasure, satisfaction, and even erotic titillation to the portrayal of a woman's submission to domination.

The viewing of ideal sculptures can be seen as parallel, at a higher cultural level, to a phenomenon rampant during the 1840s: in "opera houses" and taverns, women, erotically draped in gossamer, posed as if they were nude statues.[3] The blatantly erotic intent of these *tableaux vivants*, which were frequently raided by the police, exposes the suppressed erotic content of their upper-class counterparts. Embedding the erotic in submissive figures yokes female sexuality with dependency. As *The Wide, Wide World* shows us, women in a culture that insists on such a link not only must learn to be submissive, they must learn to find submission erotic.

The extreme masculine counterpart of such a phenomenon is, of course, sadism. It is not surprising then, that the portrayal of female submission and passivity found its endpoint in visions of women dead. Like the fainting maidens who littered the drawing rooms and novels of the nineteenth century, beautiful young dead women seemed to tumble indiscriminately out of the popular imagination. In reality the lives of many women were cut short by death, oftentimes through complications of that other idealized version of womanhood—maternity. Funereal sculpture memorializing women dead from childbirth flourished in England during this period.[4] In America, Edgar Allan Poe, dead within a year of the Seneca Falls woman's rights convention, was the premier writer of dead women. A complex personality, made more so by the deaths of his own young mother, Eliza, and his child-bride, Virginia, Poe created women whose deaths threatened to overwhelm the men who loved them. His women had the uncanny ability to erupt from their eternally passive states and return to life. But if Poe erred on the side of horror in response to the female life force, a generation later Harriet Beecher Stowe moved to the sentimental center with the death of little Eva in *Uncle Tom's Cabin*. Here the idealized beauty, purity, and innocence of the child-woman found its fulfillment in death. The dead woman was the woman par excellence— safe eternally from the corruption of the world, and silent forever. Louisa May Alcott's Beth, the sweetest of all her little women, codified the nineteenth century's ideal of the good woman. Beth, charmingly self-sacrificing, is quiet, passive, and, as a result, utterly lovable. Having renounced her own desires and her own self, she slips out of life, a victim of her own goodness, having contracted a fatal and lingering disease from the poorfolk she tends. The message is clear, and more chilling even than Poe's with his voraciously needy, unsatiated, undead women: ultimately the perfect woman—emptied of self, of needs, of voice—is the perfectly quiet, perfectly passive, dead woman.

In 1859, a successful American artist working in Rome, Harriet Hosmer, sought to conflate the stereotype of the acquiescent, vulnerable female with that of the woman warrior. She created *Zenobia,* a monumental sculpture of the powerful Syrian queen who had challenged Rome only to be captured by troops of the Emperor Aurelius. Hosmer's *Zenobia,* while captive, is—unlike most figures in the ideal tradition—fully clothed, her regal bearing and self-possession intact. Her clothing removes her from the realm of the erotic and forces a less voyeuristic claim on the viewer's attention, and her chains, imitating as they do the draping of her robe, are camouflaged to the point of becoming a mere decorative element. *Zenobia* inspired other studies of the nature of power in women. Best known today is Hawthorne's Zenobia, heroine of his 1852 novel *The Blithedale Romance.*[5] Like Margaret Fuller, upon whom she was most probably based, Zenobia is portrayed as an independent, intellectual advocate for women's rights, the reigning queen of a Brook Farm–like utopian community. The course of the novel, however, portrays the erosion of her power and, finally, her self-destruction. Hawthorne most easily imagined Zenobia as a force of influence over powerful men. "'How forcibly she might have wrought upon the world, either directly in her own person, or by her influence upon some man, or a series of men, of controlling genius!'" Her downfall is connected to her sexuality and to her erotic desires. Even the limited power that she is seen to possess is undermined by what Hawthorne saw as a feminine nature that inevitably gives primacy to love. While Hawthorne's Westervelt declares, "'Every prize that could be worth a woman's having—and many prizes which other women are too timid to desire—lay within Zenobia's reach,'" his narrator replies, [but] "'there would have been nothing to satisfy her heart.'"[6] Zenobia's power, always a function of the men around her, is sabotaged first when she gives up her feminist ideals for the man she loves, and then when she is rejected by that man. Her vulnerability is exposed, and she, love-sick, drowns herself.

In *Blithedale,* power and femininity are shown to be incompatible. "'. . . it is a woman's doom, and I have deserved it like a woman,'" cries the dying Zenobia.[7] Her end is a rather cruel twist on Margaret Fuller's death, which occurred two years earlier, in 1850, when she, too, drowned. Fuller had also suffered a failed love affair, but her response to that pain was quite unlike that of Hawthorne's Zenobia. She threw herself into her work, not into a shallow pond. She went to Europe as a correspondent for the New York *Daily-*

Tribune, and defied convention by taking a young Italian lover, Giovanni Angelo Ossoli. After Rome fell to French counterrevolutionaries, Fuller, Ossoli, and their child were returning to America when they were shipwrecked in a storm off the coast of Long Island. Fuller was returning home with what she considered to be her best work, a history of the Italian revolution. Her power—like her love life—was intact.

In *Woman in the Nineteenth Century,* published in 1844 and available to Hawthorne before he wrote *The Blithedale Romance,* Margaret Fuller articulated possibilities for alternatives to the nineteenth century's conventions concerning women. Hawthorne, unable to stretch the boundaries of those conventions, fell back upon readily available stereotypes concerning strong women. For him a woman's strength and power could be modeled only by passive endurance. "Passive and patient endurance has been often so naturalized," wrote Lydia Sigourney in 1839, "as to seem indigenous."[8] David Reynolds argues that Hawthorne, in his "innovative fusion of contrasting stereotypes" from the popular culture, was able to create "a wholly new kind of heroine," especially with Beatrice Rappaccini and Hester Prynne, who combine the sensuous dark lady with the exemplary angel.[9] Reynolds also notes, more gently than would I, that these women are still caught in a limiting angelic role. Indeed, their action upon the world is confined to their influence as female exemplars, their poison—or their sexuality—always a threat. Throughout his career, Hawthorne would keep attempting to create a multifaceted heroine who could carry moral weight, but an 1858 journal entry regarding Margaret Fuller may locate the source of his, and his culture's, limitations in their meditations on women. It seems that it is a woman's sexual need, independently expressed, which leads to her fall. Hawthorne writes in regard to Fuller that perhaps "tragic as her catastrophe was, Providence was, after all, kind in putting her and her clownish husband and their child on board that fated ship. . . . It was such an awful joke, that she should have resolved—in all sincerity, no doubt—to make herself the greatest, wisest, best woman of the age." He disparages Fuller's life with Ossoli and presumes his negative effect on her work: "all her labor [was undone] in the twinkling of an eye. On the whole, I do not know but I like her the better for it; because she proved herself a very woman after all, and fell as the weakest of her sisters might."[10]

Hawthorne's inability to see new possibilities for women which could go altogether beyond existing stereotypes was not uncommon. While Harriet Hosmer had hoped to present a Zenobia who could survive with an imperial dignity even the chains of her captors, research into the responses to Hosmer's sculpture reveals that her intentions were erased by an audience that only saw yet another captive maiden: "in 1859 not even the most iconoclastic of American sculptors could profoundly challenge the prevailing expectations about woman's nature and woman's role. Confronted with an image of power, many nineteenth-century viewers, continued to see an exemplar of powerlessness."[11]

II

The idealization of female passivity and powerlessness was a distinctly middle-class phenomenon which overlooked the realities of many women's actual lives. Working-class women, an almost invisible presence in the literature and the lives of the middle classes, never had the luxury of passivity. Women had long worked as domestic servants, and, with the rise of industrialization, the number of women in the workforce grew. In 1845 almost 56,000 men and 76,000 women worked in America's textile mills.[12] By 1870 close to 325,000 women were factory workers, many crowded into the sewing trades, "where their situation was desperate."[13] And by 1880, 14.7 percent of working people ten years old and above, or 2,650,000 workers, were women.[14] Clearly, the persistent indoctrination of female docility conveyed in many domestic novels and preached in etiquette books and tracts was specifically geared for the middle classes, which, of course, also comprised the literate readership.

Alongside literature promoting the limited sphere of "true womanhood" was a plethora of adventure novels featuring bold, swashbuckling heroines who flouted calls for domestication.[15] Perhaps the most wonderful is E. D. E. N. Southworth's *The Hidden Hand or Capitola the Madcap*, published as a serial in the *New York Ledger* the same year, 1859, that Hosmer's sculpture of Zenobia appeared. A rollicking comedy in the eighteenth-century tradition of Fielding, it has multiple plots moved and linked by wild coincidences. Capitola Le Noir, a ragamuffin girl who grows up on the streets of New York, saving herself from sexual assault by dressing as a boy, becomes a self-reliant, nononsense woman who takes on a band of "ruthless desperadoes," capturing the leader, whom "no one can take." With her axiom "cowardice is worse than death," Capitola saves herself and other women from assault and generally fills the vacuum left by the death of male chivalry.[16] As Joanne Dobson puts it so well, referring to *The Wide, Wide World,* Capitola "turns Ellen Montgomery on her head."[17]

It is important to note, however, that Capitola's freedom is intricately linked with her lower-class street life, while Ellen's confinement is a prescription for the life of a middle-class lady.[18] When Capitola is rescued from the hard life of those streets and ultimately finds herself to be an heiress, she must protect herself from a different form of assault—the patriarchal onslaught that would transform her, like Ellen, into a "true woman." In exasperation, her guardian, the blustery "Old Hurricane," asks, "'will you never be a woman?'"[19] He confides to the Reverend Mr. Goodwin that "'the wild, reckless, desolate child has passed unscathed through the terrible ordeal of destitution, poverty and exposure! . . . [But] I can't manage her! She won't obey me, except when she likes! She has never been taught obedience or been accustomed to subordination, and don't understand either!'" The Reverend Mr. Goodwin's advice on how to make out of Cap a middle-class true woman, subordinate and obedient, is to "'lock her up.'" But as Old Hurricane realizes in despair, "'Cap evidently thinks that the restriction of her liberty is too heavy a price to pay for protection and support!'"[20]

Enfolded within the fantastic adventures of Capitola Le Noir is a multiplotted domestic novel of true womanhood. Alternating with Cap's escapades are four intersecting sentimental tales of Old Hurricane's abandoned wife, his sister, Cap's mother, and, as if this were not enough, his wife's son's fiancée. Each of these four women displays a strength of character which Hawthorne had idealized in Hester Prynne, that which springs from passive endurance. For instance, Capitola's mother endures abduction while pregnant, separation from her child at birth, and confinement to attics or insane asylums for the ensuing years—all so that another can win her husband's patrimony; she explains that the last chapters of the gospel of John, "that narrative of meek patience and divine love!" is what saves her from madness and despair.[21] The hardships that necessitate such passive endurance are inflicted upon these women by men—not only evil men like the wicked Gabriel Le Noir who spends a lifetime abducting and murdering, but also generally good men like Old Hurricane, who abandons women who do not, or do not seem to, conform to his wishes.

These four women, in true sentimental fashion, seem to "float" or "glide" when they move; fragrant odors "waft" from their presence; sweetness, gentleness, humility are theirs, and, in addition—like the newly married Lillie Devereux Umsted—they sew. When the rescued Cap has the opportunity to learn the leisure-class lady's "mysteries of cutting and basting, back-stitching and felling, hemming and seaming," she almost goes mad. "'Nothing ever happens here! The silence deafens me! . . . [I am] decomposing above the ground for want of having my blood stirred;'" in other words, as she puts it, she is "bored to death."[22]

Perhaps this cliché speaks to the root cause of all those dead, silent women so beloved of the nineteenth century as well as to the patriarchal strategy for anesthetizing them. As Lillie Blake wrote in her first published essay, "the endless sewing that fills up all the leisure of woman's life . . . I know of nothing more cramping to the mind . . . of many a poor lady who . . . sees existence stretching before her an endless world of petty conventionalities and wearisome repetitions."[23] It is important to note, however, that a "true woman" was anesthetized in an explicitly sexual way. In contrast to Capitola, who fancies "men whose very names strike terror in the hearts of commonplace people," the "true woman" is dead to desire. Old Hurricane takes great pains to assure Mr. Goodwin that Cap is sexually pure. He swears on his "'truth as a man . . . honor as a soldier and . . . faith as a Christian'" that Capitola has escaped her street life "'unscathed,'" her virginity intact. "'She *has*, sir! She is as innocent as the most daintily sheltered young heiress in the country! She *is*, sir: and I'd cut off the tongue and ears of any man that said otherwise.'"[24] Indeed, the protection which Capitola is asked to pay for with her freedom is the protection of her virginity in which the middle-class patriarchy has "so large an interest." Capitola, because she is from the streets, can tease the Reverend Mr. Goodwin with innuendoes concerning her lack of purity, but Old Hurricane's wife must spend decades in celibate exile as proof of hers. Capitola seems to embody the lost vitality of womankind, which, while absent in the middle classes, is presumed to still exist in the lower classes, or at least in some middle-class fantasy of them.

While Southworth purposefully displaced both the power and the sexual nature of her heroine into a lower class where their energy could be enjoyed vicariously from a distance great enough to have little effect on the values of true womanhood, Harriet Hosmer, by clothing her female figure, substituted dignity and strength for helplessness and thereby removed *Zenobia* from the voyeurism that marked the response to so many ideal sculptures. But in so doing, she also emptied it of its eroticism. Lillie Devereux Umsted's ambitious first novel, also published in 1859, attempted a revision of assumptions regarding women's power and sexuality which would neither empty her heroine of desire nor displace that desire onto a different class. Blake tried to create a middle-class heroine who could speak her own mind and make her own way in life and still be accepted as a "true woman." But her enterprise, like Hosmer's, was doomed to failure, her heroine deemed mad. Only in the realm of comic fantasy, it would seem, could swashbuckling women be allowed to exist.

III

In *Southwold* Blake alludes to Zenobia: held captive by a social order that denies her any alternative to the marriage market, Medora Fielding exists in a "state of half slavery" like the "captive Zenobia."[25] Medora has connections to yet another sculpture, the first of the many "ideal sculptures" created during the nineteenth century in America–*Medora* by Horatio Greenough. A funereal piece, exhibited in America in the 1830s, *Medora* is a full-scale female, lying on a bier. Both Greenough's and Blake's Medora refer in turn to Byron's heroine in "The Corsair" (1814). Blake gives a single hint of her source when she remarks that Byron is Medora's favorite poet: "the passionate poetry of Byron touched more than any other a responsive chord in her heart."[26] A most faithful woman, waiting patiently at home for the return of the poem's hero, Conrad, Byron's Medora kills herself in the belief that Conrad has died in battle. Greenough and Blake pick up details from Byron's poem: Greenough's Medora holds a cluster of flowers in her dead hands; Blake's version of the dead Medora is arranged with a white robe, long fair hair, a smile.

But although she shares blue eyes and a name with Byron's heroine, Blake's Medora is more like his dark lady, the Byzantine Gulnare. While Byron's Medora is passive to the point of self-destruction, his Gulnare is a woman of appetite and action. Conrad had saved her from certain rape, and she in turn saves him from the execution ordered by her husband. She declares her love, and although she understands and values his fidelity to Medora, after releasing him from prison at great risk to herself Gulnare sails home with him. Although Byron frames his poem with descriptions of Medora—her long-suffering fidelity defining its opening and her self-sacrificial death its ending—the powerful Gulnare is pivotal to the poem's unfolding. However, for Byron, for Horatio Greenough, and for the audiences who shared their sensibility, the ever-faithful, dead Medora was the only woman worthy of attention. Gulnare remained the exotic "Other," and by the end of the poem, despite her heroic deeds, this active, assertive, and sensual woman disappears, dropping right out of Byron's range of vision. Beyond her usefulness to the hero, she is rendered invisible. We find no statues of Gulnare exhibited for nineteenth-century audiences. After all, in a context which valued a woman only in her relation to a man who had a legitimate right to her, she was merely a faithless wife.

Blake, on the other hand, looks to the exotic Gulnare in the construction of her heroine, and in so doing she attempts to undermine the restrictive stereotypes that pitched angels against bitches, leaving little room for real women. She combines Medora's passive fidelity with Gulnare's assertive sensuality and makes of the Byzantine woman's alien status a central component of Medora's social condition. Forthrightly aggressive in her expression of affection for the man she loves, and loyal to him long after he has proven himself unworthy, Medora, the nineteen-year-old daughter of an impoverished widow, is an outsider in a world run by money. A counterpart of her author in details large and small, Medora has "little taste for the feminine graces of the needle"; "restless and miserable," with "too much intellect to be satisfied with the mere frivolities of society," she is the product of a false education that drives her to focus all her energy on appearances and success in courtship games; but she holds her own in debates with men, espousing the feminist ideas that Blake would later develop on the lecture circuit. "'No man ever does anything wrong or foolish,'" Medora tells a startled dinner party, "'that people do not blame either his wife or mother.'" Medora undermines the sentimental notion of transparency with the claim that if we were not capable of "'suppressing all outward signs of feeling . . . would not our countenances be for ever distorted with the anguish of unhappiness and disappointment?'" Or again, "'How little can even the most penetrating man suspect the thoughts that are surging under the placid surface of a fair face.'" Medora disturbs the love of her devoted fiancé, Floyd Southwold, when she denies that women "'owe any special debt of gratitude to Christianity. . . . No nation has ever assigned to us so noble a rank as the ancient Scandinavians—those northern barbarians—who worshipped Odin and dreamed of the fair Alruna maidens. They regarded their wives as companions to be consulted on all important occasions. . . . I can scarcely imagine it to be necessary to the maintenance of a true faith that we should believe all the false arguments which enthusiasts have adduced in its support.'"[27]

This was rather precocious stuff for the twenty-five-year-old Lillie Umsted, whose world was populated by intellectual figures who were also Christian apologists. Her cousin Theodore Woolsey publicly lectured on the modifying and softening affects of Christianity on the position of woman in society: "Christianity deepened the obligation of justice, while in the element of reverence for the purity of woman Christianity was the more efficient cause. . . . If, then, in some regions where Christianity has spread, there has been little elevation of the female character, the reason is that only the name has been there without the essence. . . . Christianity brings a new standard of female character into the world."[28] Elizabeth Cady Stanton, who had the benefit not only of eighteen years of maturity but of more than a decade of suffrage discussions in a community of radical thinkers, had cast aspersions on women's debt to Christianity when she wrote to the Syracuse temperance convention in 1852 that "Woman has always been the greatest dupe . . . like the poor slave 'Uncle Tom,' her religion, instead of making her noble and free, and impelling her to flee from all gross surroundings, by the false lessons of her spiritual teachers, by the wrong application of great principles of right and justice, has made her bondage but more certain and lasting, her degradation more helpless and complete."[29] In 1883 Blake would declare, in her refutation of the Lenten Lectures of the rector of Trinity Church, what Medora had claimed in *Southwold,* that Christianity, "this man-made Church" has degraded rather than uplifted women.[30] In 1885, Stanton would echo Blake's lenten lectures: "The assertion that woman owes all the advantages of her present position to the Christian church, has been repeated so often, that it is accepted as an established truth by those who would be unwilling to admit that all the injustice and degradation she has suffered might be logically traced to the same source."[31] By the end of the century, Blake would collaborate with Stanton on *The Woman's Bible,* which may well have been inspired by Blake's 1883 lectures.[32]

Yet, however much Blake's confidence in her own ideas would develop, in 1859 the heroine who shares those ideas is seen as a fallen angel, her lack of religious faith a sign of her turn toward evil. As appealing as Medora is, a straight-talking feminist who defies conventions regarding passivity and guilelessness in women, she is presented as a deformity of a woman, her mind "almost masculine in its depth of thought and capability of analytical inquiry. This power is always dangerous to its possessor, but doubly so, when that possessor is a woman."[33] The narrative voice in *Southwold,* which condemns Medora as evil, repeats the cultural prescriptions of nineteenth-century womanhood which censured the very qualities—passion, ambition, and self-reliance—that would have been valued in a man and that Blake valued in herself. Blake's censorious narrator reflects her own struggle to fully accept those aspects of herself which her society deemed inappropriate. She held ambivalent attitudes toward a heroine who could possess her own desires and pursue them ruthlessly and who could make the assault on patriarchy which, at this point in her life, Blake could only dream of. In creating a woman of independence and determination, Blake strayed so far from a depiction of the ideal of passive, true womanhood that she risked being drawn to the reverse of that popular model. While clearly identifying with a heroine who presumed to control her own sexual destiny, Blake hid her empathy beneath the voice of her condemning narrator. A captive of cultural dictates and scarred by her experience in New Haven, Lillie distanced herself from her heroine lest she condemn herself all over again, this time for her radical ideas. We see in *Southwold,* however, Blake's initial attempt to transform her ambivalent feelings about herself and her heroine into a strategy that could turn contradiction into a disguise for revolutionary thought. She began to develop the double-voiced narrative she would use throughout her career: her feminist heroine—strong, passionate, trapped in a world of hypocrisy in which she has no sanctioned place—is condemned by a patriarchy whose legitimacy is questioned throughout the text.

Set during the worldwide financial panic of 1837,[34] *Southwold* has a plot fueled by the connection between marriage and money. Medora, passionately in love with Walter Lascelles, would endure a life of poverty for his love, but he, in need of a wife with money, jilts her. His obsession with her keeps him from even a pretense of love for his wife, Lucy Wentworth, who dies not long after she gives birth to a daughter. Lascelles's concomitant obsession with money leads him to bribe a nurse to keep their dead baby warm long enough to falsely establish that the baby died after the mother, thus ensuring that Lucy's wealth will pass through the baby to the father.

Marriages, because they provide either access to or consolidation of inherited wealth, are the sites of patriarchal power in much eighteenth- and nineteenth-century fiction, and *Southwold* is no exception. As a result of the rise of the middle classes, however, the financial arrangement that had long characterized aristocratic marriages became distasteful; marriage was now supposed to be the bedrock of a new domesticity rather than a perpetuation of an old aristocracy.[35] Blake critiques the aristocratic connection between marriage and money as a corruption which undermines middle-class conventions concerning the sanctity of the home as a safe haven for women. But more than this, she unmasks the middle-class exclusion of women from control of both their financial and sexual resources as parallel to the aristocratic subordination of lesser classes. She exposes the fragility of the middle-class domestic haven which, because the women kept within it do not control its source of power, can so easily be transformed into a prison. The patriarchal control of money and of female sexuality subverts the domestic idyll that the ideology of separate spheres had promised women. Lucy's home, once an idealized place of safety presided over by her benevolent father, becomes, as does her body—and the child she brings forth from it—a mere source of funding for the rapacious Lascelles.

Blake makes a frontal attack on a system that idealizes the home as a safety zone for women but is really concerned with consolidating wealth through lineage. She strips the patriarchal notion of "home" as domestic haven to reveal its reality as "house," a center of inherited wealth. *Southwold*'s title refers neither to the eligible Floyd Southwold, on whom Medora Fielding sets her sights after being abandoned by Lascelles, nor to his wealthy uncle, who controls his finances, but to the patriarchal mansion, to the "house" of Southwold. It is the patriarchal inheritance and the implications of patriarchy, which all women fall heir to, that are at stake in the novel.

Ancestral mansions are the stuff of Gothic fiction, but Blake reformulates the Gothic to position Medora in the male role of usurper. Medora is not a Gothic heroine imprisoned in a castle, trying to get out; rather, she is excluded from the domain of men, trying to get in.[36] Lacking a home and a benevolent protector, she moves with her mother from one boardinghouse to another, always on the fringe of a social sphere to which, because her father is no longer alive, she only precariously belongs.

Using her one option, the marriage market, to regain access to a world in which she is marginalized, Medora buys into the constrictive system that she had sought to combat. Her passion is transformed into cunning, and Medora becomes strikingly manipulative in her pursuit of Floyd, whose idealized goodness has no effect upon her. It is the family patriarch, Floyd Southwold, Sr., with whom she must do battle to win the hand of Floyd and, with it, her share of the promises of patriarchy. When Floyd falls in love with Medora, his uncle makes clear that if he marries his allowance will cease and he will no longer be welcome to live at Southwold. "In an instant Medora saw all that was before her—the tedious waiting for an old man's death, the false position that must always arise from slender means and great expectations, and the possibility of wasting the best years of her life, in the same struggle against circumstances of which she was already so weary."[37]

The monetary underpinnings of the patriarchal system are embodied in

Floyd's unsympathetically drawn uncle—"that self-complacent old man" who complains that democracy inevitably gives rise to the common people and who has the power to withhold the patrimony. Medora's resistance to this patriarch is to refuse him aid when he plunges headlong over a cliff. Medora "hissed" in Floyd's ear, "'Let him die!'"[38]

Both Medora and Melissa of "A Tragedy of the Mammoth Cave" act aggressively (and unscrupulously) against the men who thwart their ambitions, but they do not murder anyone. Yet the narrative voices articulate the social outrage over their aggression, deeming their actions murderous, and the heroines themselves acquiesce in this judgment. His uncle "murdered," Floyd sees in Medora "an angel who was in reality a fiend."[39] In effect, both Medora and Melissa die for their audacity. Medora topples a patriarch; her reward is condemnation and death.

Medora Fielding discovers that her only patrimony is insanity, inherited from her paternal grandmother, who died in an asylum. Thus, unlike the furious first wives of much nineteenth-century fiction, who, in a neat psychological metaphor, are safely split off from the heroines and consigned to attics,[40] Blake's heroine is herself a madwoman. Her madness manifests itself in pacing: she "paced with restless steps up and down a short distance, turning ever at a certain point and walking fiercely back to her original starting-place, as if she were confined within barriers, instead of at liberty to wander away for miles."[41] But, as Blake well knew, a woman was not at liberty to wander away; she was confined within the barriers devised by a social order which limited her actions and suppressed her desires. Insanity is indeed her patriarchal legacy; Medora's confinement is both symptom and source of her madness. When we first meet her, long before her mental illness develops, she "would pace the room like a caged tigress, with a fierce impatient longing to throw aside all the restraints of her sex."[42]

Blake would echo these words in her essay "The Social Condition of Woman," in which she depicts an everywoman who must, "if of nature too lofty to submit tamely to control, chafe fiercely against the restraints around her." Medora is an earlier version of this hypothetical young woman, so reminiscent of the young Blake:

> If she have independence, she must revolt desperately against perpetual subservience to man—as for him she must wait, and upon him depend for every pleasure or comfort. If she have honor and truth, she must bitterly loathe the system of deception that society requires of her. Ex-

pected to check every noble aspiration outside of a little set world as "unwomanly," to conceal the most sacred emotions of her heart as "unmaidenly," condemned to an endless repetition of formalities, to be content with amusements so frivolous that they are outgrown at twenty, she may for a few brief seasons be permitted the unsatisfactory and injurious triumphs of youth and beauty, but for the rest of the long years of her life she must be content to sink into utter insignificance.[43]

Like Byron's and Greenough's Medoras and Hawthorne's Zenobia, Blake's heroine dies by her own hand. However, in a significant swerve from her male counterparts, Blake portrays Medora's suicide not as a capitulation to love, but, rather, as an assertion of control over her own fate and as a resistance to dependency. Seeing signs of her inherited insanity, Medora decides to kill herself before she is made helpless by the progression of the disease. Helplessness, Blake knew, is the "female complaint" caused by the progression of patriarchy. It is the subtext of all those nineteenth-century ideal sculptures, as well as the etiquette manuals counseling dependency, the restrictive dress that inhibited breathing, the romance of fainting, the weakness which, as Hawthorne would insist, proved one to be a "very woman." Medora's final act is her supreme resistance to the dictates of feminine frailty.

If many in the nineteenth century could see only powerlessness even when confronted with images of powerful women, the alternative was to see deformity. Even Blake, while dealing with the issues of a patrimony withheld and of a woman's power and impotence in a corrupt, money-based system, distances herself from Medora's anger, shrewdness, and ambition, which the world found unacceptable in women and which Blake found monstrous in herself. If *Southwold* is not entirely successful in its attempt to revise prevailing assumptions regarding women, its very failure reveals the difficulty in imagining what at that cultural moment seemed unimaginable. The popular revisions of *Medea*, the reception of Hosmer's *Zenobia*, *The Blithedale Romance*—each reveals the difficulty of redesigning the cultural boundaries of "woman." Part of the value of a work like *Southwold* is to let us apprehend anew the struggle that took place before women could be acknowledged as multifaceted personalities possessing the same drives and desires as men.

Even Blake herself was not yet able to fully cast off the social prescriptions which condemned a woman's active pursuit of her own desires. Her sympathies still lay with the world of her parents, and in her first novel, dedicated to her mother, she ultimately sacrificed her heroine, and her self, to them. Floyd

Southwold is an idealized portrait of her father, dead when she was four. George Pollok Devereux's bachelor uncle, George Pollok, like Floyd's uncle, intended his nephew to take his family name and become his heir. For close to nine years, while living and traveling with his uncle abroad, Devereux delayed his marriage to Blake's mother. When the nephew preceded the uncle in death and left only female children, the promised inheritance was not forthcoming. Floyd Southwold lives in a family homestead in Stratford, the description of which fits Blake's ancestral home, the Johnson house. A loving younger cousin awaits him there, and clearly she, a half-veiled version of Blake's patient mother, is a better match for this faultless young man than the worldly-wise Medora. Blake's sympathy for the idealized version of her young parents made more problematic her attitude toward the character who most embodies her own authentic self.

Through Medora, however, Blake continued to undermine the stereotype of feminine frailty and purity by defying convention and reclaiming for women the capacity for violence and desire.[44] No matter how problematic her heroine and her own relationship to her, by killing Medora off at the end of the novel Blake clearly identifies the limitations imposed on women who breach culturally imposed sanctions.

IV

Blake had begun writing *Southwold* in August 1858, three weeks after the birth of her second daughter, when she was well enough to travel from the Union Place Hotel in New York City to her mother's home in Stratford. By November, the Umsteds moved back to New York to a suite of rooms—two bedrooms and a parlor—in a boardinghouse on Fifth Avenue near 8th Street. The board included private meals, and Lillie employed a wet nurse for her infant and a maid who helped with both children and did the washing. She finished her book before Christmas, and in January 1859 the manuscript was accepted by Harper & Brothers, the premier New York publisher. Harper could not publish the book until May, however, and Lillie could not wait. In the only overt statement that hints of a criticism of her husband, she wrote in her autobiography, "the pressure of want of money was beginning to come upon us and I was anxious to be able to earn something to help out our income to which my husband added little or nothing."[45]

In the midst of these anxieties, the Umsteds were forced to move once again, because of the financial difficulties of their landlady, all of whose furniture was being attached. On January 31, within hours of hearing the "appalling news"[46] that they must immediately move from their rooms on Fifth Avenue, they had packed their trunks and moved to rooms in the Carleton Hotel, where they lived for the next three months. They had a parlor with an adjoining bedroom on one floor and a nursery on the floor above. Lillie recorded as a comedy of errors the details of a panicked and exhausting move:

> It was no small matter to transport such a family as ours. The trunks were brought out and crammed full. Eliza [the maid] worked like a Trojan, Maria [the wet-nurse], lazy and dull as possible, baby rolling over and over the floor, Bessie daubing her face with raw meat and Frank running about like one distracted, putting a doll and a silver cup into his best hat and stuffing glass ware, old shoes, a pincushion and a clothes line all into a box together.[47]

Lydia Sigourney had advised that women should "endeavor to preserve cheerfulness of deportment, under the pressure of disappointment or calamity,"[48] and, indeed, Lillie's habit was to disguise difficulty with humor, turning domestic adversity into an amusing anecdote. However, the sketch of her husband's distraction and disorganization should be borne in mind in the context of later events.

Attempting to get Lillie's book published as quickly as possible, Frank dealt with editors at Appletons and at Rudd and Carleton. *Southwold* was published by Rudd and Carleton on February 5, 1859, with a second printing in press on the 12th and a third on the 19th. The book sold well enough during the spring that the Umsteds anticipated a move on May 1 to a house on 36th Street between Fifth and Sixth Avenues. The novel was widely reviewed, and while the opinions were mixed, Lillie was exhilarated by the attention. The only comment that bothered her was one of the most interesting: N. P. Willis's *Home Journal* commented that the author's character was a mystery, that she must be a tragedienne "out of place on the tame sidewalk of common life."

Blake never could accept the fact that she was not part of the ordinary world into which she tried so hard to fit. Her diary often laments days spent brooding over questions of free will and predestination.[49] Yet although her work to date was filled with tragedy and despair and her musing involved issues of meaning and purpose, Blake felt a need to apologize for her "moods" and to keep up an appearance of joy. Unhappiness was failure for a woman in a system which defined her worth in terms of her making a successful marriage and becoming a mother. Her dark concerns confused her and seemed to embarrass her. She felt it was unseemly to have the questions and yearnings that plagued her, and she found it difficult to admit to unhappiness.

But Lillie took real joy in the success of *Southwold,* and noted that since she began to write, she was far happier than before: "It seemed to me now that the object I had so long sought was found and that my life hereafter would not be fruitless."[50] She had always made a point of systematically studying and reading, and now, after caring for her children in the mornings, she scheduled an hour each for practicing the piano and reading French. Then she would go the Astor library and read for several hours. In April she was reading Carlyle's *Frederick the Great* and Voltaire's *Siècle de Louis XIV.* The spring of 1859 was a high point in her life. Productive and fulfilled, Lillie anticipated the move to the house on 36th Street (although it was not ready by May 1, so they remained in the Carleton Hotel), her portrait, painted during the winter by William Oliver Stone, was hung prominently in the spring exhibition, her book sold well, her babies grew, her husband had recently turned twenty-six: "Dear handsome fellow, handsome, active and fresh, in the very prime of all his powers."[51] On May 8, she wrote, "Spent a happy evening with my dear Frank, talking and sewing while he read to me."[52]

A muffled thump was all the warning Lillie had that her fragile burst of happiness was spent. It was enough to awaken her, to rouse her out of bed where Frank had left her, with a kiss, but a moment before. Fifteen years later she would remember:

> The early morning light streamed palely into the room. Near the window Frank sat in an arm chair with a sad smile on his parted lips. . . . His position was easy and natural, his face not even yet very pale, his right hand which rested on his knee held the pistol. On the table beside him was the box which contained the implements belonging to it. Near was the morning paper which he had apparently been reading and on the hearth-piece lay the shattered remains of a vase. The ball, after doing its deadly work, had passed on and shivered this glass to atoms.
>
> As I rushed to him, a horrible sound caught my ear, the slow drip, drip of the blood that flowed from the wound in the temple.[53]

On the day she was widowed, May 10, 1859, Lillie Devereux Umsted, author of two published stories, a poem, and a novel, was just twenty-five years old, the mother of a two-year-old child and a ten-month-old infant. The diary she kept is missing. Katherine recorded in typescript the May 14 and 16 entries ("May 14 Dead! My darling husband is dead! May 16 Oh Frank, Frank! How can I live without you?"), but she found the rest so upsetting that she could not continue: "The succeeding pages were so full of grief that . . . I did not want to dictate them, nor had I the heart to copy them."[54] She notes in her biography that her mother "spent dreadful days and nights of anguish and despair."[55] In her autobiography, Blake transcribed some of the diary entries of the summer after Frank's death, and they reveal her profound grief and loneliness. One evening, retracing a walk in Stratford which she and Frank had taken, "my heart cried out with a great longing, O Frank! Frank! But I was alone; there was no answer . . .":

> Sad and tired, I walked back over the track, now all shrouded in shadow. Suddenly, there was a low rumbling, increasing rapidly, and in another moment a train swept around the curve, came rushing toward me, on the single track upon which I stood. A deep ditch ran on each side of the track. I could only step down the sloping embankment and crouch into the ground. I had scarcely reached this place of safety when the train rolled on, deafening me with its roar, and almost blinding me with the smoke. The great cars rushed along not two feet from my head. It was a long train and as each huge mass rode by, I thought that one hair's breadth of deviation, a stone on the track, or the smallest obstacle, would [bring] the unwieldy monster down upon me and I should be crushed and really as I sat there, I did not much care.[56]

On June 17, she wrote that her memories "torture" her and the future looms as "a threatening abyss. Sometimes it seems as if my brain would give way under this terrible pressure of thought and recollection"[57] and, indeed, by August she was seriously ill and bedridden for three weeks.

The inquest into Frank Umsted's death was inconclusive; the coroner's verdict did not determine whether the death was a suicide or an accident. Blake never believed that Frank had premeditated his end. "His death may have been a sudden impulse, a mere accident in the careless handling of his weapon. I cannot say which. This only I do know, that he loved me so deeply that he would freely have lain down his life if he had cause I would be the happier for the sacrifice, and that I loved him so well that his strange untimely death cast a shadow on my heart that time was long in lifting."[58]

Several days after Frank's funeral, Lillie looked into his papers, which were "in the most hopeless confusion," and came to "the astonishing knowledge that I was penniless. Not a trace of the fair fortune I had brought to him on my marriage was to be found. It was irrevocably gone."[59] In addition, $18,000 worth of stock which Lillie's mother had given Frank to invest for her was missing. Rumors began that Frank was worse than careless. Years later, when Bessie and Katie were rummaging in a trunk looking for old clothes to play "dress-up" in, they came across the stock certificates, vindicating, as far as Lillie was concerned, her husband's honor. In her mother's biography, Katherine is protective of her father's memory. She omits all mention of the living arrangements which indicate financial stress—the Union Place Hotel, where she was born; the Fifth Avenue boardinghouse from which they had to move so suddenly; or the Carleton Hotel, where her father killed himself. She writes:

> Everything I have ever heard indicates that at this time my father was the best possible companion to my mother, and both inspiration and encouragement to her in this new field of endeavor. He was a man of education and fine feeling, cultivated in his tastes, and able to assist her with his knowledge of the world and with practical advice, while she was writing and marketing her book. He must have been as anxious for her to find an outlet for her energy, as she was for "Fame." He had many friends, and many opportunities to further her effort, and he delighted in doing everything possible.[60]

It may be that Frank was as anxious for the income which *Southwold* might generate as he was for the outlet it provided his wife. Besides his activities arising from the publication of her novel, he had recently undertaken a suit on behalf of Lillie and her sister Georgie to recover some of their patrimony. Lillie, the disciplined, organized, and ambitious member of the couple, assumed that her husband was equally responsible and deferred to his judgment. She was never able to fully see Frank's limitations, and she could never comprehend the reasons for, or the premeditated nature of, his death. Frank, as much a captive of culture as the women we have discussed, was trapped in his own prescribed role, unable to openly discuss their finances with his wife or to let her manage her own money. When her fortune ran out, still maintaining his silence, he took his life. Lillie was left abandoned without explanations.

Recoveries

4. Of Loss and War

If we could first know WHERE *we are, and* WHITHER *we are tending,*
we could then better judge WHAT *to do, and* HOW *to do it.*

. . .

"A house divided against itself cannot stand."
—Abraham Lincoln June 16, 1858

I

DURING THE WINTER OF 1859–60, a lone figure dressed in black could be seen skating across the frozen surface of Stratford's Sterling Park Pond.[1] Lillie Devereux Umsted flew fiercely across the ice as much for the feeling of propelling herself into the future as for the exercise it provided her. Two, three, even five hours at a time she relentlessly skated the pond. She needed time to think about a future that sometimes seemed a "threatening abyss."[2]

Two days after her husband's death, a man whom Lillie did not know had written to her proposing marriage. Marriage was a profession for a woman, and Lillie was out of a job. By the end of the summer three more offers of marriage had been made through intermediaries. Remarriage was the expected solution to the financial plight of nineteenth-century middle-class widows, and Blake's mother, alarmed by their altered financial situation, assumed her daughter would follow the usual course. Lillie was determined not to fall into this all-too-well-known trap. In her anonymously published essay of 1863, "The Social Condition of Woman," she would characterize marriage in a social order that limits women from other means of earning a living, as institutionalized prostitution. If all women were allowed employment, she reasoned, then no woman would "ever be reduced to the degrading necessity of marrying for a support—that is, selling herself because she sees with despair that, as society is at present constituted, and from the defects of her education, there is no hope of earning an honest livelihood."[3] Not for her that degrading necessity.

Lillie was opposed to any marriage, not just one demanded by financial distress. At the end of 1859, Henry Lord Page King, to whom she had been engaged at the age of seventeen and of whom she was most fond, renewed his suit, but she refused to marry even him. Over the next few years, she would receive numerous offers of marriage, each of which she refused. Two and a half years after she was widowed, we find her, in a letter to her mother, firmly putting off Mrs. Devereux's concerns: "It is rather hard of you to find fault with me about Mr. D. I never said I had refused him, I only said he made some advances, so he did, and I repulsed them and should again if made in the same way. . . . I am glad he has gone for you know I do not have to get married although I should not refuse a good offer."[4] That last clause is an instance of her habit of covering with an acceptable statement what was a radical and rebellious remark, "I do not have to get married." Clearly, this time around, Lillie had decided to make a life of and on her own.[5]

However, hardly a trace of her considerable fortune had survived Frank Umsted's death. Lillie felt that she could impose upon her mother for board and lodging, because under the terms of her father's will she was entitled to one third of his property. But all other expenses she would have to earn for herself. Although neither Blake nor her biographer daughter is explicit about her family's finances, land records reveal that Lillie's mother may have been more severely hurt by Frank's poor investments than they knew or cared to acknowledge. On November 29, 1859, Sarah Devereux took out a mortgage on Elm Cottage for $1,000. Two years after Frank's death, on September 30, 1861, when the country was experiencing major financial trauma as a result of the Civil War, she took out another $1,000 mortgage on the property with her cousin, Eli Whitney, Jr. Three weeks later, to cut her expenses, she closed up the house, and moved in with her younger daughter, who had married on June 6, 1861, and was living in Wallingford, Connecticut. Although this move was intended to be temporary, less than six months later, on March 14, 1862, Sarah Johnson Devereux sold Elm Cottage for $3,000 and paid off her two mortgages the next day.[6]

Shortly before his death, Frank had brought suit on behalf of Lillie and her sister against their father's brother, Thomas Devereux, alleging an inequitable settlement of their grandmother's estate. Their grandmother had inherited half of her brother's $1.6 million estate, all of which had been intended for Lillie's father, who had died so early and unexpectedly. At the time, their grandmother had settled between $50,000 and $100,000 apiece on Lillie and Georgina, a considerable fortune but far less than had been intended for them. When their grandfather died in 1840, Thomas Devereux gave his brother's daughters $200 apiece from the estate, his sister was given $20,000, and he appropriated the rest. Their grandmother's will left $25,000 to charity; the remaining $25,000 and property (which included twenty-seven slaves) Thomas also absorbed. Frank sued for one-third of that remaining property.[7] The widowed Lillie was pinning all her hopes for financial security on the outcome of negotiations with Thomas Devereux, but six weeks after Frank's death her uncle Thomas announced that he declined to reach a compromise on the suit. Lillie, still reeling from the grievous loss of her husband and the profound shock that all her money was gone, was thrown against a hard rock of despair at this news: "O, that I could find words eloquent and burning enough to express all the misery and wretchedness of my heart. I struggle on day after day, I scarcely know how, sustained only by one thought, my children. For their sakes I must live and try to be cheerful. Only for that one hold my existence would be too darkly terrible for endurance."[8]

Only a "defiant confidence"[9] in herself overcame Lillie's despondence in the face of both grief and financial ruin—a ruin difficult in itself, but one that must have complicated her grief over the loss of a husband who seemed to be the cause of her tribulation. At the end of the summer after Frank's death, having convalesced from the serious collapse which left her bedridden for three weeks, Blake seemed to have recovered some of her equilibrium, and she resolved not to be steered into remarriage, but instead to earn a living by writing. Just the year before, she had sat in Elm Cottage writing *Southwold*, dreaming of successes to come. Now, returned to her second-story room which overlooked Stratford's Main Street, Lillie distracted herself from grief with intensive study. With the 10,000-volume library of the founders of Columbia University available next door in the ancestral Johnson homestead, Lillie, through the summer, fall, and into the winter of 1860, read and wrote abstracts of histories of England, Scotland, France, Spain, Assyria, Turkey, and Prussia, which, over the next few years, she would publish in a variety of venues. She studied Latin and French; she read Irving's *Life of Washington*, Machiavelli's *Hints to a Prince*, John Lothrop Motley's *Rise of the Dutch Republic*, W. S. R. Hodson's *Twelve Years of a Soldier's Life in India*, *The Arabian Nights*, and some Locke. She read Dickens's *Pictures of Italy*, "from which I learned that his forte is not description of scenery."[10] Her response to reading the complete works of her illustrious ancestor Jonathan Edwards was "What wretched hair-splitting!"[11]

And she wrote stories. In December Blake's diary notes with discouragement that "Peterson has returned my piece as too sad."[12] She might have meant *Peterson's Magazine,* which was edited by Ann Stephens from 1843 to 1886, or, more probably, because she does not use the possessive, she was referring to the Philadelphia publisher who was part owner of the *Saturday Evening Post,* which, by 1871, would list Lillie Devereux Blake as "among the ablest writers" in its employ.[13] Two stories written in September 1859 were accepted: "John Owen's Appeal" appeared in *Harper's Magazine* over a year later, in December 1860, and, later still, in January 1861, "The Lonely House" was published by the *Atlantic Monthly.* Blake's second novel, *Rockford,* was begun during the winter of 1860 but not published until 1863. The delay in publication and remuneration at prestigious magazines pushed Blake into less distinguished venues. She found that she could more easily and quickly publish short pieces in Frank Leslie's publications, *Harper's Weekly,* the *New York Leader,* and the *New York Sunday Times.* When her work did not appear anonymously, she used a variety of pseudonyms—Essex, Charity Floyd (her great-great-grandmother's name), Violet, the romantic Di Fairfax—and later added the whimsical Tiger Lily and Lulu Dashaway.

Neither the work nor the grieving was easy. On May 10, 1860, returning home after visiting Frank's grave, Lillie wrote in her journal, "One year a widow! and what a year it has been! When I look back over its dreary course of distress, disappointment and misery, I hope earnestly that it may never be repeated, and I *wonder* that I have struggled through it as well as I have. It is rash to hope that the darkest time is past. . . . As I stood there on the hillside alone with only that cold grave beside me, I felt as if I must recall him from that desolate resting place. Oh my husband! My husband! Lost forever! Oh Frank! Frank! How can I struggle on, [make?] my weary way through this cruel deserted world!"[14] By the second anniversary of her husband's death, however, Blake had gained some emotional distance: "Today I visited poor Frank's grave. [Unreadable word] that a life should be cut off so early—Alas! that a kind heart should cease to beat—God rest his soul!"[15]

Her fiction during the autumn and winter after Frank's death obliquely reflects both her profound grief and the violent circumstances surrounding it. "John Owen's Appeal" involves the abduction and death of two young girls; "A Lonely House" chronicles a double homicide; *Rockford* opens with graveside mourning: "Along the winding shore the sea swelled in sullen rage, dashing itself with low mutterings into the sheltered bays and coves, and beating with a defiant roar on one bold promontory that stood out in the gloomy waters. Here, on a bleak hill side, was a lonely and deserted burial-ground. Over it the bitter winds swept with a mournful wail, below it the restless waves moaned a ceaseless dirge."[16] The novel proceeds to complicate grief with issues of adultery and incest. The death of George Sandys is the occasion for innuendoes regarding his sexual relationship with Claudia Rockford and the paternity of her son, Vinton, who falls in love with Sandys's daughter, Mabel. The sexual relationship between George Sandys and Claudia Rockford is never directly admitted, remaining always as the unspoken deed of the novel. Through the text's careful silence, this pivotal act becomes an absence doubling the unspeakable loss and absence caused by death.

Claudia's husband, fifteen years older than his wife, a cold man reminiscent of Hawthorne's Chillingsworth, is obsessed with his suspicions. Vengefully, he pushes for the marriage between half-brother and half-sister, trying to manipulate his wife into revealing the truth. She remains unyielding, for the truth would expose her son to the retribution of a social order built on paternal lines of legitimacy. The child of her heart would be a bastard.

In a letter from Washington, an unnamed major in the Union Army, an admirer of Lillie, wrote: "The best thing in the book are certain dramatic scenes—the breaking up of the party at the Rockfords', which is admirable, and the tête-à-tête of Lionel and Adrienne in the crimson boudoir, which is *tremendous;* but I wish the latter had been less powerful and true, for half your readers will be too prudish to approve it, though they may like well enough to read it over more than once. Our virtuous and austere dames and gentlemen no doubt enjoy their cakes and ale as well as I do, but they won't say so, and they won't welcome a George Sand in American literature."[17] Like "A Tragedy of the Mammoth Cave" and *Southwold, Rockford* is significant in its attempt to deal once more with erotic passion within a cultural code, at least on the surface, of sexual reticence.

The theme of incest was a cultural taboo. When, in 1869, Harriet Beecher Stowe published "The True Story of Lady Byron's Wife" in which she exposed Byron's "secret adulterous intrigue with a blood relation," the press "heaped a torrent of abuse upon Stowe for daring to speak publicly of incest."[18] On the other hand, adultery and seduction were the stock-in-trade of fiction. Blake's subplot involves two attempted seductions, one by a typical femme fatale, another by a just as typical rake. But the novel goes beyond stereotypes in its main plot, condemning not the forbidden relationship that existed between

George and Claudia, but the silence that must shroud their love in secrecy. The only articulation of it that the world would relish is confession and repentance. As Claudia lies close to death, having demanded without explanation that her son break his engagement with Mabel Sandys, she is urged by a minister to relieve the burdens of her heart and partake in Christ's peace: "'Such are the consolations of your religion,' answered Mrs. Rockford, wearily. 'You cannot understand how useless they are to me—how little comfort I can have in such a creed. I cannot repair the injury I have inflicted. I will not make the reparation in my power—I do not even repent.'"[19] While in *Southwold*, Medora Fielding's anti-Christian statements became negative judgments upon her, Claudia Rockford's refusal to repent reveals only the obvious depth of her character—and of Lillie Devereux Umsted's movement toward greater freedom of thought and away from the restrictions of her upbringing.

"A Lonely House," is the story of a young family "overshadowed with the gloom of sudden and violent death."[20] Poet James Russell Lowell, Blake's editor at the *Atlantic Monthly*, wrote of this story, Blake's most successful work of the period: "It is rather savage, perhaps, but I liked it for leaving the ordinary highway."[21] Drawing on the archetype of the Cain and Abel story, "A Lonely House" concerns two brothers who, filled with rage and grief, kill each other after their widowed mother dies. Although Blake never gave direct public voice to the private grief that is very evident in her journals, through the figure of the widow who sequesters herself in the house after her young husband's death Lillie was able to convert her own sorrow into a meditation on concealment and self-slaughter. She displaced both Frank's violent suicide and the suppressed rage of the story's widow into a reciprocal fratricide.

At the very end of her life, even as she is hoping her final words will bring peace to her sons, the mother of "A Lonely House" is struck speechless. In fact, she had been inarticulate during most of her life, holding tightly to an anger that manifested itself in a still and deadly sternness. But rage, not acceptable in a woman, implodes in her furious sons. They, who "wholly resembled" their mother in her grave and severe demeanor, enact her emotional life through their bitter disputes. Loss always precedes the boys' rage—the killing of a pet in childhood, the loss of a woman in young manhood, and the final loss of their mother. When they lock themselves within the house to which their mother had retreated after the loss of her husband, they become an analogue of her and of all women trapped within domestic spaces. The home is the space wherein women learn not to acknowledge those unfeminine feelings of darkness and anger.[22] So it is there that the mother's sons fight to the death, giving a horrible physicality to her unexpressed emotions. The brothers subtly become each other's doubles, "their faces, so much alike that they seemed almost reflections of each other."[23] Thus, each kills the self by killing the other; homicide and suicide are halves of a single act that shatters the ingrained nomenclature of genealogy and continuity.

This story, not published until January 1861—on the eve of the Civil War—provides a metaphorical resonance with a war that both shattered and made a nation. It eerily foreshadows national mourning over a divided civic house in which brother would kill brother. When Lincoln declared that a house divided cannot stand, he chose a biblical metaphor which employed the rhetoric of domesticity with which we have come to associate women's writing of the nineteenth century. Unlike the rhetoric of rugged individualism, Lincoln's imagery linked the worldly sphere of war, designated as masculine, to home and hearth, the province of women. The Civil War hastened the process of unraveling those gendered divisions, a process that Blake would continue in subversive ways throughout her most radical postwar fiction. In "A Lonely House," as in the nation itself, violence both causes division and is caused by the divisiveness within. Violence lies within the domestic envelope, within the house divided. As she did in her treatment of the abused Lucy Wentworth in *Southwold,* Blake pierces through the façade of sentimental and patriarchal discourses on "home" that promise women safety for the price of freedom.

II

By the summer of 1860, murmurs of the "great division" permeated the coastal village of Stratford.[24] Stratford's influx of summer visitors included those from New York, North Carolina, Georgia, and parts of New England. Men from North and South mingled in friendship and shared, if for the last time, a single clubhouse and the same round of parties. After Lillie Umsted's year of mourning, Elm Cottage, like Maple Cottage before it, had become the hub of village social life. Mrs. Sarah Devereux held receptions every Monday evening, as well as frequent dinner parties and teas where politics often dominated the discussions. The disciplined Lillie wrote every day and in the mornings walked several blocks with one woman friend or another to a small cove in the Housatonic River to swim. There, along the shore, the family had built bathing houses. Summertime in Stratford meant "long sails on the sunny seas, picnics underneath the groves, dances in bright parlors and end-less visitings and flirtation until the Autumn came and once again the sum-mer visitors flitted away and the village returned to its usual tranquility."[25]

Any tranquility the autumn of 1860 brought was not to last. By November, Abraham Lincoln had been elected to the presidency, and Lillie noted in her diary: "the great event of the week has been the election; it has gone Repub-lican by a large majority, yet after all, Lincoln is a sectional choice. It is a great pity, I think. More than that I fear some evil may come of it and if so it is destruction to our southern hopes as well as trouble and ill-feeling every-where."[26] In the draft of her autobiography, Blake carefully edited out the word "southern" from this diary selection.[27] In some regards, Lillie Devereux Umsted felt herself to be a Southerner. She had been born on the plantation of her grandfather in Raleigh, North Carolina. Her father's only sister, Frances Devereux, married the Reverend Lionidas Polk of Louisiana, who later became General Polk of the Confederate Army. One of her earliest mem-ories was of slaves laboring in cotton fields. Her northern mother was once profoundly shocked to find her daughter in a wagon to which her nursemaid had hitched six little slave boys and girls. But, although born into plantation society, Lillie was raised among abolitionists in New Haven. She saw slavery as a "horrible" institution, a "curse" for which both sections of the country were initially responsible, and she wished that a confrontation between North and South could be avoided. She held vague hopes that the South could somehow be led to dismantle slavery in a humane way.[28] The election of Lincoln portended conflict, and Lillie and her family were apprehensive. During the following winter, when the southern states followed the lead of South Carolina in seceding from the Union, their feelings of sympathy for the South changed. "For a long time North Carolina refused to follow her sisters in their madness and we were proud of the loyalty of 'the old North State,' but at last the chain of the Confederacy was complete. From the moment that open rebellion was proclaimed, war declared, our hopes and prayers were with the Union though we never to the last day of the struggle ceased to feel a regretful sympathy with the sorrows of that section of the country where we had so many friends and relatives. . . . I call them 'rebels' now; they would de-stroy the Union and they are my enemies."[29]

Lillie's patriotic fervor was deeply aligned with her own need to secede from the social scripts reserved for women. On April 12, 1861, Fort Sumter, in the harbor of Charleston, was bombarded by the Confederate Army. Lincoln called up troops and ordered a blockade of southern seaports. Lillie, in

Philadelphia with her children on an extended visit to her husband's family, reacted to news of the attack with "What a curse that I was born a woman so that I can take no active part in the great work of the day!"[30] Like many women, including Louisa May Alcott, whose initial response to the war was "I long to be a man,"[31] Blake filled her diary for the spring of 1861 with words of bitter frustration that she must wait on the sidelines:

Saturday, April 13. . . . Maj. Anderson and his gallant band of one hundred soldiers are fighting against seven batteries and ten thousand men and we must sit tamely home and have the news dribbled out to us by unreliable telegrams! Oh, it is too terrible!

Tuesday, April 16. Definite news at last. Ft. Sumter surrendered on Saturday. The President has called for 75,000 men, the border states repudiate the call with indignation and will no doubt join the South. God help us, we have no longer a country! Ruin and distress stare us in the face. Oh if I were only a man I would join the army at once, no matter for death so that I were doing something in this great struggle. Any hardship is better than this crushing inactivity.

Friday, April 19. . . . Oh wretched country! The model Republic expiring in groans and blood! All is ominously quiet in the South, no one can tell when the rebels will march on Washington or where these troops will be ordered. It is easy to talk of war at a distance but who can guess at its hours of excitement and nights of anxiety but those who have tried them. Oh it is too cruel to be shut up here in this secluded village with nothing to turn my thoughts from this one horrid theme.

Wednesday, May 8. Home again after three days of fatigue in New York. While there went with G. to the Seventh Regiment Armory and later to see the Garibaldi brigade where soldiers were being drilled in three different languages. Today went down to the Battery and saw more soldiers. The city was greatly changed, the streets gay with flags and soldiers, but deserted by the country people. . . . The financial pressure is awful. Hundreds of young men thrown out of employment, business stagnant, the first houses have failed. My friends all gloomy, many of them with penury threatening them. And I can do nothing. I am only a woman. I cannot be a soldier, I can do nothing but keep quiet and suffer.[32]

What Lillie was expected to do was to sew; the hated activity became the central business of the women of Stratford. While young men began to die— Theodore Winthrop in July's battle of Big Bethal, three Stratford boys in

August—about fifty women met regularly to make bandages for the troops. Calling themselves The Stratford Patriotic Association, they elected Lillie as vice-president after she was offered, but declined, the presidency. Perhaps it was the prospect of this seemingly endless sewing circle that pushed Lillie out into the world. She was determined to go to Washington.

Still dependent upon her family's approval, Blake somehow prevailed upon her mother for permission to leave. Perhaps she renewed her suggestions that she go on the paid lecture circuit, an idea she had floated before—to her mother's utter horror (and to her own fear of "notoriety and censure").[33] At least a female reporter wrote in private instead of subjecting herself to the promiscuous gaze of a public audience. Still, it was less than what was expected of a lady. One woman writer agreed to report on a reception for General Grant for the *New York Tribune* only after Horace Greeley promised her a male escort in evening dress so that she would not be humiliated by being identified as a journalist.[34]

It may be that financial stresses played a part in her mother's willingness to let her daughter go to Washington. However Lillie managed it, that fall she and her mother closed up Elm Cottage, and Mrs. Devereux moved in with her younger daughter, the newly married Georgina Devereux Townsend, who had settled in Wallingford. Lillie and her children temporarily took rooms nearby.

Blake traveled to New York where she contracted with the *New York Evening Post* and the *New York World* to write columns (then called letters) from Washington at a rate of ten dollars each, almost what privates in the warring armies made in a month.[35] Leaving two-year-old Katie with her mother, she left Wallingford with Bessie, now four, on November 7, 1861. Traveling by train, Blake stopped in Philadelphia where she contracted with the *Post* for letters and with *Fornay's War Press* to write fiction, a story a week related to the war. Her sister Georgie and her husband met Lillie and Bessie there and escorted them to Washington where they took rooms at the famous Willard's Hotel at Fourteenth Street and Pennsylvania Avenue. Later Blake rented two rooms in nearby G Street.[36]

Julia Ward Howe was also staying at the Willard. She had come to the capital with her husband, Samuel Gridley Howe, who had been appointed a commissioner overseeing sanitary conditions for the Union troops. On November 18, the Howes rode out toward Bailey's Crossroads, Virginia, for a troop review, but a surprise rebel attack forced civilians to turn back. The road was clotted with troops, so to pass the time, Howe and her party sang army songs. Lillie Devereux Umsted arrived at the Willard the next day, November 19, 1861, that memorable day when Julia Ward Howe rose in the early hours of the morning to write new words to the song "John Brown's Body," producing what would become the "Battle Hymn of the Republic."[37] Though in close proximity, the two writers would not meet until another decade passed.

On November 20, 1861, from Munson's Hill, Blake watched the postponed grand review of 80,000 troops, "drawn up in a huge parallelogram" at Bailey's Crossroads: "it was there that I first saw Abraham Lincoln. He struck me as being singularly awkward and ungainly in figure, but although I had been violently prejudiced against him by persons who were politically his enemies, I noted there the amiable and patient expression of his face. I have never heard this last quality mentioned so prominently as I think it should be in dwelling on a description of this trait. In all the many times that I afterwards saw Mr. Lincoln, this look of patient endurance struck me as the one most characteristic of his countenance."[38] Blake humanizes Lincoln by feminizing him, attributing to him the patient endurance so often inscribed in stereotypes of the "true woman."

Back at the Willard that evening, Blake wrote five different versions of the day's events for her newspapers. Journalism was a venue open, in limited ways, to middle-class women. Since colonial times, women had been printers and editors, publishing such papers as Rhode Island's *Newport Mercury* and *Providence Gazette,* Charleston's *South Carolina Gazette,* and Boston's *Massachusetts Gazette.* In the nineteenth century there was a concerted effort to eliminate women from the printing trade; the National Typographical Union had a policy of actively discouraging their employment. But the number of women editors continued to increase and included Lydia Maria Child, who, in 1841, became the editor of the *Anti-Slavery Standard,* Sara Josepha Hale, who edited *Godey's Lady's Book* for forty years (1838–1877), and Margaret Fuller, who edited *The Dial* in 1840–1842. Fuller was the most distinguished of women journalists, hired in 1844 by Horace Greeley for the *Tribune.* Greeley also hired Jane Grey Swisshelm, the first female Washington correspondent and an outspoken abolitionist. She wrote for five dollars a column before the war and returned to Washington in 1863, where, in 1865, she started the short-lived *Reconstructionist.* Sara Jane Clarke Lippincott, who wrote as "Grace Greenwood," and Mary Abigail Dodge, known as "Gail

Hamilton," also worked in Washington both before the war and again later during Reconstruction. Perhaps the best-known woman correspondent after the war was Mary Clemmer Ames, who for twenty years beginning in 1866 wrote a "Woman's Letter from Washington" each week for the New York *Independent*.[39] There were, however, very few women who served as Washington correspondents during the war itself, and most were anonymous. Lillie Devereux Umsted was one. Her first of many letters was published in the Philadelphia *Post* on November 24, 1861.

When war broke out, male correspondents flocked to Washington, creating fierce competition and intrigue, sometimes trading good press for government documents.[40] Women found it difficult even to gain entry to the Capitol press galleries, where they were in direct competition with male reporters; access to social events and influential people who could provide material worth reporting was the key to the woman journalist's success. Blake had arranged for letters of introduction that provided her with entré to the highest circles: Yale's President Woolsey gave her a letter to Treasury Secretary Salmon P. Chase and Navy Secretary Gideon Welles; her former New Haven neighbor, Professor (later Yale president) Noah Porter, wrote on her behalf to Professor J. Henry of the Smithsonian Institute; her mother wrote to the wealthy Washington resident Dr. Ogle Taylor.[41] Blake's life in Washington was filled with social activities that provided her with subject matter for her columns—White House receptions, Washington dinners, teas, volunteering at the hospital, day trips out to Alexandria to see the troops were all written up for her papers. She met the president, his generals, his cabinet officers. She was received into the homes of General George B. McClellan, Attorney General Edward Bates, War Secretary Edwin Stanton, Secretary of State William Seward. General Henry W. Halleck escorted her to the opening of Congress on December 2, 1861.[42] She sat next to Anthony Trollope once at dinner. He asked her for a copy of *Southwold*, telling her that he had written for ten years before anyone would read his work.[43] Trollope was, Lille wrote home, "entirely bald, with a very handsome, full, iron gray beard, or rather black, streaked with iron gray, a very red face, a squat nose and spectacles—altogether hopelessly ugly, but he is not at all snobbish, and has a pleasant hearty, loud way of talking."[44] She was escorted to several functions by her cousin, Eli Whitney, Jr., and by N. P. Willis, poet, editor, and brother of Fanny Fern, who had roomed with her mother's brother at Yale and had written a wedding poem for Sarah Devereux's marriage. Lillie referred to him in a letter to her mother as "Hyacinthe, the Melifluous."[45] Lillie was not only on the initiating end of letters of introduction, which were the only proper means of initiating social contact. William Oliver Stone, who had painted her portrait in 1859, gave Carl Leutze a letter of introduction to her.[46] Leutze was painting "Washington Crossing the Delaware" for the Representatives' gallery. When Hawthorne arrived in Washington, he described meeting Leutze at work on the fresco: "It was an absolute comfort, indeed, to find Leutze so quietly busy at this great national work, which is destined to glow for centuries on the walls of the Capitol, if that edifice shall stand, or must share its fate, if treason shall succeed in subverting it with the Union which it represents. It was delightful to see him so calmly elaborating his design, while other men doubted and feared, or hoped treacherously, and whispered to one another that the nation would exit only a little while longer."[47]

Blake was frequently at the home of Professor Henry of the Smithsonian, whose daughter accompanied her to the Capitol galleries. In February she attended the debates in the Senate over the expulsion, on the grounds of disloyalty, of Jesse Bright, senator from Indiana, who had referred to Jefferson Davis as "His Excellency . . . President of the Confederate States." Lillie often had dinner with her mother's friends the Ogle Taylors, at whose home, because they were southern sympathizers, she had had to declare her allegiances, "lest I should be misunderstood and perhaps hear what was not intended for me."[48] Their house was "a nest of Secesh," she wrote in her diary, but she enjoyed the hospitality.[49] It was there, a day or two after Senator Bright's expulsion, that she was invited to a dinner party where he was the guest of honor. The company included "Mr. Erastus Corning of Albany, Mr. Corcoran the banker, Senators Kennelly of Maryland, Brice of Minnesota, and Harris of New York . . . Mr. Bright was in excitedly high spirits and talked loudly of 'coming back to his seat in triumph,' a hope," Blake adds, "which never has been fulfilled."[50] "Don't suppose for an instant," she wrote to her mother, "that anyone thinks because I dined with Bright etc. that I sympathize with him politically. The Taylors know that I don't."[51]

Bessie, a four-year-old chaperone, was her constant daytime companion. When Lillie volunteered at the hospital, reading to soldiers, Bessie was with her, and it may have been there, in January 1862, that she contracted typhoid fever. After an agonizing six weeks of severe illness, the child survived. Not long after, Tad Lincoln died of typhoid fever. Lillie saw the president at his first public appearance after his son's death: "the President walked up the aisle quite alone. He wore . . . an old brown overcoat which looked as if it needed brushing. His hair too was in the same condition. It was rather long and hung almost in elf locks about his face. And how sad that face was! So wistfully sad and so patient! The look of suffering endured without a murmur was stamped in every line, and my heart went out in sympathy for him, as I thought of how nearly I had been called upon to bear a similar grief."[52]

Anonymously or under pseudonyms, Lillie Devereux Umsted wrote for her papers on a wide variety of topics: the Sanitary Committee, which organized the war's hospital system and arranged for all those bandages sewn in villages like Stratford to reach the appropriate destination; balloon recognizance which, during moonlit nights, brought back information on rebel encampments; instances of "rebel barbarity" especially in regard to prisoners of war, including reports of a surgeon who was captured, bound, and then shot in the leg and of two dead Union soldiers who reportedly were fed to hogs; descriptions of "contrabands," as fleeing former slaves were called, arriving en masse in Washington, many carrying babies "of all shades of color";[53] puff pieces about the prevailing "dust, pies, and spittoons," of Washington.

Often Blake wrote, for the public, opinions that belied her own. After meeting Mary Todd Lincoln, she wrote to her mother that the president's wife "was plastered with chalk, or flour," but for her papers she dutifully noted that "She was as gracious as she ever is."[54] General McClellan she found to be "a heavy-looking man with . . . a face so ruddy . . . that it gave the unpleasant effect of a countenance and hair 'all of a color,'" but for her papers he became "our brave young general . . . distinguished by his thoughtful brow and clear gray eyes, and the air of command."[55] Blake complained in her diary about McClellan's long delay during the fall of 1861 in moving his troops into action. After the July 21 defeat at Manassas, the Army of the Potomac did little other than drill. In October federal forces again suffered a humiliating defeat at Ball's Bluff, about thirty miles from Washington. Blake wrote:

> I have from my personal knowledge of events always believed that if an advance had been made immediately after the review at Bailey's cross roads, substantial advantages might have been gained. I do not think indeed that our troops would then have met any serious obstacle in taking Richmond. That unfortunate delay gave the rebels time for preparation which was what they most needed, and demoralized the national army.
>
> After that date, November 22, followed six weeks of beautiful weather

and then came a long period of storms—day after day rain and sleet fell; the soldiers, most of whom were taken from lives of comfort, sickened in the unusual hardship and the troops lost instead of gaining with every day. Those six weeks of inaction were the golden opportunity lost. To members of McClellan's staff whom I knew I would say as much. They however had ready excuses for the delay, but I fancy the gaieties of Washington life did much to reconcile most of them to the detention. The officers of out-lying regiments were not so patient.[56]

The joke around Washington, Blake wrote her mother, was that the Army of the Potomac had not yet advanced because McClellan's staff was waiting for the Willard to charge (i.e., the pun is on "charge" as both a military and commercial term; once the hotel presented them with its bill, they would have to leave town). But for her papers Blake wrote about the "confidence the whole army has in McClellan."[57] By and large, such circumspection was the journalistic rule of the day; Hawthorne spoofed the principle in "Chiefly About War Matters," published in July 1862 in the *Atlantic Monthly*, by adding his own editorial comments about supposedly omitted offensive passages: "We omit several paragraphs here, in which the author speaks of some prominent Members of Congress with a freedom that seems to have been not unkindly meant, but might be liable to misconstruction. . . . [or] . . . We are again compelled to interfere with our friend's license of personal description and criticism."[58] Abolitionists, however, did criticize President Lincoln and his appointees. Lydia Maria Child called William Seward a "'crooked and selfish hypocrite' because he had pandered to the Southern states during the secession crisis."[59] McClellan was often condemned for not aggressively managing the war. Treasury Secretary Chase was allied with abolitionists and was considered by them as an alternative candidate for president in 1864.[60] Blake, more interested in earning her living, did not discriminate too closely among her avenues to a story for her papers.

Lillie was wooed by many an army officer in Washington and was privy to confidential information. She knew beforehand when, in February, General McClellan and his staff left on a tour preparatory to an advance. When they returned at the beginning of March, she wrote home,

> Colonel Hudson came in to tell me of their trip. They made a tour of inspection through the lines, going to Harper's Ferry, then, although the stream was very rapid and much swollen by recent rains, a pontoon

page one. Front-page engravings on occasion illustrated not the latest battle, but Blake's latest plot. For instance, April 6–7, 1862, brought a Union victory in the western theater at Shiloh, one with enormous losses on both sides: the Union lost as many as 13,000 men, while the Rebels lost at least 10,000. Meanwhile, the march of the Army of the Potomac under General McClellan southward along the peninsula between the James and York Rivers resulted in the month-long siege of Yorktown that began on April 5. However, the front page engraving for the April 12 edition of the *War Press* illustrated not these latest engagements, as the readership might well expect, but the headquarters of General Edward D. Baker at Camp Observation, Maryland, just before the Battle of Ball's Bluff, which had taken place six months earlier. On October 21, 1861, federal forces had built temporary bridges to cross the Potomac at Ball's Bluff, thirty miles upstream of Washington, D.C. They destroyed the bridges behind them so that rebel troops would be unable to cross the river. It seemed not to occur to them that in so doing they left *themselves* with insufficient means to recross in a hurry. When they were routed and could not ford the river, they suffered enormous casualties, among them General Baker. Although militarily not an important battle, it was significant for its bungling and for its loss of Baker, who was a senator from Oregon and a close friend of President Lincoln. Blake's fiction for this issue of the *War Press* weaves in the fact of Senator Baker's death with the fictional death of her protagonist, and in an analogous conflation of fact and fiction, the *War Press* used its major engraving to illustrate its fiction rather than its news.

The realities of war reports and battlefront engravings intruded upon the content of Blake's stories as she moved from sentimental to realistic styles and cautiously introduced violence into her fiction. At each step there is an attempt to maintain distance, to keep death from intruding upon the domestic circle, but soon Blake wove in realistic settings and actual events, dealt with a range of social classes, and overrode sentimental evasions to write of death and loss.

On February 1, 1862, Blake published "A Ball and a Duel" in the *War Press*. This story and the next, "The Lieutenant's Courtship," published on February 8, are typical of many mid-century pieces which found their way into print. Stories of romance were of particular popularity in the papers. Gallant soldiers and bereft fiancées, heroic intentions and stalwart faithfulness predominated. When death occurred, it came complete with time out for patriotic last words. Missing were the realities of the battlefields. The gore and stench of death, the makeshift hospitals with piles of amputated arms and legs out back were replaced by patriotic pieties. The public was eager for evasions of all sorts, and many authors never made mention of the war at all. But each of Blake's fifteen stories (published between February 1862 and March 1863) is subtitled "A Story of the War," and if, in these first two, war is incidental to the plot, it is analogically significant. Possession of a woman is the gendered iconography of the civil conflict, and the war plot is closely patterned after the marriage plot. Through this analogy—ancient in the tradition of war literature—Blake took her first steps across the cultural bridge between the male and female spheres to conjoin the war's violence with the myth of inviolate domesticity.

In "A Ball and a Duel," when conflict does arise, it is in ballroom terms, with soldiers vying for a woman whose dilemma, like many in the nation, is to choose sides. The domestic plot concludes with marriage and friendship. The war plot, too, ends in reconciliation. The dueling field is the midpoint between ballroom and battleground, and conflict in the form of an organized fight allows for both the introduction and the containment of violence.

The analogy between war and duel, which might have held in the heroic past of myth, was anachronistic by the time of the Civil War and was an evasion of its brutal warfare and anonymous killing. Much of the structure of Washington social life was just as evasive. The lavish Calvalry Ball that Blake describes in "A Ball and a Duel" was typical of many given even after the outbreak of war. Harmony among the rival soldiers at the ball, which was attended by representatives of "nearly all the loyal States, and even of some disloyal ones, too," reflects the reality of the social composition of many gatherings in Washington early in the war. Mrs. Lincoln came under considerable criticism for what some deemed to be excessive spending for White House parties. Lydia Sayer Hasbrouck, editor of the reformist periodical *Sibyl*, criticized not only the continuation of balls while the war went on, but also Mrs. Lincoln's use of $20,000 for renovating the White House and her "extravagant clothes and jewels."[65]

In Blake's second story of the war, "The Lieutenant's Courtship," violence, in vague threats, is relegated to the very margins of possibility. The plot turns on no greater mishap than a woman falling off her horse after a picnic. But that is enough to introduce war tropes—rescue by a patriotic soldier, a faithful fiancée waiting at home, and home itself idealized as an edenic myth of innocence. A picnic and genteel games depict a social life that seems to lack even the wished-for violence we find in a book like *Little Women,* which, set during the Civil War, succeeds in scarcely mentioning it. And yet, although Blake's story keeps at bay fears that the wartime enterprise may be far more difficult than saving a girl from a bolting pony, it is the woman who *is* in danger, whose very innocence is jeopardized by the fact that her rescue entails a night alone with her suitor-rescuer, outside the safety of her home. Thus, this rather innocuous story transports a woman out of the domestic sphere of home and picnic grounds into the dangers of the woods and of the night, where not only is she wounded but her reputation for innocence is compromised. While catering to the public taste for evasion of the war's worst possibility—the violation of the domestic sphere and the loss of the nineteenth century's myth of an innocent eden—the story actually conceals within it that very possibility. The surface seductively assures the audience that there will always be a rescuer at hand, a gentlemanly soldier who will fix the current wrongs and put the world in order. And a woman's role is to silently assert that there will always be a loved one at home awaiting the soldier's return. Early in the war, such clichés sufficed.

IV

At the beginning of 1862, General McClellan was still organizing and drilling the Army of the Potomac. The western army was more active, but an important battle did not occur until February 6, when Major General Halleck ordered Ulysses Grant to move on Fort Henry in Tennessee. In its February 15 edition, the *War Press* included an engraving of Grant's capture of Fort Henry and that of the 22nd depicted the successful bombardment of Roanoke Island by General Ambrose Burnside. Grant next, on February 16, took Fort Donelson and its entire garrison. Amid reports of the successful Union action in the western theater, high numbers of casualties were cited in the *War Press,* and Blake's third story, which appeared on March 1, 1862, reflects not picnics and balls, but the fatal interaction between Rebel and Union soldiers.

"A Wild Night Ride" makes explicit the war's violent invasion of the domestic sphere while safely containing it within a dream. In a nightmarish chase, a young Yankee soldier flees Rebel forces, his fiancée inexplicably appears, and the couple is captured and summarily executed just as the dreaming narrator awakens. If "The Lieutenant's Courtship" had reminded the audience of the sentimental premise that the protection of home and the angels within it are why men go off to fight, "A Wild Night Ride" engages with terror the very real threats of war. Here the typically sentimental heroine gliding in white becomes an angelic martyr at the hands of Rebel forces. But because the violence is displaced within a dream, a nightmare sequence from which one can awaken, the reader is kept distant from, and in control of, its terror.

While violence is contained within the dream, the dream is contained within domestic scenes, enveloped before and after with comrades sharing a bottle of wine and the dreamer safely sleeping in his tent. This benign envelope hides within it the basic truth of war. The envelope of domesticity *contains* the story's violence in both senses of the term: it keeps it under control and holds it within itself. The imagery of Lincoln's words is again fulfilled: violence lies within the domestic space, within the house divided.

At the center of her story, within the dream of violence, Blake constructs a moment that conjoins violent and domestic elements. Enveloped by sheer terror, first of the chase and then of the execution, the sudden reunion of the soldier and his lover takes place astride a galloping horse. As his fiancée swings herself up upon his saddle, the dreaming hero—fleeing rebels—takes time to relish the unexpected intimacy of the moment: "the night was so lovely, the swaying motion was so pleasant, and I held Laura so close, that I could not realize my danger."[66] The very violence of the battle chase, manifested in the swaying motion of the galloping horse, dissolves into a sexualized moment that pierces through to complex connections between home and battleground, female space and male arena, sex and violence.

V

The engraving for the March 22 edition of the *War Press* depicts the first naval battle between iron-clad ships, the *Monitor* and the *Merrimac*. On March 8, the *Merrimac,* built in Norfolk, Virginia, had destroyed the U.S. frigates *Cumberland* and *Congress* and forced the *Minnesota* aground, but the *Monitor,* built in Brooklyn, neutralized the *Merrimac,* and subsequently a large fleet of iron-clads based on the *Monitor*'s design was built. Blake was at a Washington reception on the evening of this battle: "There was much agitation all that day over the news from Fortress Monroe of the advance of the Merrimack [*sic*] and the city was yet in suspense when I went to the entertainment. While there each guest as he arrived brought news of what had occurred, and at last Count Garouski came in fresh from the War Office with the welcome intelligence that the gallant little Monitor had driven back her unwieldy antagonist."[67]

It was not until the next day that McClellan's army began its long-delayed advance toward Richmond:

> I went home and lay awake half the night listening to the tramp of soldiers past my windows, the clattering of horses' feet over the stones as orderlies dashed here and there with orders, and the distant bugle notes of the encampments.
>
> The next morning half a dozen of my officer friends paused at my door for a hasty goodbye. They went to danger, perchance to death, and I gave them my best wishes in farewell, looked after them with eyes full of tears. Later the same day I drove with friends to the long bridge and saw the army cross.
>
> What a sight that was! Long lines of soldiers moving on, not in holiday pageantry but in the grim reality of war. Horse, foot and artillery, they filed away, those blue coated men.[68]

Much of the war's land action was still taking place in the western theater, at Forts Henry and Donelson in Tennessee, about sixty miles east and slightly south of Cairo, Illinois, where the Mississippi meets the Ohio. This nub of freedom, so crucial to the runaway Jim in *Huckleberry Finn* (1884), is the setting of Blake's fourth and most important *War Press* story, published on March 22, 1862.

Real, not dreamt, violence fills "The Rescued Fugitives." Distancing the war temporally, geographically, and racially, the story is set several months back in time, in November 1861, on the distant Ohio River, and the violence is associated with a runaway slave, Neptune, who rises up out of the river like a sea-god, much as Joseph Cinque, the Amistad African jailed in the New Haven of Blake's childhood, rose up from the Atlantic to save his comrades. Blake builds the story upon a series of contradictions in its view of Neptune, contradictions that indicate the fluid boundaries of racial stereotypes of the period. By allowing these stereotypes to clash, she subverts the racist expectations of her audience.[69] Blake, who so early in her life was provided with the heroic image of Joseph Cinque, was able persistently to suggest the black man as leader, even if, to appease her audience, she had to present her image in covert ways.

"The Rescued Fugitives" is the first of several stories in which Blake deals with race and slavery in ways that were unusual for the times. Her northern audience, and even most abolitionists, held what to early twenty-first-century readers are racist attitudes. While Blake was publishing her fiction every other week for the middle-brow *War Press*, Rebecca Harding Davis was writing for the elite, reformist *Atlantic Monthly*, and, as Sharon M. Harris points out, Davis like other antislavery advocates "did not always rise above the nation's racism, even when she was . . . at her abolitionist best."[70] Davis's "Blind Tom," published in the November 1862 issue of the *Atlantic*, recounts the true story of a young, black idiot-savant, whom Davis heard during his concertizing before the Civil War. While bringing her moving theme of "soul starvation" to bear on the caged spirits of an enslaved people, Davis describes Tom as "of the lowest negro type, from which only field-hands can be made,—coal-black, with protruding heels, the ape-jaw, blubber-lips constantly open."[71] In "John Lamar," published in the April 1862 issue, she creates an aesthetically powerful portrayal of the human desire for freedom, yet she is not free of brutal racist stereotyping. The "skulking," "blubber lipped" Ben is a "human brute," a "gorilla," in contrast to the "white dove," his mistress.[72] To be free, Ben kills his master. Giddy with the deed, he sets not a northerly course toward freedom, but, fulfilling white racial fears, a southerly one toward that white dove of a mistress whose lips his own blubber ones yearn to press.

No such cruel racial stereotypes are in Blake's work, yet they were acceptable, common, and scarcely noted by the readership of the *Atlantic Monthly*, which, though calling in April 1862 for emancipation as "the demand of civilization," had noted in the previous issue that while "a certain degree of idleness would have a charm for a time, even to an Anglo-American . . . [w]hat shall we say, then, of an inferior race, slave-born, ignorant, and undisciplined by moral influences?"[73] In the March issue a brigade of contrabands is described riding through the streets of Springfield, Illinois, "rolling about in their saddles with their shiny faces on broad grin."[74]

While they may have opposed slavery or at least its cruelties, mid-nineteenth-century citizens took for granted white racial superiority. Many questioned the very humanity of the slaves; when abolitionist icons of chained slaves ran the captions "Ain't I a Man?" or "Ain't I a Woman?" the question was posed because the answer was hotly debated.[75] The *Atlantic*, however, made an issue of calling slaves men and women, not boys and girls.[76] It is significant that Blake makes a point of referring to Neptune as "man." When her narrator first addresses him as "my man," the "my," adding elements of possession and dominance, softens for her audience the ideology implied by "man." Having introduced the charged word in this modified way, she thereafter uses it continually without modification.

The racism of many northern soldiers has been well documented, but Blake's narrator, a lieutenant in the Union Army, rushes to offer a hand to Neptune as he rises up out of the Ohio and swims to shore. The lieutenant stands in contrast to those many in the reading public who could be presumed to share the feelings of Miss Ophelia in *Uncle Tom's Cabin*. She, although an antislavery proponent, could not bear to touch a Negro. As Davis writes in "Blind Tom": "Southerners know nothing of the physical shiver of aversion with which even the Abolitionists of the North touch the negro."[77] But Blake's lieutenant, without hesitation, gives Neptune a drink from his own flask.

The lieutenant's charity toward Neptune, whom he refers to as the "forlorn creature," is not only an ideological nod toward the slave's humanity, it is also symptomatic of the kindhearted superiority of mid-nineteenth-century romantic racialists, who saw in black slaves the long-suffering martyrdom of the ideal Christian. Good deeds displayed the humanitarian nobility of a privileged elite, which carefully maintained safe, if compassionate, distances.[78] The lieutenant is the spokesman for a series of racialist descriptions: the "splendid-looking" Neptune is the only man subjected to a detailed physical inspection. The need for comment on his obvious intelligence suggests the prevailing racist presumption of a slave's lack of intelligence and is countered by a comment regarding his obvious ignorance. References made to "some admixture of patrician blood" leave no doubt that Neptune's "higher" qualities derive from an interracial heritage. And a mention of tears forming in his eyes conveys the popular notion that blacks were both infantile and emotional. Thomas Wentworth Higginson, best known today as Emily Dickinson's editor, was an abolitionist, an antislavery preacher, a member of the Boston Anti-Slavery Vigilance Committee, one of the financial backers of John Brown's revolt at Harpers Ferry, and the commander of a black regiment during the Civil War. In "Gabriel's Defeat," in the *Atlantic*'s September 1862 issue, Higginson recovers the history of a slave insurrection in Virginia. Sixty years before John Brown's revolt, a thousand armed slaves were led by the heroic Gabriel. Yet, in his 1870 memoir, *Army Life in a Black Regiment*, Higginson invariably refers to his men as children, docile and lovable, who made good soldiers because of their boyish enthusiasm.[79]

The remark, during the lieutenant's initial questioning of Neptune, that "the African is slow of speech" is especially revealing of how romantic racialism worked to hide what whites feared to know about slaves: that they would never volunteer information or, under questioning, give any more than was necessary. However, this form of resistance was interpreted by the dominant culture as childlike ignorance or as stupidity. In effect, by viewing the black as a symbol of only that version of Christianity which valued unquestioning passivity, romantic racialists were able to quell any apprehensions they might have had concerning the dangers for themselves which lie waiting to erupt from beneath any oppressive institution. Here lies the value of Rebecca Harding Davis's story of Ben who, even while loving his master, kills him for his freedom.

Blake not only taps into her audience's view of the slave as childlike, docile, and dependent, but she also engages their fears concerning his potential danger. Neptune convinces the band of Union soldiers to return with him behind enemy lines to retrieve his wife, Rose, and their child. During the maneuver, with no anxiety of conscience, he kills a Rebel sentry. He is eagerly aggressive and twice "begged to be the attacking party." His aggression is tinged with overtones of elemental evil: he is described as snakelike: "gliding flat on his face across the muddy path, and so stealing down the bank, and dropping quietly into the water." Later, he, "noiseless and sudden as death, glided up the bank." When he kills, the white soldiers "shudder." Here the mutually sustaining stereotypes of the menacing black and the conscience-sensitive whites cater to the fears and the patriotic vanities of the audience.

Other details of the text, however, subtly expose the racism and the hypocrisy of these stereotypes. Throughout the story, Blake presents and contradicts stereotypical views of the character of blacks and of the behavior of whites. Her allusion to "black possibilities" refers ironically to the white practice of raping slave women. And while Neptune's victim is termed "the unfortunate sentry," his killing dubbed "the murder," and much is made of his actions, the whites who "shudder" at Neptune's deed are in fact soldiers who are "well armed," and the narrator himself tells us that he "took aim as well as [he] could in the darkness at the nearest guard. He fell wounded or killed." Such details subvert the foregrounded stereotype and serve to question the consistency of attitudes which not only viewed whites as morally superior to blacks, but blacks as closer, however unwittingly, to the "redemptive" mode of Christian suffering than whites, and which saw, for example, blacks as both docile and aggressive, innocent and evil, long-suffering and vengeful.

As it sifts through racial stereotypes, one often undercutting another, the story gives evidence of the societal struggle with changing cultural codes and values. Blake's most compelling image of Neptune, one that subverts existing stereotypes, shows him as a capable leader in a dangerous situation. Neptune is "wise on the subject" of river currents, of Rebel troop organization, of the territory to be traversed. The lieutenant, in a question that suggests that he is at a loss as to what to do next ("'Now, how will you get them out?'"), turns over the responsibility of the rescue to the runaway slave, and by the end of the expedition Neptune is the leader, with the white men following him to the river. If Blake wanted to be published, she had to cover up and complicate this view, which ran counter to the racist narratives more comfortably familiar to her readers. As in a puzzle built on contradictory reconfigurations of its elements, her counterview of Neptune is most accessible as a textual contradiction. The image is submerged in and by the text. A variety of racial stereotypes camouflage it. Her audience could account for Neptune's expertise by perceiving it through their notions of the black's radical "Otherness": to the narrator, indeed, Neptune seems almost animal-like, if not supernaturally gifted, in his rapid running, his absolute noiselessness, and his uncanny knowledge of every spot on river or land. Immediately after Neptune has successfully assumed leadership of the rescue operation, as if to cut the impact and distract the reader from its significance, Blake inserts a stock episode which diminishes Neptune's authority and uses racist gags to reassert the dominant white hierarchy which has been challenged by Neptune's superiorities. It is a scene that has been made familiar by Twain's use of it twenty years later in *Huckleberry Finn,* when he has Huck and Tom play upon the supposed superstitious fears of the Negro; here Neptune leads two soldiers in frightening a black guard, whose "eyes rolled up till they displayed the whites." Many examples of this racist scene can be found in contemporary prose, cartoons, and illustrations. It would have provided the audience with a safe, familiar portrayal of blacks as infantile and easily terrified, and would, therefore, serve to hide Blake's inscription of an alternative narrative, one in which the black is a capable, superior leader of white men.

While most of her audience would be incapable of imagining such a black leader, they, like the lieutenant who can pity a "forlorn creature," would be able to form emotional connections with the plight of slave families.[80] Abolitionist texts tended to draw upon white middle-class empathy by scripting portraits of slave families ruptured through sale and disbursement. Thus,

Blake further complicates her view of Neptune by merging and contradicting the stereotypes of the almost animal-like slave and the slave as adolescent jester with one that combines elements of the Noble Savage and the idealized family man: on the return home, Neptune emerges "carrying the baby on one arm, while with the other he tenderly sustained his dusky Rose." Within half a sentence, moreover, Blake can alternate her contradictory images, moving Neptune out of one stereotype into another, tapping into one emotional pool of her readership and then another: "Handing the baby to Rose, wary and agile as a snake, he stole upon his victim . . ."

Throughout Lillie Blake's career, her technique would be to acquiesce in the presumed attitudes of her audience but, under the cover of inconsistencies, to dismantle those very attitudes. In "The Rescued Fugitives," the piling up of stereotypes that offer conflicting views of Neptune's character suggests both the fluidity of the boundaries of these stereotypes at a moment in history when events had thrust them into question and the confusion that is concomitant with struggles in the popular culture to reenvision the slave as freedman.

VI

Blake did well financially during her stint in Washington, making enough to pay all of her living expenses for the entire year. She was making a mark as a writer and longed to continue, but her mother, who only reluctantly approved of Lillie's work, pressured her to return to her second child, left behind in Wallingford. Blake wrote to her mother that "I have a reputation to make as a newspaper writer which may be of great help to me in the future," and requested that her summer clothes and Bessie's be sent to Washington.[81] But apparently her mother prevailed, because in April Lillie was back in Connecticut. Twenty years later, she finally admitted that she was hampered in her move into the world by, among other things, her mother: "I who desired to advance with a free step must only pace on slowly with fetters on my ankles. If anyone wonders that I did not defy these restrictions, I would remind them that my rearing and associations were especially hampering, and that I had an adored mother whose conservative views I could not think of outraging."[82]

But Blake persisted in her dream of becoming an independent woman and a writer. Her plan was to work out of New York City, now an easy train ride from Connecticut. Meanwhile, during the summer of 1862, to escape the heat inland, she took her mother and children to North Hampton and then to Sachem's Head on Long Island Sound. She continued her annual spring and fall visits to New Haven, staying for a week or two with the John DeForests, and she proceeded with her writing, completing her series of stories begun that winter in Washington for the *War Press.*

In December 1862, Lillie Umsted left her two children under the supervision of her mother and in the care of her Wallingford landlady in whose home she had taken rooms and went to New York City. For three weeks while she sought correspondence work, Lillie stayed with friends in a house near Stuyvesant Square. A battle raged at Fredricksburg, where Henry Lord Page King was fighting, and she longed to see him. Instead, she spent her days making the rounds of publishers, meeting with little success: "Could not see Mr. Godwin at the Evening Post, could not get the money I needed, found I had lost a room I had engaged. In the afternoon saw Mr. D. from whom I had hoped to get work and found that hope also had failed. I am sick of this mortifying, heart breaking, crushing struggle!"[83] A solution to her crisis presented itself two days later in the usual form: "Mr. H. sent me a splendid basket of flowers and then called and laid his hand and fortune at my feet. He is an excellent man, I know, but I cannot marry him."[84]

The next day Lillie returned, discouraged, to Wallingford, and on the day after, December 24, she learned that Henry King was dead on the battlefield at Fredericksburg. Her grief was profound, but, as grief almost always would for Lillie Blake, it reactivated her courage and her determination. In January 1863, she returned to New York and began writing for the *Evening Post,* the *Leader,* Frank Leslie's publications, the *Home Journal,* and the *Weekly Mercury.* Blake rented two "tiny rooms" on the top floor of a boardinghouse on the corner of Irving Place and Fourteenth Street. There, she was "absolutely alone" for the first time in her life.[85]

5. Reconstruction:
The Making of a Radical Reformer

The Pilgrim mothers not only had to endure all
that the Pilgrim fathers suffered, but had to endure
the Pilgrim fathers as well.
—Grace Greenwood

I

In the spring of 1863, Lillie Umsted was among the throng of people waiting to hear Anna Dickinson, "the 'Joan of Arc' of the abolitionist movement," deliver a lecture titled "The Conduct of the War" at New York's Cooper Institute, where she gave several speeches that season. The hall overflowed. Blake's diary recorded that her escort had reserved seats, but the crowd was so massive that they could not get inside.[1]

Anna Dickinson was a new phenomenon on the lecture circuit: scarcely twenty and beautiful, she was a charismatic speaker who maintained an acceptable feminine demeanor.[2] Blake was thrilled by Dickinson's power to influence crowds of people: "Standing there, I surveyed the scene, that mighty multitude hanging on the lips of a woman! My heart beat exultant as I looked on and I thought if I too could ever take my place like her, as an active worker, how glorious it would be."[3] Fifteen years later, on June 3, 1878, it was Lillie Devereux Blake who had to be dragged through the crowds extending far out into the street, pressing into Cooper Institute, filling the aisles, and overflowing the platform upon which *she* was to make a speech.[4]

Perhaps inspired by Dickinson, who also spoke on women's issues, in May 1863, Blake published in the *Knickerbocker,* anonymously, "The Social Condition of Woman."[5] Its radical premise is that gender identity is secondary to human identity. Blake insists that people share a common nature, but are trained in gender roles—in other words, that gender is socially constructed and historically contingent. She maintains that women as well as men have a need for self-fulfilling action in the world and require an equal education to reach their human potential. The historian of journalism Frank Luther Mott called the essay "a startling article . . . demanding for women 'entire equality on every point—politically, legally and socially.'"[6]

Although it may seem innocuous to the contemporary reader, Blake's premise countered the very heart of nineteenth-century woman's culture, for underlying the ideas of "woman's separate sphere" and "woman's moral superiority" was the presumption that the sexes were radically different. Lillie Blake can be aligned with a small minority of suffragists who saw the dangers for women's progress in emphasizing gender differences. Elizabeth Cady Stanton was a leading member of this group. As Lori D. Ginzberg writes: "Unlike most nineteenth-century woman's rights leaders . . . [Stanton] believed that the ideology of female moral superiority could ultimately benefit only those who opposed their cause."[7] Ellen Carol DuBois places Stanton in a radical line stemming from Mary Wollstonecraft and Frances Wright, who based their suffragism on the principle that women and men share a common nature and thus must share common rights.[8]

Throughout the nineteenth century there were notable voices arguing for equality. The Grimké sisters brought biblical passages to bear on the issue. There was no distinction between men and women "as moral and intelligent beings," wrote Angelina Grimké in an 1837 letter to Mary S. Parker, president of the Boston Female Anti-Slavery Society, a letter which was published the following year in *Letters on the Equality of the Sexes, and the Condition of Woman.*[9] Margaret Fuller, in *Woman in the Nineteenth Century* (1845), also stressed that women must fulfill their *human* potential through self-development. Their position harkened back to the eighteenth century, which had produced not only the American democracy, but thinkers like Mary Wollstonecraft, who based her suffragism on Enlightenment principles of natural rights. In 1790, two years before Wollstonecraft published "A Vindication of the Rights of Women," Judith Sargent Murray's essay "On the Equality of the Sexes" appeared in the *Massachusetts Magazine.* Both the British Wollstonecraft and the American Murray argued that the miseducation of women renders them inferior and that their dependence on men prevents them from sharing in the rights that should be common to humanity.

Nineteenth-century thought, however, emphasized sexual polarity and the primacy of biology over culture. Darwinian theory, stressing the inevitability of sexual differentiation in the evolutionary process, bolstered these beliefs. Women, perceived to have smaller brains and immense reproductive systems, were presumed to be less rational and educable than men and more subject to their biological functions. After the rhetoric of universal suffrage, which was based on natural rights, had failed to win women inclusion in the Fourteenth Amendment, suffrage leaders began to base their demands on nineteenth-century arguments that stressed women's differences. A woman's influence was idealized as a force that radiated out from the domestic space into every area of the social order. "The influence of woman is not circumscribed by the narrow limits of the domestic circle. She controls the destiny of every community. The character of society depends as much on the fiat of woman as the temperature of the country on the influence of the sun," wrote Henry Wright in *The Empire of the Mother over the Character and Destiny of the Race*.[10]

These ideas not only functioned to keep women in their proper place by circumscribing and idealizing it, but also made more acceptable women's work for the rights of others—in the abolitionist movement—and against the moral improprieties of drunkenness and the resulting hardships for (other) women and their families—in the temperance movement and in other philanthropic activities. In fact, calling for reform was women's work. Men of the patriarchy, forced into the corruption of the world, depended upon the moral sensibilities of women to fight against flaws in the social order.

Such notions were useful to the woman's movement because they bypassed the issue of inferiority by stressing difference. They authorized women's claim to a role in political life and valorized the bonds of women's networking for the good of others.[11] For the most part American suffragists followed the line of thought of Catharine Beecher and others who emphasized the distinctive nature of woman, her special needs, and unique role. They sought to elevate woman's role within the domestic sphere and to extend that role into the public world.[12] Even Elizabeth Cady Stanton, whose radical ideology Blake admired, at times articulated mainstream thought on gender differences. In an 1868 review of a speech on the identity of the sexes, which had been made before the British Association for the Advancement of Science and had created a furor in the London and Dublin press, Stanton wrote,

> . . . it matters not whether women and men are like or unlike, woman has the same right man has to choose her own place. . . . We started on Miss Becker's ground twenty years ago, because we thought, from that standpoint, we could draw the strongest arguments for woman's enfranchisement. And there we stood firmly entrenched, until we saw that

stronger arguments could be drawn from a difference in sex, mind as well as body. But while admitting a difference, we claim that that difference gives man no superiority, no rights over woman that she has not over him. We see a perfect analogy everywhere in mind and matter; and finding sex in the whole animal and vegetable kingdoms, it is fair to infer that it is in the world of thought also.[13]

"The Social Condition of Woman" was also radical in its discussion of marriage. Blake clearly identifies marriage, in a social order that excludes women from other means of earning their livelihoods, as institutionalized prostitution.[14] It was six years later, in May 1869, that Stanton declared marriage between unequal partners as "nothing more nor less than legalized prostitution."[15] Ellen DuBois writes, "At first Stanton's insistence that feminists declare for individual freedom and equality in marriage as well as in politics was not well received. The notion that woman should have 'sovereignty' over her sexuality, that her own wishes should take precedence over her husband's or that of any other external authority, seemed even to some feminists to spell the end of marriage and the family."[16] In fact, another century would pass before a woman's right to exclusive ownership of her body would be legally recognized, for even in recent decades husbands were still protected from prosecution on the charge of marital rape.

In the same month that "The Social Condition of Woman" appeared anonymously in the *Knickerbocker,* Elizabeth Cady Stanton and Susan B. Anthony founded the Woman's National Loyal League, a feminist-abolitionist group. On May 14, 1863, at the Church of the Puritans in New York City, Stanton and Anthony held their first meeting of the group that was to become a prototype for their postwar woman's rights organization: it was national rather than local, it stressed petitioning as a strategy for attaining political influence, and, most important, it was run by women. While women were the bedrock of the significant reform movements of the century, heretofore they had infrequently held positions of leadership. Even the 1848 Seneca Falls convention, which produced Stanton's famed *Declaration of Sentiments,* was chaired by a man. The formation of the League "signaled," writes Wendy Hamond Venet, "the passing of leadership to a second generation of abolitionist women, a generation as dedicated to feminism as they were to antislavery."[17]

Although she was closely allied ideologically with the burgeoning feminist movement, as "The Social Condition of Woman" demonstrates, Blake did not meet Stanton and Anthony in May. She had left the city and was not aware of the establishment of the League. It would be six more years before their paths would cross. Meanwhile, the "startling" ideas of "The Social Condition of Woman" would remain anonymous for a hundred and fifty years.

After her three-month sojourn in New York City, Blake had reunited with her children, taking them and her mother for the spring and summer to Orange, New Jersey. For the next five years, her life would rotate around winter lodgings, summer rooms, and long visits with friends. Her nomadic form of living was not at all unusual among the middle classes in New York City:

> Soaring land prices put single-family twenty-five-foot-wide row houses out of reach. Middle-class salaried employees making two thousand dollars a year could seldom afford a ten- to eighty-thousand dollar town house. . . . Many abandoned private ownership altogether and became boarders. As commerce marched into Union Square, the rich decamped northward, and their elegant town houses along lower Fifth and Madison avenues were subdivided and converted into respectable boardinghouses for doctors, lawyers, professors, and smaller merchants. Rooms here might cost from twelve to fifteen dollars a week in 1869. Hotels were another option, and those willing to settle for modest accommodations had a wide choice.[18]

In her summer quarters in New Jersey, Lillie complained about the heat and the mosquitoes. The publication of *Rockford* was delayed until July, when the book market was flat. "The country," she wrote, "was in the agonies of its deadly struggle with the rebellion; the advance of the enemy into Pennsylvania, the contest on the Mississippi, were the events which were followed with absorbing interest, and my literary venture, in common with most of those made during this unhappy year, was a failure."[19]

Despite the mosquitoes and the discouragements, Blake was safer out of New York during the summer of 1863, when bloody riots broke out over the draft.[20] For $300, which was a year's income for a laborer, a draftee could be excused from serving in the army. He could also pay for an alternate to take his place. Many men of means, including Emily Dickinson's brother, Austin, took advantage of this way out of conscription.[21] Even dedicated abolitionists like Theodore Tilton, who had been an outspoken proponent of the draft, hired a substitute.[22] The draft thus fell most heavily upon the poor. After the Battle of Gettysburg, on July 14, workers throughout the city went on informal strikes and began marching with "No Draft" placards; the riot broke out at the draft office in Manhattan and began spreading. The police, wealthy Republicans along Lexington Avenue, and blacks were the objects of brutal attack. Mobs lynched blacks and burned the Colored Orphan Asylum on Fifth Avenue. The front page of *Frank Leslie's Illustrated Newspaper* for August 1, 1863, is filled with illustrations of the burning of ships in New York harbor, battles between police and rioters, and the pillage of Brooks Brothers Clothing Store. The center spread depicts the murder of Colonel H. F. O'Brien outside his residence, the destruction of the Weehawken ferry-house, the lynching of an unnamed black man, and battles just blocks from Blake's 14th Street boardinghouse: on Second Avenue and 22nd Street, at Seventh Avenue and 28th, and on 36th Street between Seventh and Eighth Avenues.[23] Over the course of a week, a hundred people were killed, perhaps up to a thousand wounded, and regiments from the Army of the Potomac, right from the battlefields at Gettysburg, had to be called in to restore order.

Inside this same issue of the *Illustrated Newspaper* is part I of Frank Leslie's Prize Story, "The Tenant of the Stone House," by Mrs. Lillie Devereux Umsted. During this time, the *Illustrated Newspaper* was a publishing venue for women who have remained better known, such as Julia Ward Howe and Louisa May Alcott. Blake would publish "The Gloved Lady," another Prize Story, on August 22, 1863, as well as "A Visit to a Fortuneteller" in the July 1864 issue.[24] These potboilers, as Blake would refer to the work that she dashed off for the papers, are well written, fast-paced, and atmospheric. "The Tenant of the Stone House" is a gothic tale of female imprisonment for male economic gain. The mysteriously forlorn Alice Lindon has been shut up for three years as a raving maniac by an uncle who has control of her fortune. In the course of proving her sanity, she falls in love with her rescuer, and, after complications and deferments, they are united in marriage. "The Gloved Lady," on the other hand, is a tale of a wily femme fatale whose seduction of the naïve, yet quite willing, narrator is played out in a sensuous scene of disrobing:

> Her hair, partly deranged by the removal of her hat, fell on her shoulders, so that one long ringlet touched my trembling fingers; she looked so pale and lovely, and as I bent over her I was so agitated that my fingers were very clumsy and it was some time before the pin was removed. As I laid the elegant garment away on a chair, I seated myself beside her and held out my hand.
>
> "Now for the gloves."[25]

And so he removes, finger by finger, her right glove. The story plays upon undressing; the final uncovering is of Josephine's secret, which lies beneath her left glove.

By the fall of 1863, Blake was financially stable enough to rent rooms in New York on 27th Street near Lexington Avenue, where she, her mother, and her children remained for the winter, united amid their furniture from Elm Cottage. It was the first home she had been able to make since the death of her husband. To support her family, she calculated that she needed $28 a week, less than $1,500 a year, and it was hard-earned money:

> How I dreaded my trips to newspaper offices to sell manuscripts or even to ask for money that was due me! I always felt like a beggar and an intruder, and there were men who took advantage of my forlorn situation to insult me. "A fatal gift of beauty" it may well be called! My unfortunate appearance caused my visits to be remembered, caused men to try to take advantage of my request for work and above all perpetually set me up as a mark for gossip. More than one editor refused to receive my pieces unless I would receive his visits, and I grew at last so nervous about going into an office that I would walk half a dozen times past a door before summoning courage to enter it.[26]

Blake would later use these incidents of sexual harassment in her feminist novel *Fettered for Life,* in which Laura Stanley, having taken a job as a bookseller, is ridiculed, insulted, and almost raped by potential buyers.

During the winter of 1863–64, Blake wrote *Zoe; or, True and False,* a model of the polarities in sentimental discourse on women, the true and the false. Sold to the American News Company for $100, *Zoe,* which did not appear until 1866, deftly mixes murder and betrayal along with devoted self-sacrifice. Bessie Fairfax manages to get herself into fixes, such as stepping off a collapsed bridge into a raging river, which call up the rescuing instincts of Ralph Bayard, who has "'always loved anything that appealed to me for help.'"[27] They become engaged. Ralph, however, has a flaw: although he recognizes the pure transparency of Bessie Fairfax, he prefers the stylized over the natural, whether it be in the arrangement of flowers or in the lures of a painted woman. Enter Zoe Radcliffe, who weaves her spell and, to be free, murders her husband. However, after she throws herself at Ralph's feet in a disgusting display of helplessness, to which he does not respond, she understands that she has only herself to rely on. Zoe, even when she isn't murdering or stealing other women's men, is by far the most vital woman in the novel. With the police hot on her trail, she disguises herself as a man and manages to elude them for some months. But, alas, she is knocked off her horse in a freak accident with a pedlar's [*sic*] van, and, although rescued and nursed by the broken-hearted Bessie, Zoe dies as she lived, "'free, and utterly fearless of man or fiend!'"[28] To be free and fearless—and a woman—meant, of course, to be ruthless and calculating and damned. Only the enduringly patient Bessie, who broke her engagement when she thought Ralph might be happier with another and who would have lived her life in silent sorrow, is rewarded with that self-same Ralph, who *did* prefer another, but who now learns to love her better every day. Lillie Umsted undercuts her sentimental plot with this ending of flawed love. She, who, like Zoe, was attempting to live a free and fearless life, would never have settled for marriage with anyone who had to learn to love her better every day.

II

After years of turning down proposals and causing other women a degree of heartache by her flirtations, in the spring of 1864 the almost thirty-one-year-old Lillie Devereux Umsted fell in love with Grinfill Blake, then only twenty-four, a native of Maine who worked in New York City for Washburn and Moen, an iron and steel manufacturing company based in Worcester, Massachusetts. During her lifetime, the discrepancy in their ages was never noted in public documents, and she never specified how much younger her husband was. As her young narrator in "The Gloved Lady," published the year before, acknowledged, "I had consciousness, amid all my infatuation, that it would generally be considered rash for a man of my age to become engaged to a widow several years my senior."[29]

Theirs was a passionate love match on both sides. On the first of May, Lillie, her mother, and her children had left their rooms on 27th Street and, for the interim before going to a summer resort, moved for a few weeks to a boardinghouse near Fifth Avenue, where her sister and her sister's husband were staying. "One day as we sat at the crowded dinner table, a slender, dark-eyed young man came in and took a seat opposite to us. After he had been in his place for a few moments, I glanced towards him and our eyes met. Whether I should recollect all this if we had never met again I cannot say, but it always seemed to both of us that from that moment we were attracted to each other."[30]

Lillie made sure that they would meet again. Grinfill Blake had taken rooms for the summer in Flushing, and Lillie, who protests in her autobiography that she had already almost decided to spend the summer there also, asked for a recommendation for a boardinghouse. Grinfill supplied the address of his own, and when Lillie went with a friend to look for lodgings, she found the house "Mr. Blake had recommended so superior to any other that I at once secured rooms in it."[31] Under the watchful eye of her mother and her sister, whose family had rooms less than a mile away, Lillie and Grinfill courted:

Mr. Blake was an enthusiastic sailor and I very soon became his companion in long expeditions on the quiet waters near the shore or out into the Sound. "The Fanny," a trim little yacht, was our favorite boat and many a summer afternoon or moonlit evening we floated away on the beautiful sea, realizing before the season was over Shelley's lovely lines

> One boat cloak did cover
> The loved and the lover,
> Their hearts beat one measure
> They murmured proud pleasure
> Soft and low, soft and low

What is there to tell of such a summer as this? It was a dream, a delight, an enchanted period in which my cares and troubles seemed all to fade away, as I felt at last that I had found one whom I could love as he loved me.[32]

That summer, Lillie wrote one of the most biographical of her stories for the papers. It was as if falling in love had opened up the future once more and shifted her many difficulties into the past, where they could be safely enumerated from a distance. Rosa Templeton of "A Visit to a Fortuneteller" is clearly a fictive version of Lillie Devereux Umsted:

. . . she had already endured such suffering as does not often afflict one person in the course of a whole life. Three years ago she had been as happy a creature as ever lived; the idolized darling of a home where her lightest will was law . . . surrounded by luxury . . . herself the reigning belle of the town, a favorite with her young companions and adored by the young men, her position was indeed an enviable one, and she had enjoyed it to the full; naturally of a bright and cheerful disposition, the present had been all sunshine, and the future had seemed all promise.[33]

Lillie's difficulties are displaced among Rosa's—a mother rather than a husband dies; a fortune is entirely lost by a father, rather than a husband, who is denounced in public as a scoundrel: "his once honored name whispered with indignation and contempt." In the closest she ever came to acknowledging the possibility that Frank Umsted's death was suicide, she has Rosa's father, despondent over his lost fortune, "discovered one morning dead in his bed, and by his own hand." Like Lillie, Rosa had to leave her elegant home and live in cheap lodgings where "none of their former friends could or would visit." And like Lillie, who went to Washington with only $200 between herself and poverty, Rose "had only two hundred dollars in the world with which to face the future." On "Rosa's brow was the crown of those who can 'suffer and be strong,'" the same motto with which Lillie had begun her diary in 1860. In her despair, Rosa would have preferred to die, but, like her author before her, she had responsibilities—Lillie Umsted had two small children, Rosa Templeton, a younger sister called Lily.

Although she feels that she may be cheating her sister out of the prospect of security, Rosa, like Lillie Umsted, gives up the offer of a marriage of convenience and holds out for love. Lillie's description of falling in love with Grinfill Blake is echoed in Rosa's story:

> She had had a score of suitors with whom she had laughed, and perhaps sometimes flirted, but not one had touched her heart, until she met Robert Marchmont. From the moment when she first saw his handsome, manly face, and looked into his earnest eyes, up to the time when he whispered to her this strong, deep love, it was all a wild delightful dream, and life was such a golden aspect that sorrow and death seemed the greatest unrealities.

When Lillie returned to New York at summer's end, she was engaged to be married. She made yet another temporary home for her mother and children on East 30th Street, where Grinfill Blake was her "only privileged visitor." He relieved her of the burden she found so onerous, that of going to the newspaper offices to make her publication arrangements and to pick up her payments. In fact, he took over all her business affairs, and consequently, Lillie reported, she had "from this time more steady and remunerative employment. . . . I can gratefully say that I never again was so hopelessly wretched as I had been in bygone years before I had this loving companionship and this prospect for the future."[34]

Grinfill and Lillie planned to marry in the fall of 1865. However, his company merged with a larger one and he lost his job. In keeping with the times, they decided to postpone the marriage until his job prospects were more certain. Lillie returned to New Haven in July for her yearly visit and, later in the summer, along with Alice Vinton, Hattie de Forest, and other New Haven friends, spent five weeks in Amherst, Massachusetts, where Grinfill visited her often. "There were lovely drives over the beautiful hill country around us, visits to the top of Mount Holyoke, and long mornings under the trees on the college campus. And so the last summer of my widowhood passed away."[35]

The fall of 1865 was greatly unsettled for Lillie Umsted. The health of her sister's husband, Mr. Townsend, had failed, and the family had given up their house in Wallingford. They, along with Lillie's mother, had rooms in a hotel in Middletown, Connecticut, for the winter. Lillie placed her daughters in a school in Kent, some miles away, and she took a temporary room in the village there, to be close to them for as long as possible. Her physician had advised her to keep the delicate Katie, now seven years old, out of the city and in the fresh air of the country. The school, run by the Hatch sisters, had an excellent reputation and the expense was modest, but Lillie had difficulty parting with her girls. They spent each afternoon together, "but these visits were brief and seemed to renew every [day] my grief that they were no longer with me and under my care as they had been."[36] Grinfill had been ill and was still unemployed, so their marriage plans had not been settled, yet when he visited her, her happiness was palpable. Social decorum, however, kept them apart. Lillie could not think of going back to New York: "I ought not to be so near Grinfill in our present uncertainty."[37] Instead, she began to make plans for another winter in Washington.

There she stayed in one room of a suite rented by a Mr. and Mrs. Richards, with whom she had become friendly. That winter the de Forests from New Haven were also in Washington, and she was reunited with her old friends. Her escorts around town included the de Forests; the Ogle Taylors; and her first husband's cousins, Nellie and Benjamin Boyer, the latter now a member of Congress from Pennsylvania. Her many reminiscences of the time include that of the new president, Andrew Johnson, who had been born in Raleigh and knew her family by reputation. Lillie adds with a dose of social elitism that "as he was in a tailor's shop at the time he left there, it could have been only by reputation." Johnson was most cordial to her, but "he always seemed to me, if I may so express it, a shrewd, dull man at once cunning and slow. His daughters who received for him always acted as if they were frightened, appearing singularly ill at ease in their exalted position."[38] General Grant she met on several occasions; she admired him, but found "the unsmiling little man" always in earnest and unable to engage in the slightest bit of humor.

Blake had been engaged by the New York *Sunday Times* and the *Evening Post* and by Philadelphia's *Press* for letters from Washington and by the *Weekly Mercury* and the Philadelphia *Saturday Evening Post* for as many stories as she could produce. In a typical week, she would make the round of receptions, including those at the White House, go to the Capitol to listen to debates, and write over 100 pages—eight newspaper articles and a couple of stories. During her two-and-a-half-month stay in Washington, Blake finished several novels: *Josephine Peyton* was sold to the *Weekly Mercury* for $250 and, combined with *Blanche Grafton*, appeared there in 1866–67 as *The Orphan*.[39] *Ireton Standish* and *Dead or Alive?*, which she thought was one of the best pieces she had yet written, also appeared in issues of the *Weekly Mercury* that year, which, unfortunately are not extant. However, Blanche Grafton is the heroine of *Forced Vows*, published in 1870 by the house of Beadle and Adams—mostly likely *Blanche Grafton* under a new title. *Ireton Standish* was dramatized in 1880 by Edgar Fawcett as *The False Friend;* Katherine Blake writes that her mother "never received credit for the unusual plot, but it was unmistakably hers."[40] Thus, we have the text of *Blanche Grafton,* and we can infer from *The False Friend* the broad outlines of *Ireton Standish.*

Fawcett's play mixes familiar Blake motifs of disguise, secret identity, and incest in a plot that begins at the end of the Civil War, when Lucian Gleyre— or Ireton Standish—an emotionally frigid Confederate captain and despotic slaveholder, finds his plantation in utter ruin. He travels to California to seek his fortune and there marries an heiress, Nina Chauncey. Fast upon the wedding, however, Nina's father dies in financial ruin, and Gleyre divorces her. His search for gold takes him to Mexico and Australia, where he befriends a wealthy Englishman to whom he bears a remarkable resemblance. When it seems that his English friend, Cuthburt Fairfield, has died, Gleyre assumes his identity and "returns home" to England, convincing Cuthburt's sister, Edith, that he is her long-lost brother. Even when Cuthburt reappears, along with Gleyre's cast-off wife, Nina, Gleyre is able to bluff his way through their attempts to unmask him. His downfall is precipitated by his increasing, uncontrollable passion for Edith, his supposed sister, who becomes suspicious of his rather ardent kisses and fervent, unbrotherly embraces.

Blanche Grafton of *Forced Vows* is a Snow White of a woman, as bland as goodness and the cult of true womanhood could make her. The timid Blanche, "constitutionally a coward" and afraid of horses, arouses the passion of Ralph Dangerfield, who finds it "infinitely delight[ful] to be able to protect such a lovely trembler."[41] Once more, Lillie Devereux Blake, who loved horses and took pride in her own courage, is secretly allied with Blanche's counterpart, Zella Dangerfield, a woman of "strong character," and a "superb horsewoman."[42] Zella is cast as the heartless flirt and evil calculator and is also, perhaps, overly fond of her brother, but, still, she serves to puncture the pieties of nineteenth-century stereotypes. To Zella's brother, Blanche is an angel. "'An angel!'" scoffs Zella. "'Ralph, you are excitable! . . . Her inanity bores me.'"[43]

Forced Vows multiplies the familiar nineteenth-century motif of female confinement. While Blanche, along with Ralph's secret first wife, is abducted and imprisoned in the upper reaches of a desolate house, Blanche's mad stepmother is confined within her own home. When the stepmother escapes, she stalks the flirtatious Zella, who has Blanche's father under her spell, and, "with a low growl," hurls her over a cliff. So ends the life of yet another powerful woman. Ultimately, Zella is a victim of the nineteenth century's relentless portrayal of women who dared to control their own lives as evil.

<h1 style="text-align:center">III</h1>

Blake returned to her mother in Middletown in the middle of March and was reunited with her children. On May 9, 1866, in St. Luke's Chapel of the Berkely Divinity School in Middletown, she and Grinfill, whom she loved "with my whole heart,"[44] were married by her brother-in-law, John Townsend.[45] "Very different was this wedding from the former one. There was no display or show. My new dress was a travelling costume of grey trimmed with blue, and a straw hat ornamented with a wreath of blue violets. My bridesmaids were my two little girls in white marseilles dresses, my witnesses only a few dear friends, but better than all outward glitter was the deep, abounding happiness which filled two hearts as being, after so many trials, united forever, a happiness so intense that it rendered that fair spring day absolutely the brightest of my life."[46]

Grinfill and Lillie had a three-day honeymoon ("three days of intense happiness that seemed to have been cast in an enchanted land").[47] They took the train to Boston, with, because the dining car had not yet been thought of, a stop in Springfield for dinner. After driving to Grinfill's home state of Maine, they returned south to Worcester, where they had the bridal suite at the local hotel and were entertained by the Washburns and the Moens, for whom Grinfill was once again working. They arrived in New York to rooms at 51 East 29th Street.

Lillie had struggled for many years to support herself and her family. It is not an exaggeration to say that she could have married for money at any time, but she had refused to follow cultural dictates and give up her hard-won independence. Many years later, she reflected on her autonomy and the effect of her marriage upon it:

> Although I was married, I had no idea of giving up my literary labors, but continued them industriously, as I was resolved not to be a burden upon my husband and should have been miserable, indeed, if condemned to a routine of life without literary occupation.
>
> As I have said early in this sketch, above all other things I cherished my independence. The dread of lessening it had for a long time prevented me from contemplating a second marriage with any favor and had even been one thing which had made me reluctant to pledge myself to the man I loved. Long before my wedding I realized, however, that a union with him would be what a truly happy marriage should ever be, an equal partnership with no thought of mastership on either side, and at the end of many years of a singularly harmonious wedded life, I can truly say that my independence of thought and action has never for a moment been fettered, and that my happiness has been a thousand-fold increased by my union with a most kind, excellent and devoted husband.[48]

After a summer in Greensport the children returned to school in Kent, and Lillie and Grinfill, on October 21, rented rooms on Fourth Avenue near 30th street. But on March 10, 1867, Lillie's beloved mother died suddenly at the age of seventy from "typhoid pneumonia."[49] Lillie's grief was deep. "Life goes on," she wrote in her diary, "and I drag through the weary days, but there is no mother. Grinfill has been all that the kindest, most affectionate man could be, but oh, there is this aching void in my heart, this yearning for that love of that dear heart that is stilled forever."[50] Lillie fell into a depression that lasted well into the summer: "black nights and days . . . followed. A horror of great darkness overwhelmed me and the sunshine of my existence seemed buried in her tomb. . . . the weeks dragged by in a sort of despondency that it seemed for a long time impossible for me to shake off. Life looked to me an utter black failure. . . . For long months after her death I could not put pen to paper. The awful shock I had sustained seemed to have dried up my brain. I had no power to compose, no imaginings left, and I mourned day and night as one who could not be comforted."[51]

The Blakes spent the summer first in New Brunswick, New Jersey, where Grinfill's family was then living. Lillie kept herself busy giving her girls, now ten and eight, French and history lessons. Later they went to Northport on Long Island, where she taught them to swim. On August 12, she wrote in her diary, "My 34th year begins today and I feel as if I were a century old. My heart has so entirely lost its elastic hopefulness. I have never for a moment been the same that I was before mother's death and I do not think I ever shall be. Life has suddenly grown so indifferent to me. I wish to live of course for the sake of the children and Grinfill, but all the time my heart is heavy, heavy as lead. I do not care half so much how I look or what becomes of me as I did. I cannot write anything."[52]

Returning to the city in September, Grinfill rented one-half of a house on Lexington Avenue near 27th Street. Lillie had longed to make a home for her children and husband, and this half of a house at least temporarily served the purpose: "When the children came home with a kitten that had been promised them, and we sat down to our first dinner of beef steak, we drew a long breath of relief, and I almost felt that I agreed with Bessie as she clasped her hands and exclaimed, 'Isn't this bliss?'"[53] Their near bliss, although blighted by Lillie's continuing grief over her mother's death, was deep enough to create a new family. Grinfill was a kind and indulgent father to her girls, and they, along with Lillie, took his name. Lillie taught the girls at home rather than placing them in school, and in the spring of 1868 they all went house hunting, in search of a place where they could finally settle down and cease the yearly changes of residence. By May they had still not found a suitable, affordable home, so they moved for what was to be only a few days into a boardinghouse. But Grinfill, who had lost several members of his family to consumption, was stricken with a lung hemorrhage and spent six weeks near death. Lillie scarcely left his bedside.

Not until late in June was the family able to leave the city boardinghouse for a summer hotel on Staten Island near Clifton Landing. At the end of the summer of 1868, Lillie's sister Georgie took the girls for two weeks, and Lillie and Grinfill took a trip to Port Jervis and the Delaware Water Gap. "The atmosphere was deliciously invigorating, the weather cool, and in a day or two Grinfill was so much better."[54] The couple hiked and sailed, repeating the favorite activities of their courtship, luxuriating in their time together. Theirs was a passion which had been evident immediately and was sustained, through their years together, by an intellectual partnership. It would endure financial hardship and lengthy separations caused by Grinfill's recurrent invalidism. After twenty-five years of marriage, Grinfill wrote to Lillie with his characteristically teasing tone:

My darling Wife:

Knowing, as I do, that you have a just appreciation of your own value, I am sure that you will not be unduly excited if I, who have loved you ever since I first saw your dear form in a green silk dress at the Lewis House more than twenty-five years ago, say that I never meet you without, when leaving you, wondering why I have ever been blessed with such love as you have given me.

It is impossible for me to give you any understanding of my feeling for you as I bade you good-bye last night. It seemed as if the constantly growing love of all these years was concentrated in the kiss I gave you, and as long as I live I shall remember how sweet and lovely you seemed to me. Don't think me absurd, my dear Lillie, but I cannot resist telling you that I have never loved you as I do now. . . .

Yours,
Grinfill[55]

When fall came, the Blakes, having been unable to find a house which suited them in the city, decided on a flat in one of New York's first apartment buildings, on the corner of 55th Street and Fourth Avenue (now Park Avenue). While moving in and unpacking trunks that had been in storage for years, the children came across their grandmother's stock, which their late father had been accused of misappropriating. "Mamma," shouted Katie, "I think I've found a fortune."[56] The $10,000 worth of Humphreyville stock netted the family $6,000, a large sum of money which could have eased considerably the anxious years of struggle during which Lillie Umsted lived on $28 a week.

The Blakes were pioneers in apartment living. The "French Flats," as they were called after the palatial apartment buildings of Paris created by Georges Haussmann in the 1850s, were not "socially certified" for the respectable middle class until the mid-1870s. They were luxuriously large and filled with light, unlike older apartments that often had windows only in the front and back rooms.[57] The Blake apartment had seven large rooms—a parlor, dining room, kitchen, four bedrooms, closets, and a bathroom all on one floor with windows on three sides, which overlooked a landscape of squatter shanties, goats, and geese. They were well out of the city, which took another decade to catch up with them. Another pioneer in north-side living was Mary Mason Jones, the aunt of Edith Wharton and the model for Mrs. Manson Mingot in *The House of Mirth*. She "abandoned her venerable Waverly Place establishment and moved to the Northeast corner of Fifth Avenue and 57th Street. The locale, despite its proximity to the new Central Park, was still undeveloped and filled with shantytowns, slaughterhouses, charitable institutions, the unfinished Catholic cathedral, and, at Fifth and 52nd, the home of abortionist Mme. Restell, now known as the 'wickedest woman in New York.'"[58]

Whatever the surroundings, Katherine Devereux Blake declares in a chapter of her mother's biography entitled "Home at Last," that "we were a happy family in that 55th Street home." Katie described the dining room, which seems to have been the center of life for the family:

> On one side was a mahogany sideboard loaded with old family silver which it became the painful duty of my sister and myself to keep shining. . . . Across one wall a built-in bookcase held 1,500 books. Many of the shelves held a row of books behind those you saw. In one window stood my grandmother's rocking-chair, my mother's favorite seat, and under the other window an ancient divan.
>
> The center of the room held the dinner-table. At that dinner-table my mother and my stepfather discussed their own affairs and the affairs of the nation. I loved to sit and listen while older people talked, and those conversations between my mother and Mr. Blake make a deep impression on my mind. . . .
>
> It was through her conversations with my stepfather that I first became acquainted with the treatises of Darwin, Spencer, and Huxley. She read those scientific treatises with no less eagerness than she seized upon a new novel by Dickens, Hardy, or any other distinguished story-teller.[59]

Lillie Devereux Umsted Blake was, indeed, "home at last." Only Maple Cottage vied with 55th and 4th as Blake's longest place of residence. She and Grinfill lived there for eleven years while New York City grew out around them and Katie and Bessie grew from little girls of nine and eleven to young women of twenty and twenty-two.

At 55th and Fourth Blake introduced her weekly receptions, reminiscent of her mother's, to which would come such luminaries as Susan B. Anthony, Elizabeth Cady Stanton, Matilda Joslyn Gage, and Isabella Beecher Hooker, along with African explorer Paul Du Chaillu, writer Bret Harte, publisher Mrs. Frank Leslie, and French writer Max O'Rell, the pseudonym for Paul Blouët. In *Jonathan and His Continent (Rambles through American Society)*, O' Rell introduces a chapter titled "The Emancipation of Woman—Extinction of Man . . ." with a reminiscence of Lillie Devereux Blake:

> I was talking one evening with Mrs. Devereux Blake, the chief of the movement—a middle aged lady, of a fluent, agreeable conversation, who has declared war to the knife against the tyrant man.
>
> "You must excuse me," I said to her, "if I ask questions, I am anxious to learn. I have submitted so many times to the interviewing process in your country that I feel as if I had a right to interview the Americans a little in my turn. The American woman appears to me ungrateful not to be satisfied with her lot. She seems to rule the roost in the United States."
>
> "No," replied Mrs. Blake, "she does not, but she ought."
>
> "But she certainly does," I insisted.
>
> "*De facto*, perhaps, but *de jure*, no."
>
> "What do you want more?"
>
> "The right to make laws."
>
> "What do you mean by that?"
>
> "The right of voting for candidates for Congress, and even the right to a seat in the House of Representatives."
>
> "This appears to me a little exacting, and almost unfair," I observed timidly. . . . I felt a little out of place in this energetic lady's drawing-room, almost like a wolf in the fold.[60]

If Maple Cottage had shaped the sensibilities of Lillie Devereux, 55th and Fourth was the site of her reconstruction into the indubitable Lillie Devereux Blake, a powerhouse in New York reform efforts.

IV

When she was seventeen years old, Lillie Devereux had heard a speech delivered by Susan B. Anthony. In her autobiography, Blake remembers that "the scene made a vivid impression upon me, although I laughed at some of the actors in it with the gay thoughtlessness of my age. Miss Susan B. Anthony was reading an address when we went in, but after sitting less than an hour it was time for an afternoon drive." Blake's daughter remembered a less bowdlerized version of the story, one which, out of loyalty to Anthony, Lillie never told outside the family: At Saratoga, Katherine writes, "for the first time, she beheld Susan B. Anthony, attired in a bloomer costume of *pink dotted swiss!*"[61]

Eighteen years later, in the summer of 1869, venturing into the Woman's Bureau at 49 East 23rd Street in New York City, Blake met Anthony, who this time was dressed more unobtrusively in a gray traveling suit.[62] Blake's decision to enter the Woman's Bureau was not an easy one. She had seen woman's rights activists caricatured as grotesquely masculinized and hopelessly ridiculous. Even her own husband, who encouraged her to join the meetings at the Woman's Bureau, referred to Susan B. Anthony as "that cantankerous, cross-eyed old maid."[63] Blake's first publications in Stanton and Anthony's newspaper the *Revolution,* which ran between 1868 and 1872, disclosed her own concerns regarding the ridicule and social excommunication caused by entrance into the movement. "Only those women," she wrote, "who have very superior firmness of character have had the courage to come out as champions of their sex. . . . all the newspapers of the day have combined in one common impulse to vilify the women of the Suffrage movement until it has become a martyrdom from which any woman may well shrink to try to aid the cause in any way."[64]

Three times Blake passed by 49 East 23rd Street before "with sudden desperation, [she] walked quickly back, in at the gate, up the steps and rang the bell. . . . 'Is it Mrs. Stanton?'" she asked the gray-suited woman who answered the door; "'My name is Anthony,'" was the reply.[65] That day Blake also met Elizabeth Cady Stanton, Charlotte Wilbour, and Elizabeth Phelps, the philanthropist who had purchased the building specifically for woman's causes: "I looked with awe at them all, but especially at the fine intellectual head of Elizabeth Cady Stanton whom I saw for the first time. How grand a thing it must be to have won the name and fame which that small lady had attained!"[66]

Blake understood that her decision to join the woman's movement would cost her many of the social connections that had been hers since birth, and, indeed, after 1870, when she began lecturing for the movement, she was cut from society, and even her relatives, with the exception of her sister, refused to maintain contact with her. Her daughter Katherine remembered:

All these things I heard discussed between my mother and my stepfather. I was learning much. One thing I learned in those early years, and my experiences through a long life have only emphasized it:

Society will forgive either lack of wealth or radicalism. If one is poor, and conforms, society overlooks the poverty. If one who is wealthy elects to be a radical, society condones the defection from type. But if one who is poor embraces radicalism in any form, there is no forgiveness. One is pushed out; the ranks close up.

That is what Lillie Devereux Blake had to learn. When she married a poor man, and wrote to supplement her income, she was still invited and accepted as before in the society she had known all her life. Her poverty made little difference to anyone but herself. But when, in addition to being poor, she espoused an unpopular, radical movement, her friends no longer invited her to their "functions;" she was no longer included in lists of those asked to the Charity Ball, or asked to be patroness of this or that philanthropic activity. Worst of all, her relatives practically declined to see her. Only her faithful sister remained loyal.[67]

Indeed, women who appeared or spoke in public paid a public price. While Nathaniel Hawthorne worried about women writers displaying their "naked minds" in public, women like Sarah and Angelina Grimké who, in the late 1830s, publicly lectured against slavery were vilified in the press with innuendoes concerning the sexual impropriety of "exhibiting" themselves. As an antislavery orator, Lucy Stone, one of the most revered of the first generation of suffrage workers, was doused with water from a fire hose, pelted with eggs, "dried apples, smoked herring, beans, and tobacco quids," and hit over the head with a hymnbook.[68] By the time of the Civil War, women appearing in public forums had become a more frequent feature of American life, and where once only a woman's marriage and death were considered appropriate for a newspaper notice, their activities and achievements began to take up space in the press.[69] However, it was with much anxiety that Blake reasoned: "I am almost thirty-six years old, I have a right to arrange my life as it pleases me, I will not be deterred from giving my hearty support to a cause in which I thoroughly believe, by any nervous fear of what may be said."[70] Her friends, she noted, disapproved, "some remonstrated, some censured, a few grew cold,"[71] but her husband, who had first told her about the Woman's Bureau, and who believed in the cause, encouraged her.

William Oliver Stone, *Portrait of Lillie Devereux [Umsted] Blake*, 1859.
Columbia University in the City of New York.
Gift of the Estate of Florence L. Robinson

Sarah Elizabeth Johnson (1798–1867), great-granddaughter of Jonathan Edwards, granddaughter of Pierrepont Edwards, and mother of Lillie Devereux Blake. From Katherine Devereux Blake and Margaret Louise Wallace, *Champion of Women* (New York: Fleming H. Revell Co., 1943); with permission of Baker Book House Company.

George Pollok Devereux (1795–1837), great-grandson of Jonathan Edwards, grandson of Eunice Edwards, and father of Lillie Devereux Blake. From Katherine Devereux Blake and Margaret Louise Wallace, *Champion of Women* (New York: Fleming H. Revell Co., 1943); with permission of Baker Book House Company.

Above: The Johnson Homestead, built in 1799 by William Samuel Johnson for his son, Samuel William Johnson, maternal grandfather of Lillie Devereux Blake. With thanks to the Stratford Historical Society, Stratford, Connecticut.

Below: Maple Cottage, built in 1836, where Lillie Devereux spent her formative years amid New Haven and Yale's cultural elite, is pictured here under Yale University's proprietorship in 1999. Grace Farrell photo.

Lillie Devereux at fourteen, the year after she began writing her diary. From Katherine Devereux Blake and Margaret Louise Wallace, *Champion of Women* (New York: Fleming H. Revell Co., 1943); with permission of Baker Book House Company.

Pages from Lillie's 1854 diary that mention "Barnes" and contain pressed violets "From Mr. Georges Lampsen." With permission of the Missouri Historical Society, St. Louis.

June 13. Went to the opera exhibition with Mrs. Lampson.

June 19. Had a large party at home all young people very pleasant.

June 21. Party at Henry Whiting's Esq

July 4. Picnic to Lake Saltonstall

July 14. Boating party of the Halcyon.

From Mr George Lampson

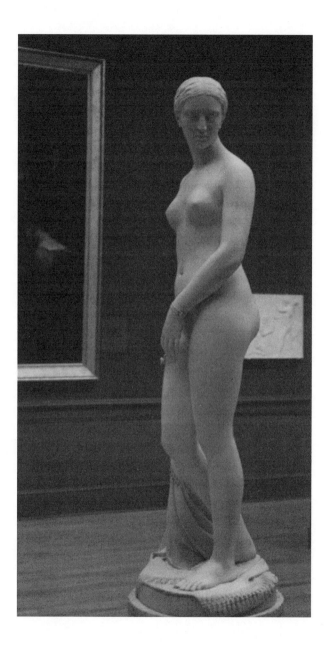

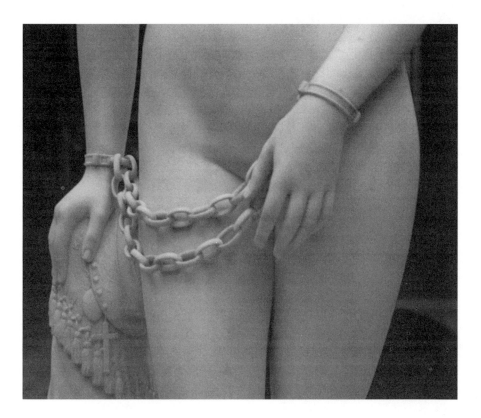

Opposite and above: Hiram Powers's *The Greek Slave* (1841–43), centerpiece of the Yale Art Gallery's Trumbull Room, celebrates the nineteenth century's patriarchal narrative of chains over female genitals. Grace Farrell photos.

Left: Harriet Hosmer's *Zenobia*, 1859, cloaks the stereotype of the vulnerable female with that of the woman warrior. From Lorado Taft, *The History of American Sculpture* (New York: Macmillan, 1903).

Below: Horatio Greenough's *Medora*, a funereal piece illustrating Byron's *The Corsair*, was exhibited in the United States during the 1830s. With permission of the Mayor and City Council of Baltimore, on extended loan to The Baltimore Museum of Art (BMA R.11168).

Elm Cottage, Stratford, built by Sarah Johnson Devereux in 1856. Here Lillie Devereux Umsted wrote her first novel, *Southwold*. Grace Farrell photo.

Participants in the founding meeting of the International Council of Women, March 25–April 1, 1888. As president of the New York State Woman Suffrage Association, Blake organized a three-day conference for foreign delegates arriving in New York and accompanied them to Washington, D.C., for the Council.

FRONT ROW (*beginning fourth from left*): Susan B. Anthony; Isabella Begelet, France; Elizabeth Cady Stanton; Matilda Joclyn Gage; Alexandria Gripenberg, Finland; Mrs. Ashton Dilne, England.

MIDDLE ROW (*from left*): Rev. Ada C. Bowles; Rev. Annie Shaw; Frances E. Willard; Lillie Devereux Blake; (*fourth from right*) Rev. Antoinette Brown Blackwell; (*continuing second from right*) May Wright Sewall; Margaret Moore, Ireland.
BACK ROW (*beginning second from left*): Rachel G. Foster; Bessie Starr Keefer, Canada; Sophia Magelsson Groth, Norway; (*continuing third from right*) Alice Trygg, Finland; Alice Scatherd, England.

With permission of the Nebraska State Historical Society.

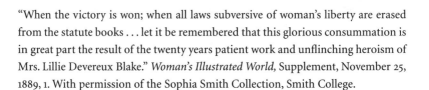

"When the victory is won; when all laws subversive of woman's liberty are erased from the statute books . . . let it be remembered that this glorious consummation is in great part the result of the twenty years patient work and unflinching heroism of Mrs. Lillie Devereux Blake." *Woman's Illustrated World*, Supplement, November 25, 1889, 1. With permission of the Sophia Smith Collection, Smith College.

For President

of the

National American Woman Suffrage Association

MRS. LILLIE DEVEREUX BLAKE

of New York

In view of the retirement of our honored leader, Miss SUSAN B. ANTHONY, from the Presidency of the National American Woman Suffrage Association, we urge the election of Mrs. LILLIE DEVEREUX BLAKE as her successor, for the following reasons:

1.　She has great executive ability.

2.　She is an admirable presiding officer.

3.　She is a woman of high culture, and fine presence, and in all respects well fitted to honor the position.

4.　She has been in active service for the cause over thirty years; longer than any other candidate.

5.　Through her efforts mainly, women were appointed

　　a.　Census enumerators in 1880 and 1890.

　　b.　Granted pensions as war nurses.

　　c.　Made eligible to civil service positions.

6.　To her efforts mainly we, in the State of New York, are indebted for the passage of the laws:

　　a.　Granting school suffrage to women.

　　b.　Making mother and father joint guardians of their children.

　　c.　Enabling a woman to make a will without her husband's consent.

　　d.　Providing that there shall be women as trustees in all public institutions where women are placed.

　　e.　Providing seats for saleswomen.

7.　She originated and sustained the agitation for the appointment of Police Matrons, and that for placing women on Boards of Education, and advancing the salaries of women school teachers.

Kindly give these facts serious consideration before casting your ballot for the next National President.

> ELIZABETH CADY STANTON,
> DR. MARY PUTNAM JACOBI.
> M. OLIVIA SAGE.

Flyer circulated in the campaign for Lillie Devereux Blake to succeed Susan B. Anthony as president of the National American Woman Suffrage Association, 1900. With permission of the Sophia Smith Collection, Smith College.

Maple Cottage, May 8, 1999. A second attempt at demolition of Blake's childhood home by Yale University becomes a metaphor for the suppression of women's literary tradition. Photographs by Anstress Farwell.

Blake entered the suffrage movement at an explosive point in its history. After the Civil War, having put their own suffrage concerns in abeyance, many women who had organized for abolition expected that women would be a part of the new postwar voting citizenry. But they were mistaken. The success of the abolitionist movement resulted in a serious setback for female suffrage. Abolitionists considered support for woman suffrage a liability and an added burden that might imperil the fight for black male suffrage.[72] Woman suffrage was a threat to the existing system of political bosses and to those opposed to prohibition who feared a women's voting bloc might support temperance measures. Republican supporters of woman's rights turned against the movement, calling this the "Negro's Hour."

Woman suffrage reformers were divided over the issue of the Fourteenth and Fifteenth Amendments. In May 1869, Stanton and Anthony split with the American Equal Rights Association when it supported the Fifteenth Amendment which excluded women from the vote, and they formed the New York–based National Woman Suffrage Association (NWSA), the purpose of which was to secure a constitutional amendment that would give women the vote. In the fall of that year, the Boston-based American Woman Suffrage Association (AWSA) led by Lucy Stone and her husband, Henry Blackwell, was formed. The AWSA retained its alliances with the abolitionist movement and supported black male suffrage while vowing to work state by state for universal voting rights. History, bequeathed to us primarily through the *History of Woman Suffrage* controlled by Susan B. Anthony, minimizes the role of the AWSA and distorts the disagreements between the two groups, figuring the AWSA as conservative and the NWSA as radical.[73] Although housing some of the most radical voices in the woman's movement, including Elizabeth Cady Stanton, Matilda Joslyn Gage, and Lillie Devereux Blake, the NWSA and the unified association, the National American Woman Suffrage Association (NAWSA), were increasingly conservative throughout the last quarter of the century. Speculation on the relative conservative or radical nature of the two associations serves to distract us from what were really the two major distinctions between the groups: first, the narrowing of focus which the NWSA increasingly insisted upon and second, its abandonment of abolitionist ideology.

Two years before forming the NWSA, Stanton and Anthony had traveled to Kansas to stump for two Republican referenda, one for black suffrage and one for woman suffrage. When they discovered that the Republicans were endorsing only the black suffrage referendum, they allied themselves with Democrat George Francis Train, who was given to antiblack tirades and whom abolitionist William Lloyd Garrison called a "rack-brained harlequin and semi-lunatic."[74] Stanton and Anthony partook of the racialism common to mid-nineteenth-century America when even abolitionists took white superiority for granted. With Train at their side, their anger at women's exclusion from the vote was cast in racist tones. Blake, who never participated in the short-lived alliance with Train, and who publicly disagreed with the NWSA stance against the Fourteenth and Fifteenth Amendments, met Train only once, in 1875, and remarked in her diary that he is "mad as a march hare, I should judge."[75]

In this charged, politicized atmosphere, Blake entered the offices of the NWSA at 49 East 23rd Street in Manhattan in early summer, 1869. At the first formal meeting that she attended, Phoebe Couzens of St. Louis, articulating the NWSA position, spoke against ratification of the Fifteenth Amendment. But Blake immediately proved to be a maverick who spoke her mind no matter the politics of those around her, and her very first public speech was an impromptu rebuttal of Couzens's remarks. Blake stressed the need to work directly for woman's rights rather than dissipate energies in a fight against Negro suffrage. She was noted in the next day's newspapers, and her name became quite quickly linked to the cause of woman suffrage.

Blake was invited to participate in her first suffrage convention to be held in Newport on August 24, 1869. Scheduled to speak alongside Elizabeth Cady Stanton, Susan B. Anthony, Pauline Wright Davis, Isabella Beecher Hooker, and Theodore Tilton, she wrote two speeches, practicing her delivery until the speeches were memorized. Almost overcome with stage fright, she pushed herself to speak and found her vocation as an orator:

> . . . stifling one wild desire to rush away from the scene, I rose and advanced to the front of the platform. I laid my manuscript on the table and turned to face the people who greeted me with some applause. Up to that moment I had been faint and sick with nervous dread, but on the moment it vanished and I began my declamation with a feeling of absolute enjoyment. At every word this increased. A thrill of intense excitement rushed through me as I saw how my audience was giving me their best attention. I never looked at my manuscript. I never thought of embarrassment or fear, one only wish possessed me, the desire to con-

vert my hearers to my views. While a new delight and a new joy swelled in my heart, surged in my veins, I uttered my appeal with passionate earnestness and sat down at its close glowing, intoxicated and triumphant with the knowledge that I had a portion of heaven's divinest gift, eloquence!

I knew it from that moment with an absolute certainty. . . . My bitter regret is in the realization that while I come of a line of statesmen, of ancestors who all were speakers, yet until now I had wandered past this road to success, not because I was not fitted for it, but because I am a woman.[76]

Blake's self-assessment, not moderated by any false modesty, was attested to many times over by her audiences and by the press. She quickly became an important player in the suffrage movement, acknowledged as a powerful speaker, in turn ruthlessly logical, bitingly sarcastic, utterly charming, and funny. After her success at the NWSA Convention in Newport, Anthony asked her to speak in Wellsville, New York, in November, and her career was launched.

Blake challenged herself by preparing material but speaking extemporaneously. She researched her topics thoroughly and worked at her speechmaking, honing it to perfection. She took elocution lessons and even gymnastics "to expand my chest and so strengthen my voice."[77] She knew when she was good, and exulted; she knew when she faltered, and agonized, determined to do better. And until his health utterly failed, Grinfill was always there to discuss the issues with her and usually to see her off to her conventions and welcome her home with a warm embrace.

Her first lecture on a topic other than suffrage was "The Dignity of Labor," delivered at the Working Woman's Association on October 28, 1869,[78] and she spent much of 1870 lecturing for the suffrage, labor, and peace movements in Saratoga, Providence, Philadelphia, Stamford, Newark, New Brunswick, and, like Anna Dickinson before her, at New York's Cooper Institute. Less than a year and a half after joining the movement, Blake gave the opening speech of the January 1871 NWSA Convention in Lincoln Hall, Washington, D.C. That summer she began what would be an annual routine of speaking throughout New York State on peace, temperance, and woman suffrage. During the fall of '71, she expanded her terrain, lecturing in Richmond, Virginia; Philadelphia; Danbury, Connecticut, and throughout Dutchess County.

Grinfill's salary had been cut from $2,500 to $1,800, and Lillie was desperate to earn money. Lecturing provided her with an income. She would collect anywhere from ten to fifty cents at the door or pass the basket after her speech. After paying for a hall, advertising, circulars, and travel expenses, she might make $5 to $10 a week; sometimes she would only break even. She continued writing once a week for the *Free Press,* the *Evening Mail,* the *Globe,* and the *Society Journal.* She wrote anonymously or under a new pseudonym, "Tiger Lily," the flowerlike name camouflaging and containing an assertion of her new-found ferocity. Over the next few years, she spoke on working women, capital punishment, equal wages for equal work, and the Fourteenth and Fifteenth Amendments. Her titles included "The Dignity of Labor," "The Jury Question," "Woman's Sphere," "Heroines of History," "The Justice of Our Cause," "Soldier and Victim," and "The Importance of the Ballot for Working Women." Her speech "Women Murderers" argued the injustice of hanging women, who, politically, were classed with idiots.

Blake's reputation grew, and with it came greater opportunities to speak. She was offered the generous sum of $50 a night to speak in support of the 1872 Democratic candidate for president, Horace Greeley. But, although Blake badly needed the money, she refused the offer to stump for Greeley, "the man who had openly declared himself opposed to giving women any political equality!" Instead she supported the reelection of Republican President Ulysses S. Grant. By 1880 the Republicans offered her $50 *not* to speak for the Democrats.[79]

In May 1878, Blake was invited to that university which today remembers her only through the vicious rumor of a jilted lover. She lectured at the Divinity School at Yale College as part of "a Sunday course of lectures."[80] She describes the new chapel built with money donated by the Sterling family of Stratford: "a new building, not the old brick horror I knew in my youth, but it was like a visit to a mausoleum to me, for all along the walls were memorial tablets to the members of the faculty who had been in their prime when I was a girl." The loss of her own Maple Cottage in 1999 may have provided protection against a similar fate for the Divinity School buildings; Yale University had planned to demolish four of the buildings around the Sterling Quadrangle but reversed its decision in the wake of controversy and litigation over its destruction of Maple Cottage.[81]

Early on in her suffrage career, Blake worked for reunification of the two strands of the movement. On March 25, 1870, she presided at the NWSA session at which Theodore Tilton proposed a meeting "with a view to harmony" between the National and the American Associations.[82] Later she noted: "For the purpose of affecting a union, a conference of several of the principle [*sic*] advocates was held at the Fifth Avenue Hotel. It resulted in nothing, however, and in May two Woman Suffrage Conventions were convened."[83] Lillie attended both. On May 10, after lunching with Elizabeth Cady Stanton, Susan B. Anthony, and Theodore Tilton, and after a "stormy" afternoon debate, Blake carried through a motion that would coalesce the two societies. But it would be twenty years before the two groups merged into the National American Woman Suffrage Association. Hostility between the groups ran deep, and, for example, in October 1870, abolitionist Thomas Wentworth Higginson tried to prevent Blake from speaking at the Rhode Island Woman Suffrage Society annual meeting in Providence, where she was the guest of Pauline Wright Davis. Two years earlier, Higginson had founded, with other woman's rights reformers who supported the Fourteenth Amendment, the New England Woman Suffrage Association "to counter political initiatives being made by Stanton and Anthony."[84] In her autobiography, Blake writes, "a prominent man from Boston, whose name I will not be so unkind as to give, declared that I ought not to be heard. His demand was, however, voted down in committee." In the typescript of her diary, however, she is more explicit: "Col. Higginson acted the part of a scoundrel today, abusing me and saying that I should not speak."[85]

V

Hardly had the first year of Blake's public life ended when she was embroiled in a new controversy within the woman's movement—an attempted takeover by the free-lovers Victoria Woodhull and her sister Tennessee Claflin. Woodhull, or Mrs. Satan as she was dubbed in the nineteenth century, was a spiritualist, financier, free-love advocate, publisher, and presidential candidate as well as a con artist and probably a blackmailer and prostitute.[86] Victoria's marriage at fifteen to the alcoholic Canning Woodhull ended in divorce, although he lived on with the Claflin clan. After the Civil War, with carnivalesque road shows featuring the sale of sham medicine and communication with the dead, Woodhull and her sister supported an extended family, which included parents, in-laws, and her ex-husband. Later Woodhull earned her family's keep by going on lecture tours preaching woman suffrage and free love. Maintaining a level of notoriety kept the gate receipts high.

Woodhull's second marriage was to James Blood, whose initial meeting with her resulted in a trance out of which she announced that they were destined to marry. She and Blood later divorced, remarried, and divorced again before her move to England, where she married a wealthy banker, John Biddulph Martin, convincing him that she had been the leader of the woman suffrage movement in America.[87] Her marriage with Blood involved free love and a *menage à trois* with her first husband, or so testified her mother during one of the many family feuds that landed them in court. Blood directed Woodhull's entry into the worlds of finance and reform. Early in 1870, Woodhull and Claflin attracted the attention of the recently widowed Commodore Cornelius Vanderbilt, to whom they passed on stock tips garnered via their seances. Vanderbilt, who was probably Claflin's lover, set them up as the first female stockbrokers.

The Blakes had one, and only one, social engagement with the new stockbrokers. On Lillie's birthday, August 12, 1870, she and Grinfill went to Woodhull and Claflin's "where we had a curious time," she wrote in her diary. Katherine remembers "vividly" that the next morning at the breakfast table her mother said, "'Grinfill! You know you behaved disgracefully last night!' His reply was, 'Well, Lillie, my dear, if you will take me to a house where there are not chairs enough to sit on, so that a pretty plump young lady with nothing on but a Mother Hubbard comes and sits on the arm of my chair and leans over me, you must expect me to put my arm around her.' Mr. Blake did not usually behave in that way,'" Katherine adds.[88]

In her 1871 novel *My Wife and I,* Harriet Beecher Stowe, characterizes Woodhull as the "bold[ly] intrus[ive] . . . Miss Adacia Dangyereyes."[89] And although Blake reports that "up to this time [Woodhull and Claflin] had never been connected in any way with the Woman Suffrage Movement," Woodhull was able, briefly—for about a year—to insinuate herself into the movement by gaining a hearing before the House Judiciary Committee on the same day, January 11, 1871, that the NWSA Convention was held in Washington. It is probable that Woodhull slept with the Massachusetts congressman General Benjamin Butler in exchange for her invitation to address the committee—an invitation which suffrage leaders had for years tried to gain. In response, as Blake saw it, the suffrage leaders had but two choices: "either let Mrs. Woodhull appear as the sole representative of the reform, or go with her before the Committee and themselves plead for the cause with such grave and judicious arguments as they knew so well how to employ." The suffragists appeared at the hearing. Woodhull's position, that a voting rights amendment was unnecessary because, under the wording of the Constitution, women already could vote, had earlier been voiced by Elizabeth Cady Stanton and had been argued against by Blake.[90]

Subsequently, quid pro quo, Woodhull was invited to speak at the NWSA Convention. She read the "memorial" which she had presented before the House Judiciary Committee and was followed by Blake, who lectured on whether women should be denied the vote because they do not participate in the army. This was an important post–Civil War topic. The rhetoric of equal rights had swerved to discussions of the duties and rights of citizens. Soldier-citizens, the ranks of which included many black males, had proven, it was argued, their right to vote. "Equating soldiering with citizenship," of course, "easily excluded women, who were barred from soldiering."[91]

Because of the presence of Woodhull, Blake refused to speak again, and when the spring conventions were planned, she "was resolved to appear on no platform where the advocates of the horrible doctrines of free love were permitted to come as prominent partisans of our cause."[92] She went so far as to remove her name from the list of officers of the NWSA, and she met with Stanton, Anthony, Wilbour, and others with whom she "had a long talk in which I plainly gave my views regarding their most ill-advised espousal of Woodhull and Claflin."[93] She and Charlotte Wilbour were denounced by Dr. Mary Walker, the first woman ever to receive the Congressional Medal of Honor.[94]

During the spring of 1871, Blake began meeting with others in the movement who were as concerned as she about the intrusion of Woodhull and Claflin into woman suffrage. On May 25, ten years after her missed encounter at the Williard Hotel in Washington with Julia Ward Howe, the two women met to discuss the issues raised by Woodhull's entry into the movement, but Blake was suddenly taken ill.[95] As she would several times over the last decades of her life, Blake had worked herself into a complete collapse. She was bedridden for six weeks. When she was able to travel, the family rented a farmhouse in the hills near Poughkeepsie where she stayed with her daughters, visited frequently by Grinfill, until mid-September.

Upon her return to the city, Blake immediately devoted her time to the suffrage movement. The identification of woman suffrage with free love was so persistent that many supporters had retreated. In fact, only when droves of women began boycotting NWSA meetings, vowing to hold out until Woodhull was no longer invited, did Susan B. Anthony, always sympathetic to the unconventional and initially charmed by Woodhull, begin to pull back and try to distance Woodhull from the NWSA. In New York, Dr. Clemence S. Lozier, one of the first woman doctors in the country, was president of the city's Suffrage Association; Blake served as chairman of the Committee on Public Meetings. To keep the free-lovers at bay, the association decided to hold private, rather than public, meetings every other week. Blake's strategy was to intersperse these "parlor meetings" with carefully controlled public gatherings, geared to specific constituencies: "the leisured women" as well as working women, city dwellers as well as suburbanites.

The featured speaker at the first public meeting that Blake organized for "fashionable" ladies was Julia Ward Howe. It was a shrewd choice of speaker. The Bostonian Howe had been late to enter the suffrage movement, believing, as did many women of her class, that it was unladylike. However, she became, as Venet points out, "an enormous asset to the suffrage cause, for she was a paragon of gentility. 'Your mother's great importance to this cause,' one blue-blooded Bostonian told Julia's daughters, 'is that she forms a bridge between the world of society and the world of reform.'"[96]

Blake often drew her speakers from the ranks of the Boston association. Her series of meetings for working women featured Jennie Collins, "an indefatigable worker from Boston, [who] had founded a home for working girls known as 'Boffin's Bower.'" Collins and Blake, whose topic was "The Importance of the Ballot to Working-women," repeated their speeches in Harlem, Bayonne, and Poughkeepsie.[97] On the occasion of at least one of these meetings, Victoria Woodhull arrived uninvited to circulate her newspaper, *Woodhull and Claflin's Weekly*.[98] Blake's third public meeting was a general conference with a goal of weakening the persistent identification of woman suffrage with free love and coming out forcefully for the institution of marriage. Her strategy of targeting women of different classes combined with her skillful and conscientious organizing was successful in revitalizing the New York movement.

During this time, however, Blake began to receive "mysterious hints" that there would be repercussions if she persisted in her anti-Woodhull activities and that, in fact, her life was in danger. On April 18, 1872, Blake reports that she "received a vile attack from Woodhull on Tuesday, a printed slip containing scurrilous articles about all the ladies here who do not act with her."[99] An anonymous note demanded $500 or her divorces would show up in *Woodhull and Claflin's Weekly.* Katherine recalled clearly "my mother walking up and down [in our parlor], wringing her hands, while I tried to comfort her, protesting, 'But, Mamma, you never have been divorced, so it won't matter if they do print that.'" But Lillie remembered the New Haven scandal of 1854: "During her girlhood she had had one personal experience with unfounded scandal," Katherine wrote, "so she cried, 'Yes, it will matter! The truth never catches up with a lie! The lie runs too fast.' When Mr. Blake came home she threw herself into his arms, crying, 'Grinfill, what shall I do? What shall I do?'" Grinfill advised ignoring the demand, which she did, and there was no further incident.[100]

In 1865 the Claflin family had been forced out of Cincinnati after accusations by neighbors that they were operating a brothel and after Tennessee was named in an adultery and blackmail suit. It was assumed now that Woodhull and Claflin were behind the attempted blackmail of leading suffragists, including Blake, Elizabeth Phelps, Laura Curtis Bullard, and Susan B. Anthony.[101] Woodhull wrote in her *Weekly* that for women blackmail was the "only method of righting themselves" and "aveng[ing]the oppression of [their] sex."[102]

In January 1872, Anthony had begun to marginalize Woodhull in the suffrage movement. Stanton and Anthony alone appeared before the Senate Judiciary Committee, and Woodhull was limited at the NWSA Convention to a speech on spiritualism. Blake met with Stanton and Anthony on May 6 and again on May 8 to express her views of Woodhull. She noted in her diary, "Had another long talk which resulted in nothing definite. They are evidently all sick of Woodhull, but don't know how to get rid of her."[103] The next day was the opening of the NWSA Convention. Knowing that Woodhull intended to turn the meeting into a nominating session for what she called the People's Party, Anthony refused to allow her to speak at all.[104] Earlier, in Anthony's absence, Woodhull had prevailed upon Elizabeth Cady Stanton to sign the names of the leaders of the NWSA (Stanton, Anthony, Hooker, and Gage), to a joint announcement of the conventions of the NWSA and the People's Party. Anthony and Stanton had a major falling out over this incident; as a result, Anthony presided over the convention and assumed the presidency of the NWSA. Blake witnessed the scene as Woodhull "behaved very badly and quarreled with Miss Anthony, who is a grand and noble woman."[105] Anthony persistently refused to recognize Woodhull, who finally seized the podium and refused to be silenced, whereupon Anthony ordered the lights turned off and the hall emptied.[106] Leading the People's Party contingent, Woodhull marched to Apollo Hall, which, it seems, she had already rented for the purpose, and there became the first woman nominated for president of the United States, with Frederick Douglass as her running mate. After reading in the next day's paper of his nomination—made without his knowledge or consent—Douglass declined it. He, like Anthony, Stanton, and other suffrage leaders supported Grant for reelection. Woodhull and the People's Party left their bills to be paid by the NWSA.[107]

On May 16 Blake attended the closing meeting of the convention, which was held at Dr. Lozier's home, where strawberries and ice cream were served. "Rather a contrast to [the] former meetings," Blake dryly noted in her diary.[108] We are "happily rid of Victoria Woodhull."[109]

They had not, however, heard the last of Woodhull. Shortly after the May convention, she was arrested on charges of using the postal service for the distribution of obscene material and jailed for six months. Blake's diary of October 31 records what happened when those six months were up: "Those horrible women, Woodhull and Claflin, have at last printed their infamous story about Henry Ward Beecher and Mrs. Theodore Tilton. There is an intense excitement."[110] Theodore Tilton, with whom Blake had worked in the early attempt to unite the Boston and New York suffrage associations, was the wounded party in the biggest sex scandal of nineteenth-century America. Henry Ward Beecher, the well-known and extremely popular minister who played important roles in the abolitionist and woman suffrage causes, was accused of seducing Tilton's wife and, yes, lying about it publicly. When it was clear that she was being edged out of the suffrage movement, Woodhull threatened to expose the affair in *Woodhull and Claflin's Weekly* if Beecher did not support her. She demanded of Beecher a public apology for adultery or a declaration that he, like Woodhull, was an advocate of free love. When Woodhull was released from jail, she took her revenge. By the evening of November 2, 1872, copies of *Woodhull and Claflin's Weekly* were selling for $40 a copy.[111] In 1874, at his own initiative, Beecher was investigated by his church and found innocent; in 1875, Tilton brought civil charges against him, but the jury was unable to reach a verdict. Woodhull published transcripts of Beecher's 112-day trial. And if this were not enough to make a potboiler steam, Woodhull declared that she and Tilton had become lovers in 1871, when the infatuated Tilton was writing an adoring biography.[112] During the 1875 trial, Tilton maintained that the biography was written to appease Woodhull and to keep her from breaching the secrecy of the Beecher affair. In response to his cross-examination as to why he, in fact, had on at least one occasion spent the night at Woodhull's, Tilton explained that, exhausted from working on the biography (which was a thirty-three-page essay), he had fallen asleep on the couch.

Publicity surrounding the Beecher trial had a negative impact on the woman suffrage movement. "As if we were responsible for the shortcomings of a man who had once been president of a branch of our Society!" fumed Blake; "It would surely have been more reasonable to hold Congregationalism responsible than Woman Suffrage."[113]

VI

In February 1872, in the midst of this convoluted, real-life intrigue, Blake began writing her heavily plotted novel *Fettered for Life*. Inspired by her work in the woman's rights movement, she wanted it to portray "forcibly and powerfully" the sufferings endured by her sex.[114] The novel was unabashedly political, depicting, through a cross-section of social levels, the consequences of female subordination in the home and in the workplace. Although its publication was delayed by a financial panic in 1873, when it finally appeared on March 28, 1874, it was an instant success, selling 1,300 copies on its first day in print. When Susan B. Anthony read aloud to her ailing mother, the book she chose was Lillie Devereux Blake's brand new novel. "It will stimulate every girl reader to have something beside marriage to depend on for support," Anthony recorded in her daybook for Sunday, April 5.[115] She was not alone in praising *Fettered for Life*. Nathaniel Parker Willis's Philadelphia *Home Journal* declared it a "thrilling story . . . a powerful book," and the *New York World,* "among the most readable and notable books of the year." Its twentieth-century critics have called it "a feminist classic," and "the most comprehensive women's rights novel of the nineteenth century."[116] By April, the Fifth Avenue library had thirty-five copies in constant circulation, and it went into several editions during the spring of 1874 and was reissued again in 1885.[117]

Fettered for Life interweaves women's rights, abolitionist, and temperance issues with the plight of urban working women (especially poor women), and problems of women's personal freedom. It addresses in detail the post–Civil War status of women, including the restrictions on their use of public space, whether on the lecture circuit, on public streets, or in newspapers; issues of women in the workforce, their housing arrangements, and their limited vocational options; the various forms of sexual harassment to which they were subjected; their educational options; and the push for reform in matters of property rights and marriage and of female attire and exercise. The novel documents broad social concerns resulting from industrialization, immigration, and an increasing urban population.

The title is a conflation of allusions to nineteenth-century reform movements. "Fettered" was a familiar code word for black slavery, a word that came to signify for antislavery feminists their own link with their sister slaves,[118] and it also refers to marriage, with the novel's subtitle "Lord and Master" doubling both meanings and the theme of female constriction and imprisonment underscoring them. A third meaning of "fettered," which emerges thematically with Blake's exploration of disguise and the freedom gained when a woman appears in male form, is that of femaleness itself as a fetter which, in a patriarchal social order, enchains a woman for life, limiting her fulfillment as it circumscribes her freedom. In the post–Civil War milieu, when feminist disappointment over the denial of universal suffrage was keen, Blake resurrected in "fettered" a word sure to inflame feminist anger as well as to encode anew both the historical affiliation of the suffrage, temperance, and abolitionist movements and the forms of enslavement each fought against.

Blake makes the writing of male cultural stories and the erasure of female voices the central political trope of her novel. In the opening chapter, a chorus of old men in a New York City police court gaze at Laura Stanley, shaking their heads knowingly at "the old, old story." That old story, the old men's story, is the titillating patriarchal story of seduction and possession. Blake became very much aware of the realities of that story when, in April 1870, she joined a committee to look into the treatment of women in police custody. She discovered variations of this old story playing out in police stations throughout the city: stories of rape and abuse of female prisoners at the hands of a totally male police force. Most of the women, she discovered, were homeless, some were innocent of any crime, many were young girls, all "were at the mercy of the policemen. No doubt many of these were worthy and well meaning men, but in the course of my investigations, I heard many a dark story that suggested possibilities which it would not do to mention publicly."[119]

Later, Blake would prepare a resolution adopted by the New York State Woman Suffrage Association calling for the presence in all police stations of "police women, reputable persons of strong physique and good health, who shall receive the same compensation as policemen."[120] She was immediately attacked in the newspapers; the term "police woman" was ridiculed as the utmost absurdity, and Blake was wildly caricatured, "dressed as a policeman, brandishing a club and running after an inoffensive man."[121] She engaged a lawyer to draw up a piece of legislation, which she delivered (with "police woman" replaced by "police matron") to State Assemblyman John G. Boyd, and she spoke before the Assembly's Committee on Grievances. The Police Matron's Bill was passed and vetoed in May 1882 and passed again the following January. It, too, was vetoed.[122] It was introduced again in 1883, in 1888, and in 1890, but was always vetoed. Blake persisted, and finally, in 1892, the bill was signed into law. Blake then began lobbying for equal pay for the police matrons. She worked on this issue with Theodore Roosevelt, first when he was police commissioner and then while he was governor.[123]

The opening scene of *Fettered for Life* foregrounds the issue of female containment within the legal space of patriarchy. The novel's antagonist is a police-court judge by the name of Swinton, who runs a racket abducting young women entering New York in search of jobs. Questioned by Judge Swinton as to why she is in the city and where she plans to stay, Laura Stanley is befriended by Frank Heywood, who promises to keep her name out of the papers and warns her not to let anyone know that she had spent the night in the police court. Later in the novel, Guy Bradford, her otherwise unremarkable suitor, exiles himself on a trip abroad rather than face the uncertainty of Laura's whereabouts on her first night in New York. Unaware of the depth and breadth of the social restrictions imposed upon women, contemporary readers may be puzzled as to what all the fuss is about. However, an account of an actual event dating from almost a generation later illustrates the depth of those restrictions and the implications for a nineteenth-century woman to be out alone, particularly at night. Twenty-one years after the publication of *Fettered for Life,*

> on the night of December 6, 1895, the police of New York City arrested Lizzie Schauer, a young working-class woman, on a charge of disorderly conduct. She had, according to her own account, been looking for the house of her aunt and had stopped to ask directions of two men. This behavior—as well as the fact that an unaccompanied woman was out at night—was presumptive evidence that she was soliciting prostitution in the eyes of the arresting police officers and of the judge who sent her to the work house. . . . [She was released] only after a doctor's examination had shown her to be a "good girl."[124]

Such medical and judicial intrusions into a woman's very person as well as into her personal life are indicative of the level of social control exercised over her. The marriages which Blake exposes in *Fettered for Life* are the private manifestations of such public norms. When Ferdinand LeRoy tells his reluctant bride Flora that he has the right of entrance to all parts of his house, the sexual implications and the pervasiveness of control are clear; a married woman did not belong to herself. In the latter half of the nineteenth century, "'self-ownership,'" writes Margit Stange, "signified a wife's right to refuse marital sex—a right feminists were demanding as the key to female autonomy."[125]

When projected onto the larger canvas of the novel, the picture that Blake draws of Laura, detained against her will in the police court, implicates society as a whole in a broad range of actions that seek to control women. Laura has had to "escape" her father; in his attempt to procure her for Judge Swinton, John Bludgett, threatens to drag her into his house; and later she is kidnapped. But these are only the more violent forms of imprisonment that she faces; sexual harassment of any degree restricts a woman's freedom, and just the threat of being the object of the Judge's unwanted attentions results in Laura's self-confinement: "She made it a rule to be at home every day before twilight fell, and avoided going out, except on the ordinary round of her duties." When she tries to earn a living as a book agent, the harassment she endures just entering commercial establishments is enough to force her to give up the job.[126]

Laura Stanley is one of five young women who begin their adult lives in the city—each from a different class, each with a different strategy for survival. Both Rhoda Dayton and Laura Stanley are the objects of Judge Swinton's abductions. He is successful with the one, but not with the other, whom he harasses at every opportunity. Both Maggie Bertram and Flora Livingston are the objects of the wealthy Ferdinand LeRoy's obsessions: the first he seduces and betrays, the second he marries. While Maggie is left to waste away in a garret, Flora is expected to do much the same, but in more regal apartments. The fifth woman, also once the object of Judge Swinton's designs, escapes only by disguising herself as a man. With this character, Blake presents a woman—as talented and successful as any man might hope to be—who can function in the world only when, by cross-dressing, she literally steps into a male script and allows herself to be read as male.[127]

The world in which these women find themselves is one in which they are prey. Written the year after the famous meeting of another pair named Stanley and Livingstone, the novel makes clear that the primitive Congo which Blake's Laura Stanley and Flora Livingston enter at the risk of their own selves is that of American society at large. Within the heart of Flora's Fifth Avenue home lies a conservatory filled with exotic flowers and jungle birds, a gorgeous yet primitive enclave, which provides ironic comment on her parents' practice of the barbarous but socially sanctioned ritual of enslaving their daughter in a cruel marriage.

Blake's work with the Woman Workers' Association and her professional relationship with Jennie Collins, the activist of Boston's settlement house movement, had enlarged Blake's view of the plight of working women. In her novel, women across class lines suffer various forms of degradation. Molly Bludgett is a long-suffering, romance- and Bible-reading, battered housewife who takes in boarders who are really young women her husband procures for his boss, Judge Swinton. Maggie Bertram and Rhoda Dayton, seamstresses forced to take second jobs as barmaids, are trapped in an economic system that denies them living wages and are harassed by men who rape and then, in another instance of male scripting, scorn *them* as fallen women. *Fettered for Life*, like "The Social Condition of Woman" before it, makes clear that there is little difference between the sweatshop seamstress, so underpaid that she is forced into prostitution, and the wealthiest of wives, who is permitted no activity save sewing and who, if married to a tyrant, soon finds neither her life nor her body is her own.

Like Laura Stanley, other women experience various forms of confinement. Molly Bludgett is not allowed outside her home. In despair at the control her employer has over her, Rhoda wonders if she is "to be forever an utter and abject slave!" Wife and mother, Agnes Moulder, by metaphoric implication, is a caged bird whose escape throws her husband into a murderous rage.[128] Mrs. Livingston colludes in the patriarchal socialization of her daughter, Flora, although she "had at one period of her life protested against her destiny as bitterly as did ever any revolted slave; but having for years past been contented with her chains, she could endure no thought of revolt in others." Flora Livingston is imprisoned like a pinned butterfly, and then "bartered away" by her parents, who "if they had read an account of how certain savages deck out their young daughters with beads and feathers, and then offer them to some great chief for sale, . . . would probably have been shocked at such unchristian and barbarous practices." Ferdinand LeRoy calls her "my sweet trembling little prisoner," and Flora is "unable to escape." She is drawn through elegant salons like "some fair Grecian captive led in chains to adorn the triumph of a victor." Not only is the social order constructed in such a way that women are always in need of protectors, but those protectors—fathers, husbands, judges—are often the very people from whom one must escape. Only the woman who has disguised herself as a man has unharassed access to the city any time of day or night.

Covering up her womanhood protects the novel's cross-dresser from, among other things, male proprietary gazing, which Blake constructs as another form of fettering.[129] It is the men of power who impose upon women the unrelenting, possessive gaze of patriarchy. Ferdinand LeRoy watches Flora "with a gaze which never relented. She was gay with her gay companions, she laughed with the rest; but there was with her all the time, a feeling of oppression, a sense that she was not one moment free from that cold, yet devouring regard." Laura is violently startled when Judge Swinton gazes at her, but even after she turns away from him he looks after her from his position of power, amused and "with a smile on his lips." Men look upon Laura as she stands before the police court, and an "almost imperceptible glance of intelligence" is exchanged between the judge and his procurer, John Bludgett. A power network exists among these men, filled with "knowing winks," so that often not a word need be spoken for an exchange to take place.

If the power of men is so great that words can be dispensed with, the suppression of women's voices, on the other hand, is a central form of patriarchal control. To be fettered in this society meant not only that women were confined in various ways, and not only that they were objects of intrusive viewing, but, in addition, that their freedom to speak was restricted. Although women were encouraged by a culture that valued the "feminine" orientation toward working for the good of others, it was clear that they were to be unobtrusive in doing so; they were to be neither seen nor heard. "'Women should be shrinking and modest, avoiding the public gaze,'" Mr. Glitter, the principal of a school for girls, informs Laura Stanley. To gaze at a woman is a possessive act reserved for a privileged male. *Fettered for Life*'s most obvious allusion to the question of a woman's lecturing in public occurs in a confrontation between Laura and Mr. Glitter, who maintains his position that woman's place is in the home and not at the podium even as he sends his overworked wife out of the home and into the rain to run all his errands.

The real issue involved in the appropriateness of women speaking in public concerns the source of control over language, and *Fettered for Life* presciently plays out this concern in themes that reflect contemporary feminist issues of voice and authorship. Laura points out to Mr. Glitter that his position implies that while an actress is socially acceptable because she repeats other people's words, a female orator is not because she repeats her own words. The power of words, and the ownership of that power, are made clear when Judge Swinton abducts Laura. Chloroformed, she is "quiet as a lamb." Frank Heywood's threat to use words, to give voice to Laura's outrage by reporting it for his newspaper, is sufficient to foil the Judge, whose only response is the utterance of yet another word, "a very ugly word, which he gave under his breath, but with great force as he turned on his heel."

Giving breath to any word with great force was not considered appropriate to women. When Laura first appears in the novel, she is described as "quietly self-possessed," but ultimately *Fettered for Life* reveals that phrase to be an oxymoron; to be quiet, to give up one's voice, is finally to give up oneself. One can only be quietly dispossessed. Laura may "prefer the quiet paths of art and study to the angry strife of politics," but her very choice of that quiet path of art *is* political, for when it is explained that Laura wants to be a serious artist, the idea is greeted with laughter. It seems that there is no quiet way for women to possess themselves. To be quiet, whether out of fear or the need to please another, is to erase one's own desires and to give up the power necessary to script one's own life. Out of fear of displeasing her father, Flora Livingston suppresses her desire to be more than an ornament. Molly Bludgett, who spends her days reading sentimental fiction, like "Berenice the Beautiful," knows that to give voice to her dreams will result in nothing but a brutal beating. Indeed, to break the silence can be terrifying, and in several incidents, when Laura has incited her friends to speak up for themselves, she herself is frightened by the sounds they make and seeks to silence them. "'Oh do try to be more quiet,'" Laura urges Agnes Moulder after her husband has killed her uncaged bird; "'It is perhaps better not to speak hardly of him,' Laura said quietly" to the newly married Mrs. LeRoy, leaving Flora silent and alone to guard "the secrets of the prison-house."

Female silence is essentially a matter of the erasure of the female self. The most powerful and lordly of men, Ferdinand LeRoy, makes clear that men of his ilk demand quietness in women. With the dehumanizing gaze of one who possesses a new toy, he looks at Flora "as one might at a doll one was attiring," and says, "I can see that your nature is quietness itself!" When her father tells her that "a true woman is willing to lose her own identity in her husband's," Flora's "suppressed wrath . . . burst[s] forth into words." When she declares that her marriage has killed her, and her mother cautions her, "Don't say such wild words, and the doctor has forbidden you talking much," Flora replies, "They are not wild words, and it will not hurt me to talk." Words are what Flora chooses as the instrument that will make her life her own, but upon the appearance of her first publication, her husband burns all of her remaining manuscripts. When she pleads with him, saying "I need an object in life," LeRoy's response is "women should be quiet." The burning of Flora's manuscripts, like Laura's humiliating job of bookselling, becomes a trope both for the erasure of women's attempts to write their own lives and for the suppression of women's literary tradition.

Blake's motifs of voice and quiet, words and books, converge with the death of the female self when the silenced Flora, after dismissing her maid with a request to go to a bookstore to get a book, any book, walks to the sea, follows the voice of the waves which she hears "calling to her, calling to her, with their hollow voices," and with her own "strange wild cry" tries to drown herself. Suicide reduces the self to silence. When Flora dies, "there was silence in the room; silence except for the faint sigh of the wind, and the chant of the waves that was like a requiem!"

And when Molly Bludgett's life violently ends, it is significant that she is silenced with a boot heel in her mouth. Her life brutally connects the motifs of words and books, voice and silence. From her first appearance in the novel, Mrs. Bludgett alerts us to the fact that, for a woman, reading is a subversive activity. A voracious reader of sentimental stories, she quickly and guiltily hides from her husband whatever novel or illustrated story paper she happens to be reading. "Bludgett he don't like it," she explains. The last book she hides from her husband is "no showily-covered romance, but a poor, worn copy of the Bible," the appearance of which "seemed to stimulate his rage to madness; he snatched it from her and smote her down again, silencing that pleading voice by a stamp of his heavy boot-heel on the helpless mouth."

Blake was able to write with impunity of behaviors such as drunkenness in husbands and abuse of seamstresses because these abuses were under attack in the mainstream society by temperance societies and the settlement house movement. Her middle-class readership, positioned at a superior distance, could accept her depiction of brutality in lower levels of society. She could even expose the sexual corruption at the heart of middle-class institutions— of the judicial and marriage systems. *Fettered for Life*'s revelations were readily accepted by a readership familiar with allegations of political corruption during the early 1870s reign of Boss Tweed in New York City, which split the Republican Party, as well as the sensational allegations about the sexual improprieties of Henry Ward Beecher. In its May 6, 1874, review of *Fettered for Life*, the *Home Journal* emphasized the accuracy of the novel's portrayals:

> While the story makes several startling statements, and draws some very dark pictures of men, we believe none of them are stronger than the truth. The great merit of this story is its startling reality, its truthfulness to every day life. Mrs. Blake writes of what she knows and some of the characters introduced to the reader are easily recognized by people acquainted in New York. Those who once commence to read the story of Laura Stanley's struggles, trials, and triumphs in this city will hardly close the book until the end is reached. In describing such a place as Bludgett's den, Mrs. Blake must have taken council of some of her gentlemen friends. The Judge Swinton she puts upon the canvas is far more of a representative man than most people suspect, while Flora Livingston is one out of many of the unfortunately married belles of Fifth Avenue. "Fettered for Life" is a powerful book in its motive, and is too true to be easily upset.[130]

While perhaps "startling" or "dark," Blake's polemics on the serious political corruptions of the day presented no serious threat to the status quo. However, *Fettered for Life* moves beyond popular reform issues to give a narrative explication of the ideological position concerning gender identity articulated in "The Social Condition of Woman." Blake's belief that gender differences are socially constructed called for a reconception of the nature and status of woman. While *Fettered for Life* overtly exposes political corruption and social disorder, because her agenda pushed against the boundaries of nineteenth-century ideologies of womanhood she had to present her ideas concerning the nature of women more covertly.

Attuned to the attitudes and expectations of her readership, Blake used strategies for satisfying her audience even while articulating radical revisions of the status quo. Blake's was a prose of disguise, layered with carefully hidden agendas which undercut commonly held perceptions regarding women. Thus disguise lies at the heart of her fictional enterprise. She cross-dresses her fiction, outfitting it with traditional plot elements and a conventional ending palatable to her readership, giving it the acceptable patina of the patriarchal script. However, her novel contains a hint for the reader that hers is a "cunningly-devised fiction," as the cross-dresser says of her "dear little [fake] moustache." With the use of the phrase "cunningly-devised fiction," Blake challenges her readers to see beneath her novel's camouflage. The hidden premise within *Fettered for Life* is that men and women are essentially the same; and the hidden story within *Fettered for Life* is the story of the man who is a woman. Blake's use of the gender switch implies that gender itself is a surface detail, and that the profound differences between the sexes, used to create a hierarchy and to justify social inequities, are themselves not preordained givens, but social constructions.

This, her most radical agenda, Blake kept well hidden not only from her middle-class readership but also from her sisters in the suffrage movement. Cornelia D'Arcy, M.D., the novel's leading suffragist and seemingly the model for what any woman might be, given both freedom and education, is the spokesperson for mainstream suffrage thought, not for the more radical ideology of suffragists like Blake and Stanton. She voices the nineteenth-century conception of woman as radically "other" vis-à-vis man. The differences between the sexes "'are radical and God-ordained,'" Mrs. D'Arcy says. "'Man represents in the world, the element of strength and force; woman that of love and spirituality; the cooperation of both is needed to form a perfect society or government.'" When Mrs. D'Arcy voices these mainstream suffrage sentiments, Laura Stanley remains mute; she does not agree—nor, as she made clear in the anonymous "Social Condition of Woman," did Blake. But her radical vision was not a welcome one, even to many within the suffrage movement. Only a "small minority," writes DuBois "called for radical transformation in women's lives . . . the great majority of suffragists . . . intended no such challenge."[131]

In its focus on women and work, *Fettered for Life* was one of many novels of the last third of the nineteenth century that participated in an intense social debate concerning the changing status of women. Louisa May Alcott's *Work: A Story of Experience* (1873) provided a survey of various professions available to middle-class women. Alcott's insistent interpretation of women's work in the public world as a continuation of their duties in the home reasserts the notion that woman's essential nature is connected to a separate domestic sphere and skirts the issue of the appropriateness of women working outside that sphere. Only when Alcott's heroine, Christy, sacrifices herself to save another can the reader begin to answer Alcott's central question: "A fine actress perhaps, but how good a woman?" We watch as illness and misfortune bring about a passivity in Christy, and we are told that her better self is emerging. When Christy looks back over her life, her proof of its success is her dead husband's presumed approval, her subordination of her own work to his and the self-sacrificial nature of her endeavors. Alcott's need to domesticate her public women is indicative of the dis-ease with which the middle class approached any change in the status of women.

In 1873, Fanny Fern wrote a piece titled "Lady Doctors" that plays on stereotypes of the petty envy and vanity of women: "Before swallowing her pills (of which she would be the first), I should want to make sure that I had never come between her and a lover, or a new bonnet. . . . If I desired her undivided attention to my case, I should first remove the looking-glass." Fern concludes, "While I am in my senses I will never exchange my gentlemanly, soft-voiced, soft-stepping, experienced, intelligent, handsome doctor, for all the female M.D.'s who ever carved up dead bodies or live characters—or tore each other's caps."[132]

William Dean Howells's *Dr. Breen's Practice* (1881) rehearsed what had come to be standard fare in the novelistic treatment of women physicians, who were seen as stunted emotionally because of their inability to find husbands. Howells's Grace Breen enters medicine "in the spirit in which other women enter convents"—that is, in response to an unhappy love affair, her fiancé having married her best friend. She is seen as strong only when she admits to her failure in love and allows herself to be rescued, through marriage, from the ridiculous predicament of having a profession. Only then can she complete her arrested development and fully mature into a married woman. Elizabeth Stuart Phelps's *Dr. Zay* (1882), a response to Howells's novel, depicts a fully mature, self-possessed professional, a new type of women who "demands a new type of man" if the conflict between marriage and a woman working is to be resolved.

In *Fettered for Life*, Blake insists that beyond economic necessity, work is a vital activity for women as well as for men, for it brings meaning to life and definition to self. This idea countered the notion that women should work only for the good of others and not of self, it undermined the primacy of marriage in the fulfillment of women's lives, and it posed a threat to the dominance of husbands through whom wives were supposed to be defined. Blake's ideology was a precursor of that which enabled the next generation of writers, like Charlotte Perkins Gilman and Kate Chopin, to depict with sympathy women who awakened to their own selves and desires in the face of a culture that acknowledged in them no needs beyond fulfilling those of others, and no voice save that which the patriarchal culture might script for them.[133]

VII

Within the male-inscribed and predatory world of *Fettered for Life*, a covert circle of female storytellers creates a community of women which, at least temporarily, breaks through both the borders created by the hierarchical class lines of patriarchy and the silences imposed upon women. Laura Stanley asks Molly Bludgett, "tell me all about yourself," and so begins a secret solidarity based on women's storytelling. Frank Heywood asks for Laura's story; she asks for Rhoda Dayton's and gives hers to Cornelia D'Arcy. Flora Livingston is a poet, the crossdresser loves to write; each speaks out of a silence that imprisons her. Everyone is careful to whom she tells her story, for in the patriarchal order a woman is not to have her own story. The most secret story, the hidden story of disguise, becomes emblematic of the novel itself; not only does the novel keep its most subversive story well hidden, but it makes clear that the very act of writing the self is a woman's most subversive activity.

Lillie Devereux Blake had not been ready to fully script her own life until her mother died. Only then, out of that death and the prolonged depression that followed it, did Blake begin again the reconstruction of self that she had undertaken after Frank Umsted's suicide. In the woman's movement, she found not only compatible minds and meaningful work that utilized her extraordinary rhetorical and organizational skills in a cause to which she was wholeheartedly committed, but also a means to achieve significance in the world. She had always been ambitious for fame, and through her suffrage work she would achieve it.

6. Beneath The Suffrage Narrative

Miss Anthony has one idea and she has no patience with anyone
who has two. I cannot sit on the door just like Poe's raven,
and sing suffrage evermore. I am deeply interested in
all the live questions of the day.
—Elizabeth Cady Stanton, letter
to Clara Colby, circa 1895

I

IN HIS ESSAY "Ought Women to Learn the Alphabet?" published in the February 1859 *Atlantic Monthly*, Thomas Wentworth Higginson posed the question asked rhetorically by, among others, Elizabeth Cady Stanton, Lillie Devereux Blake, and Margaret Fuller and, before them, by Mary Wollstoncraft and Judith Sargent Murray—are not the male and female brain the same? In the 1870s, President Charles W. Eliot of Harvard University responded for the majority when he answered, "No. . . . Sex penetrates the mind and the affections, and penetrates deeply and powerfully. . . . there is a fundamental pervading difference between all men and all women which extends to their minds quite as much as to their bodies."[1] Later, Eliot worried that "girls are being prepared daily, by 'superior education' to engage, not in child bearing and house work, but in clerkship, telegraphy, newspaper writing, school teaching, etc. And many are learning to believe that, if they can but have their 'rights,' they will be enabled to compete with men in the pulpit, the Senate, the bench."[2]

In 1873, Edward H. Clarke, M.D., former professor of medicine at Harvard and Fellow of the American Academy of Arts and Sciences, wrote that the growth of the female reproductive system unfortunately coincides with a girl's education: "The growth of this peculiar and marvelous apparatus, in the perfect development of which humanity has so large an interest, occurs during the few years of a girl's educational life." Overtaxing the system by trying to develop the brain while Nature is developing the reproductive organs, Clarke reports, has resulted in the growth of many an excellent female scholar with undeveloped ovaries. "Later they married, and were sterile," or, worse still, they suffered progressive invalidism and even consignment to lunatic asylums.[3] In *Plain Talk about Insanity*, T. W. Fisher, M.D., cites incidents of girls studying to the point of insanity. For example, "Miss C———, of a nervous organization, and quick to learn; her health suffered in normal school, so that her physician predicted insanity if her studies were not discontinued. She persevered, however, and is now an inmate of a hospital, with hysteria and depression. . . . A certain proportion of girls," he advises, "are predisposed to mental or nervous derangement. The same girls are apt to be quick, brilliant, ambitious, and persistent at study, and need not stimulation, but repression."[4]

Girls may beat boys in "unraveling the intricacies of Juvenal," but only, Dr. Clarke warns, at the risk of consumed blood and worn brain tissue and arrested development. Moreover, any woman "who has been defrauded by her education" runs the risk, if not of chronic disease, then of the development of "more muscular tissue than is commonly seen, a coarser skin, and, generally, a tougher and more angular makeup. There is a corresponding change in the intellectual and psychical condition,—a dropping out of maternal instincts, and an appearance of Amazonian coarseness and force. Such persons," Dr. Clarke concludes, "are analogous to the sexless class of termites."[5]

"It were better not to educate girls at all between the ages of fourteen and eighteen, unless it can be done with careful reference to their bodily health," wrote Dr. S. Weir Mitchell.[6] Mitchell, a prolific writer of poetry and fiction, as well as medical monographs with such titles as *Fat and Blood* and *Wear and Tear*, is now best known as the doctor who prescribed the famously debilitating "rest cure" for both the narrator of *The Yellow Wallpaper* and its author, Charlotte Perkins Gilman. The recommendation was for girls to be educated in programs requiring two-thirds the amount of study that the programs for boys demanded and enforcing rest for "constructing a reproductive apparatus . . . [and] every fourth week, there should be a remission, and sometimes an intermission, of both study and exercise."[7]

Given the fact that such powerful voices were brought to bear against the higher education of women, it is not surprising that only two institutions, Oberlin College and Butler University, were coeducational by mid-century.[8] Mount Holyoke was founded in 1837, Vassar in 1865, Wellesley and Smith in 1875, and Michigan, Boston, and Cornell Universities admitted women by the 1870s. On October 4, 1873, beneath portraits of her ancestors, Blake delivered an application to President F. A. P. Barnard of Columbia University for admission of five female candidates. She met with the president and faculty, showing them the college charter which stated that the institution was founded for "the instruction of youth," and did not specify youth of only one sex. At Barnard's request, Blake wrote a plea which, on October 6, he presented to the board of trustees.

Columbia's board referred Blake's proposal to a committee headed by the Reverend Morgan Dix, rector of Trinity Church, who was fiercely opposed to coeducation. "Nature herself forbids co-education and protests against it," he wrote. Dix could support only that education "which develops the true ideal of womanhood, as distinct from that of manhood."[9] His committee tabled the proposal. As a result of Blake's initiative, however, President Barnard would renew her plea over the course of several years, and individual professors began to allow women into their classes (although this practice was eliminated in 1879). In 1883, as a first step in the process toward coeducation, women were admitted to the Columbia Collegiate Course for Women. Women could receive a certificate of achievement, and, after 1886, they could receive a bachelor's degree, although, while women took the same final exams as men, they could not attend the lectures upon which the exams were based.[10] The movement toward coeducation was halted in 1889 with the founding of Columbia's female affiliate, Barnard College. Blake was opposed to the formation of Barnard, because she wanted women to be admitted to Columbia on an equal footing with men, not relegated to a separate institution.

Most histories of Columbia and Barnard College exclude or minimize Blake's role in opening higher education to women at Columbia, and they do so in a way that illustrates how political controversies can be elided, and controversial people erased, in an attempt to present an uncomplicated history that has the mien of inevitability. In an 1891 account of the founding of Barnard College, Annie Nathan Meyer acknowledged that in 1873 Lillie Devereux Blake made a plea to the Columbia faculty on behalf of several qualified young women, but Meyer, a proponent of affiliate schools for women rather than coeducation, proceeded to disparage the push for coeducation.[11] Much later, she wrote another account omitting mention of Blake's work altogether and beginning the history of women and Columbia with the effort to create an affiliate college.[12] In so doing, she obliterated fifteen years of the history of opening higher education to women in New York. Moreover, she silenced the arguments of the opposition and erased the issues that in themselves were the real history of the movement.

Following Meyer's lead, in their 1939 history Alice Duer Miller and Susan Myers write:

> In 1879 President Barnard's report [to the trustees] discussed for *the first time* [emphasis mine] plans for the admission of women as students at Columbia, supported by petitions that had been twice made by Sorosis, the great and active woman's club of New York. . . . For five successive years thereafter Dr. Barnard set forth in his reports reasons and arguments in favor of admitting women. . . . He was uncompromising in his belief that coeducation, in the commonly accepted sense of receiving women into the classrooms with men, was the best method of achieving the desired end.[13]

In fact, Barnard first presented his proposal, which was written by Blake, in 1873, and Sorosis, whose annual dinners and breakfasts Blake attended, put forward a proposal to admit women some three years later.[14] Marian Churchill White, in her 1954 history, dates the first attempt to open Columbia to women with the Sorosis proposal of 1876.[15] A third history published in 1964 replicated the errors of the previous volumes and continued the exclusion of Blake from its narrative.[16]

Annie Nathan Meyer was opposed to coeducationalists and radical feminists like Blake. The argument between Blake and more conservative postwar women who worked to establish affiliate institutions for women reflects the argument between those nineteenth-century feminists who wanted women integrated into the public world without regard to sex and those of the majority, who emphasized gender differences in their struggle for women's rights. It was the argument that struck at the heart of Blake's feminist philosophy and at the core values of women like Meyer. No wonder, then, that Meyer minimizes Blake's and emphasizes her own role in the fight for higher education for women by eliminating a fifteen-year context. "The woman who first approached the Trustees of Columbia College with a plan to found an affiliated college for women was," writes Annie Nathan Meyer, "Mrs. Annie Nathan Meyer. . . ."[17]

Meyer visited Morgan Dix, knowing that his support was crucial to the formation of the female affiliate. Her 1935 reminiscence is almost worshipful in its approach to the "learned divine": "My knees were wobbling, and I could scarcely bear to think what my voice would sound like, if and when I could control it sufficiently to be heard at all."[18] Meyer makes reference to the Reverend Dix's Lenten Lectures, which Lillie Blake, not at all wobbly-kneed or awestruck, had countered with her own series of lectures in 1883. Blake was enraged by Dix's first lecture, which idealized maternity, circumscribed female freedom, and argued that the status of women was elevated by the teachings of the Christian church. Blake referred to him as "this clerical dictator."[19] By the time of his third Friday sermon, she had rented a hall, publicized her own lecture, and was ready to respond to him on Sunday evening. Each Friday in Lent Dix would give his lecture, and each Sunday Blake would respond. She refuted him on historical fact and peppered her own history of woman's condition with citations from Livy, Quintilian, and Valerius Maximus. She correlated the contraction of woman's status with the rise of the celibate priesthood, arguing that in order to sustain "this hideous doctrine . . . women were declared to be by nature inferior, to be unfit to associate with men, to be unworthy and degrading in their influence." She proceeded to reinterpret Genesis, showing how only a male reading of the text can conclude that woman is the inferior of man. Each week her audiences grew until the hall "was packed to suffocation, hundreds going away unable to gain admittance."[20]

Within a fortnight, she had offers from publishers to print her lectures, but she had delivered them from notes. With help from newspaper accounts of what she had said, and "by desperate efforts," she compiled a manuscript and was reading proof in less than three weeks.[21] The book was out before the end of April, and by May 2 she was getting reviews. *Woman's Place To-Day,* her daughter noted, "was widely sold, and became a handbook of arguments for woman suffrage workers on both sides of the Atlantic. . . . In a month she had become one of the most quoted and best-known women in the country."[22] Elinore Hughes Partridge writes that *Woman's Place To-Day,* "created a sensation in the contemporary press and did much to awaken women into active workers for suffrage."[23] Blake confided to her diary:

At last, it has come. Recognition. When I stand today one of the foremost women of the nation. Every paper has some notice of the controversy I am carrying on. Fame, trumpet tongued, is uttering my name. So long I have dreamed of this, even far away in my childhood, but for years I thought it was but a vain dream. Now, however, I have achieved a place I may honestly be proud of. The notices of me are innumerable in every paper, personal descriptions, etc. My picture and biography is printed by Schoppel's Association, a pictorial press, and sent all over the country. I have letters of congratulations from friends and strangers and work is coming, work that will pay, articles, etc.[24]

"On the whole," Annie Nathan Meyer concedes, "the redoubtable Mrs. Lillie Devereaux [sic] Blake . . . had rather the better of the argument."[25]

The Reverend Dix was not opposed to a separately financed institution for the education of women, but he disapproved, writes Meyer, of "'wild women . . . of unwomanly tactics, of creatures who are not men and certainly not women.'"[26] Meyer's implication is that Mrs. Blake was just such a woman. Acknowledging that there was opposition to the "annex movement," Meyer dismisses it with the remark that its "battle-cry might have been almost said to have been 'Co-education or no education.' . . . But the wiser policy," she insists, prevailed, "and it was acknowledged by the majority that 'those co-educationalists who ignore the annex project are butting their heads against a stone wall when a nicely swarded path lies before them.'"[27]

Ironically, Barnard College was named in "grateful tribute to the late President Barnard," although Barnard had himself been a coeducationalist who firmly maintained that the establishment of an annex was desirable *only* if "considered as a step toward what I think must, sooner or later, come to pass, and that is the opening of the College proper to both sexes equally." Naming the annex after Barnard erased the significance and silenced the argument of the opposition even as it appropriated him, regardless of his own intentions, to the narrative of the majority. Meyer fully acknowledged Barnard's position, but maintained that "the affiliated college is not always a mere 'step toward co-education.'"[28] Blake, then president of the New York Woman Suffrage Association, remarked that the annex was "another proof of the injustice with which the 'unfortunate sex' is so generally treated."[29]

II

The historical treatment of Blake at Columbia would be, in small, the same as that which would be accorded her in the official records of the suffrage movement. As a dissident, she would be sacrificed in favor of a grand narrative with a smooth surface. The woman's movement was never exempt from internecine warfare. In this it was clear that women did indeed share a common humanity with men. The battles could be vicious, personal pride often taking precedence over the good of the movement. The major strategy was one of exclusion; those who threatened one's own position of prominence were not invited to speak or were allotted five minutes at the podium instead of an hour, or their contributions were not acknowledged in the written records. At the Woman's Congress, held in New York City on October 15–17, 1873, for example, Elizabeth Cady Stanton publicly complimented Blake's campaign to enroll women at Columbia. However, the Congress was arranged by Charlotte Wilbour, who had excluded Blake from the platform.[30] Once, to prevent Blake from speaking, Isabella Beecher Hooker actually stepped in front of Susan B. Anthony, who had just introduced Blake, and announced another speaker.[31] During almost forty years of activism, Blake would win many skirmishes, but she ultimately lost the battle for her rightful place in suffrage history. She quickly learned that her ideal of female solidarity was more difficult to achieve in the competitive world of suffrage politics than in the pages of her feminist novel.

Lillie Devereux Blake was not innocent of using exclusionary tactics herself. Her 1871 strategy in New York had been based on excluding Victoria Woodhull from meetings of the New York City Woman's Suffrage Association. She was particularly averse to giving Dr. Mary Walker any opportunity to gain access to the platform. Dr. Walker, who always wore masculine attire—usually a trousered suit, tie, and top hat—had been an assistant surgeon in a Civil War regiment. She attended many woman suffrage conventions, attempting to speak from the platform even when not invited to do so, sometimes parading about on stage while others spoke. Blake had first seen Dr. Walker, or "poor Mary Walker" as she called her, at the New Year's reception at the White House in 1862: "I was immediately preceded by an odd little figure in bloomer costume. It was that of a very thin woman, plain of feature and apparently about twenty-five. She wore a dress consisting of a long cloth polonaise or basque, trimmed on the front with military braid, and a pair of trousers. Apparently there were no skirts at all under the basque which reached about half way between the knee and foot. On her head she wore a hat and feather and her hair was arranged in long ringlets." Although she herself could create a sensitive portrait of a successful cross-dresser, Blake considered Walker "a harmless monomaniac," and, always sensitive to public opinion, she wanted Walker off the platform, because "her grotesque appearance invariably excites a laugh and brings us into ridicule."[32] When she was in charge of the 1877 NWSA annual spring convention, Blake refused Dr. Walker entry to the committee room, through which she had to pass to get onstage. Blake even resorted to leaning against the door to keep out Walker, who was pushing hard from the other side. Later Blake employed a policeman to stop "the little doctor," as she patronizingly referred to the first woman ever given the Congressional Medal of Honor, from entering.

Attempts to exclude Blake from the inner circles of the suffrage movement began almost as soon as her rhetorical strategies brought her publicity. On October 7, 1872, Blake, along with Susan B. Anthony, Matilda Joslyn Gage, and Isabella Beecher Hooker, was on the platform at Cooper Union in support of the Grant-Wilson Republican presidential ticket. As Blake concluded her speech, rolls of applause broke out each time she named a state:

> We have all stood on the ocean shore and seen the tide come in. The waves steal on little by little sometimes advancing, sometimes seeming almost to recede, but ever gaining in strength. So it is in this election. A great breaker comes tumbling in, like the first echoes from Vermont. A lighter one ripples along the beach, like the August wave in North Carolina. As it dies away, a huge billow swirls up from Maine, while New Hampshire follows leaving its shining record high along the sands. Tomorrow the great rollers will come, tossing in from Pennsylvania and Ohio, from Indiana and Illinois, until in November next around all the shores of the republic will swell the high tide of victory![33]

The crowd went wild and would not stop until she came forward again. Blake wrote in her diary that "it was an intoxicating moment, all that vast crowd swaying, shouting and calling for me. . . . This kind of triumph is delicious as any I ever tasted."[34] It also, she noted in her autobiography, created enemies, who "from that moment swore to me an undying hatred.[35]

A month later, on November 14, 1872, Blake and Dr. Clemence Lozier, who had, during 1871–72, revitalized the New York City Woman's Suffrage Association in the face of wholesale abandonment by women who refused to be associated in any way with the free-love politics of Victoria Woodhull, were summarily dislodged from office. "An unworthy trick was played upon me," writes Blake, "and I was thrown entirely out of the management of the Society. . . . I had labored hard in the previous winter and only asked to be permitted still to work; this my enemies did not intend to allow. My prominence had brought the inevitable accompaniment of envy and those who were jealous of me wished to put me on the shelf. It is a sad, sad picture of human weakness that comes before me as I write, and I cannot go into any details of events I would willingly forget."[36] Blake mentions no names in her autobiography, but in her diary she identifies Charlotte Wilbour as the person who pushed her and Dr. Lozier aside and assumed the presidency for herself.[37] Two months later, Blake wrote with determined spunk rather than sadness that Mrs. Wilbour "has tried to crush me. She can't do it. I carry too many guns for her. She might as well try to put out a volcano with a petticoat."[38]

On February 17, 1873, the New York suffragists spoke before the state's Constitution Commission. Always eloquent, Blake delivered an address which the Albany *Express* printed in full.[39] In it she brings to bear the standard suffrage argument that if women have a separate sphere, it is one of responsibility and purity that will only enhance the value of their votes to society; but her primary argument is based on the perspective argued ten years earlier in "The Social Condition of Woman" and imagined in *Fettered for Life*— that gender is a detail of difference that should be irrelevant to politics: "Why, only imagine that half the men of the State were denied the right of suffrage, for no fault of their own, but simply for some physical accidents of weight or coloring."[40] Blake reports in her diary that "Mrs. Wilbour was quite angry that she was not even noticed [by the papers], and told me that she didn't 'like to be the tail to my kite!'"[41]

Charlotte Wilbour continued to try to diminish Blake's prominence. She refused to take part in further state Assembly meetings on New York constitutional reform, and when Blake agreed to appear again before the Assembly Judiciary Committee, Wilbour, as president of the city Association, declared that she had not authorized anyone to appear. The *New York Times*, always delighted by a cat fight, laughed: "Thus, if Mrs. Blake comes up at the appointed time and argues for her fellow-women, the committee is required to remember that nothing she says is authorized by Mrs. Wilbour."[42] Blake defied Wilbour and did speak before the committee. The following year, in January 1874, Blake, along with Susan B. Anthony and Matilda Joslyn Gage, were the only speakers to address the Judiciary Committee, and Blake's speech was again reported in full in the New York papers.[43]

Charlotte Wilbour also tried to cancel the city association's annual spring convention in 1873, but Blake appealed to the authority of Susan B. Anthony who insisted that it be held. Blake arranged for the May 6 meeting at which Anthony spoke about her arrest for voting in the 1872 presidential election. Blake was determined to continue her work in the movement, no matter the opposition, so when, on June 17, Anthony was found guilty of illegally casting a vote and was fined $100, Blake, outraged, staged a series of "indignation meetings" in New York City, Milton, Poughkeepsie, and Yonkers. She draped United States flags in mourning and closed the meetings with her characteristically rousing rhetoric:

> And this mockery of a trial was held on the 16th day of June, the anniversary of the battle of Bunker Hill! On that same day, one hundred years ago, our ancestors struck the first blow for personal liberty. At the end of a century, a summer's day not less fair hears the sentence pronounced which declares that the personal liberty for which they fought they gained for only one half of their descendants?
>
> The anniversary of the Independence of the men of this country is at hand. My country women, where are our own liberties? The Judge who, usurping the functions of the Jury, pronounced Susan B. Anthony guilty, classed the women of this land with idiots, criminals and lunatics and declared it a crime for them to claim their freedom!
>
> Heretofore it has been the custom to portray Liberty in female form and Columbia, the fair genius of our country, is a woman. What a mockery men have made of all this! Hereafter the graceful form should be portrayed with fetters on her wrists.[44]

By 1879, Blake was more systematically developing women's political power. She established the New York State Woman Suffrage Association (NYSWSA) with Matilda Joslyn Gage and served as its president from 1879 to 1890. She immediately organized the association in a campaign to defeat Governor Lucius Robinson in his bid for reelection. Robinson had vetoed a bill to allow women to vote for and serve as members of local school boards. Blake had worked hard during several sessions of the New York State Assembly to gain passage of this bill, and she was furious when the victory was canceled by the governor's veto. She wrote letters, published circulars, rented halls, raised money, and organized a speaking tour throughout the state. She elicited promises from the other two candidates for the office to sign the school board bill that Robinson had vetoed. When Robinson was defeated, women were given the credit; newspapers ran this riddle:

> Who killed Cock Robinson?
> We, said the women,
> With our little tongues,
> We killed Cock Robinson.[45]

On February 15, 1880, the newly elected Governor Alonzo B. Cornell signed the bill giving women the right to vote in school elections. The next month the NYSWSA presented a gold pen to the governor, and he in turn gave the organization the pen with which he had signed the bill. Before election day in November, Blake embarked on a strenuous speaking tour across the state, urging women to vote in school elections. In several towns, whole slates of women were elected.

Blake's power was steadily growing. The defeat of Governor Robinson had a wide impact on both women and politicians, and it was long remembered. When, in 1882, Blake was granted a meeting with President Chester A. Arthur, who had succeeded to the presidency after the assassination of James Garfield, he received her, she wrote, "with marked cordiality," reminding her that he had not seen her since the anti-Robinson campaign in 1879.[46] The president said, "'I was sorry that our national nominations did not please you as well as our State,' alluding to my taking up the cause of [General Winfield S.] Hancock [instead of Garfield, for president in the 1880 campaign]. I smiled and said that I had always maintained that he, the President, was in sympathy with our question. He replied that he was not there to make pledges but thought that when the time came for action we would not be disappointed in him."[47] In 1886, during Grover Cleveland's first term, Blake again went to the White House, presented her card, and, she reports, "I entered the Library where were seated many men waiting to speak to him. In a few moments the gentleman with whom he was talking when I entered left and the President signified that he would see me next."[48] Clearly, when organized to effect elections, women did have enough political clout to catch the attention of presidents. And just as clearly, Lillie Devereux Blake was perceived, at the highest levels, as a woman of power.

Since the formation of the Woman's National Loyal League by Stanton and Anthony in 1863, the suffrage leadership had concentrated on petitioning as a strategy for attaining political influence. But at the 1880 NWSA Convention in Washington, encouraged by the defeat of Governor Robinson, Blake proposed a major new strategy for giving women political access. Her plan was to dispense with petitioning and to organize women to campaign for the 1880 presidential candidate most favorable to their issues. Her views, Blake reports,

> were accepted, though not with the enthusiasm I would have liked. Miss Anthony and the other older workers have so long labored in this cause as a mere moral reform, and having learned their first lessons in the

anti-slavery agitation, cannot realize that this question of ours can be made a living political issue.

To my mind at this time the greatest danger threatening our cause was that it should drift, high and dry, into the ranks of respectable indifference, small meetings of nice old ladies in churches who assemble to listen to long winded arguments becoming the mode of carrying on the movement. My great wish has been for a year past to gain political influence and, consequently, power, and I tried hard to impress these views on the others.[49]

Blake proposed that delegates attend both Republican and Democratic presidential nominating conventions in an effort to affect the party platforms, and she traveled to Chicago and Cincinnati to make her voice heard. She combined this trip with speeches in Indianapolis, Lafayette, and Terre Haute, Indiana; Bloomington, Illinois; and Grand Rapids, Michigan.[50] She organized a delegation which met with the Democratic candidate, General Hancock, on August 8, 1880. He was noncommittal regarding suffrage, saying that he could not go beyond his letter of acceptance of the nomination. Blake's diary records the following exchange:

"We will abide by that, General, and rest satisfied if you will answer us one question. Do you think women are people?"

"People?"

"People," I said, "You think women are people, do you not?"

"Certainly," he said, "Women are people."

"Then," I went on triumphantly, "We will hold you to your letter of acceptance in which you say you believe in 'a full vote, a fair count, and a free ballot for the people,' that is, for women as well as for men."

"That's it, that's it!" exclaimed the General, his face lighting up with pleasure. "I will take my stand on that, ladies, you may say I believe in a full vote and a free ballot for *all* the people, women as well as men."

The NWSA campaigned for the Democrats. Susan B. Anthony and Lillie Devereux Blake split New York between them, Anthony canvassing the western counties, and Blake the eastern.[51] When Garfield was elected, she wrote in her diary, "I mourn for my country."[52]

Blake continued with her strategy of organizing women as a political force and pressing for legislation, such as the school board bill, which would gradually give women the vote, if only in limited arenas. In her view, such gradual steps would complement the push for a woman suffrage amendment. Blake's method was to write legislation, find sympathetic assemblymen to introduce her bills, and then tirelessly lobby for their passage. During her career in New York State, Blake organized legislative action which proved instrumental in modifying many laws that discriminated against women. Through her leadership, Civil War nurses became eligible for pension benefits, women became eligible for civil service positions, mothers were made joint guardians of their children, and for the first time women could serve on school boards and work in all public institutions where women were incarcerated. Blake labored for twenty years to have policewomen hired in New York City and then lobbied for equity in their pay, promotions, and benefits. She met with General Francis A. Walker, chief of the Census Bureau, to lobby for women enumerators, and, after winning his approval, began a newspaper campaign to alert women to this avenue of employment, and she lobbied heads of local bureaus to look favorably on applications from women. The NAWSA acknowledged her influence, writing of an article she wrote for the *Woman's Journal:* "'Women as Census Enumerators' brought letters from women anxious to secure the position from nearly every State in the Union."[53] In 1886 she reorganized the New York City Woman's Suffrage Association into the New York City Woman Suffrage League and served as president from 1886 until 1897; thus for four years Blake presided over both the city and state associations. She chaired the Committee on Legislation at the national level, traveling around the country to teach workers in other states how to effectively promote legislation favorable to women.

Blake relished the achievement of her childhood ambition for fame, and she was not at all averse to the limelight. In 1886, she headed a women's delegation which, protest banners unfurled, sailed out to the Statue of Liberty, newly arrived from France, to point out the hypocrisy of having a female statue of liberty at the gateway of a nation in which women were not free. When the Executive Committee of the NYSWSA had met at Lillie's, they learned that the cheapest steamer they could rent was a cattle barge, which, they were assured by the captain, would be scoured to eliminate the smell of cattle.[54] The day of the statue's dedication was "wet and wretched." The *John Lennox* had not been scoured. Overcome by the smell, several women refused to board the cattle barge. There were "no camp chairs, no warmth; wretched; mist and dampness everywhere," Blake writes in her diary, but "at last we got underway." Katherine writes in an attached note, "I remember how we all admired my mother's daring."[55]

Over the course of her suffrage career, as Blake's sphere of influence broadened, so too did the compass of her traveling. Her journeys were not easy. Trains, stagecoaches, and ferries brought her sometimes to the homes of new friends and other times to hotels that were no more than saloons with a room or two in the back. One night a rat ran over her bed.[56] Once, when her train broke down in an area where no stage coach was available, she began to walk toward the village where she was to speak, found a woman who agreed to ferry her across a river, and so made her way to her engagement.[57] Blake turned difficulties into opportunities. When returning from a speaking tour in Philadelphia, she took a train to New York at three in the afternoon, but because of an accident, she did not reach the city until ten; she headed straight for the *Times* office and wrote a report of the accident.[58]

In 1882, Susan B. Anthony wanted Blake to campaign in the West, so she embarked on a six-week tour of Nebraska for $30 a week plus expenses. She was ill during this trip, but managed to speak in a different town almost every day. When she arrived by train at Kumard, she was so sick that she had to lie on the bed of the station agent's wife all afternoon. For this she was reprimanded in a telegram sent by Anthony's lieutenant Rachel Avery.[59]

She found the typical Nebraskan town "miserable . . . with houses dropped on a prairie, no trees whatever and of course no fences. Wide streets, absurdly wide enough for a great city thoroughfare, plank walks, houses all one story or a story and a half, no blinds, no comforts, water undrinkable, and so hard that I have not had clean hands since I left Omaha." At one stop, there was no one to meet her and no instructions from headquarters in Omaha, so she hired a team and drove to Ord, then the furthest point west, the "last settlement before the sand hills." When she returned home to New York, she had made $150 from her Nebraska trip "which made me quite comfortable for the winter."[60] She also had material for stories. In "Lost in a Blizzard," which she published in 1893, she evokes the Nebraskan prairie:

> Across the level plains of wide Nebraska a storm was sweeping straight from the ice fields of the north; the wind came cold, biting, furious, laden with frost, tearing on madly as if it would freeze everything with the stark death of the arctic regions.
>
> Above there was no sky, below there was no earth; nothing anywhere but snow. Not level reaches of snow or white banks of it as there are in New England, but snow blown and tossed into blinding clouds by the

chill breath of the blast, rising, falling, whirling the fresh flakes descending from the sky, and the old drifts uptorn by the savage scoop of the wind, mingling together in the frantic dance; nothing to be seen anywhere but the pale spray of a wide ocean of snow driven into writhing flight by the relentless scourge of the gale.[61]

In the summer of 1888, Blake's travels took her to Colorado, Arizona, Utah, California, Michigan, Minnesota, and the Dakotas. These trips were in addition to her annual summer and fall speaking tours, all of which took their toll on her health. Frequently, she would return home exhausted and even feverish to the point of delirium. "Brain fever" it was called, and it would confine her to bed for weeks. She had an attack in 1872 after her tireless fight against Victoria Woodhull, and again in 1881 after weeks on tour: "I thought I should very likely die. I whispered to poor Katie who sat beside me my last instruction. Had no fear of death, no desire for prayer, thought I had had perhaps the best of life, that if there was another existence I should no doubt be happy; if not, then I was content."[62] After this episode, Blake was subject to colds, fatigue, and fever, but she managed to continue her grueling summer and fall speaking tours, her legislative campaigns in New York, presidential campaigns every four years, her work for the National Association, and her presidency of the New York State Woman's Suffrage Association and of the New York City Woman Suffrage League.

III

Speaking tours were Blake's primary source of income. Grinfill, who continued to work in management and sales in the steel industry, fell on hard times on several occasions. It was in January 1872, when his salary was cut by almost a third, that Blake began her career on the speaker's circuit. In mid-1875, after seven years in their "French flat," Grinfill's company, Washburn and Moen, let him go because of financial reverses, and he was many months without any income. His father paid their rent for a year, and Lillie redoubled her newspaper correspondence. During the summer she wrote columns from "country places" for the *Evening Mail,* so she and Grinfill had a series of paid mini-vacations, and she was able to earn some money freelancing.[63] On May 9, 1876, the Blakes celebrated their tenth wedding anniversary with a gala party, their rooms hung with chains of tin,[64] but by the fall Lillie was forced to sell her silver in order to pay the rent. Luckily, by that time both Bessie and Katie had graduated from normal school and found teaching positions with salaries of $41.75 each a month—less than $10 a week.[65]

In July 1878 Grinfill found a lucrative job with the Gautier Steel Company. "The position is a splendid one," wrote Lillie. "It seems as if the dark days are really over." Flush with success, the Blakes moved the following May to a luxurious duplex apartment at 666 Lexington Avenue. The year before, they had been joined by Frank Umsted's nephew, James, a reporter for the New York *Tribune*, who became a regular member of the family, living with the Blakes for the next ten years. Blake wrote that 1879 was "one of the happiest periods of my life. Grinfill was doing so well in his business, had his salary raised January 1st; the girls were well and happy, and Jimmie, full of life and spirits, made with the girls such a gay household for us. I gave my usual receptions and we went out very much, the time passing gaily and always happily."[66]

Unfortunately, in June Grinfill's business was reorganized and his job was eliminated. The following spring, the Blakes were forced to give up their new home and move to a third-floor apartment at 163 East 49th Street. The next year, while Lillie was delirious with "brain fever," Grinfill, exhausted from caring for her, suffered violent lung hemorrhages and was taken by his brother-in-law, Dr. English, to his family home in New Brunswick, New Jersey, where he could be cared for around the clock and be away from the "dampness and fumes of the city." He returned home, but suffered repeatedly from consumptive attacks, and during the winter of 1882–83 returned again to New Brunswick. He was never able to work again.

> He rallied a little after the first [of the year], but he never grew really well again, and all through this year [1883] was away from home. Sometimes he would come in for a few days if he felt pretty well. When I could, I went to see him, but it was very sad. A dark cloud had come over my life and brought with it not only the sympathetic sorrow I must feel for his sufferings, but also the terribly significant fact that I must now depend entirely on myself for my support. I had found it a hard matter to struggle for myself in former years and the problem that was difficult of solution at twenty-five seemed still more formidable at fifty.[67]

At the end of 1884, Grinfill sailed to Bogota, Colombia, where the pure, high mountain air was said to be curative, but, because of political unrest there, he returned within but a few months. By 1886 he was often bedridden, but whenever he felt well he would return to New York for a few days, or Lillie would visit him in New Brunswick.

Family life continued with its inevitable changes. In the fall of 1885, Lillie moved to 149 East 44th Street, where she lived for ten years. At the end of 1885, Bessie married John Beverly Robinson, architect, reformer, and, later, professor at Washington University in St. Louis, and in April 1887, Bessie had twins, Lillie and John—the Equal Rights babies, their grandmother's friends called them.[68] Jimmie married, but his wife, Pauline, was unstable, and in June 1889 she disappeared, only to be found in the Brooklyn Hospital where she had been taken after being arrested for shooting herself four times with a "toy pistol." "Raving" mad, Pauline was committed to the Cromwell Sanitarium where Lillie, Katie, and Jimmie visited her often, always finding her condition unimproved. In 1897 she disappeared from the sanitarium and was not found until after she had bought and swallowed ammonia and had collapsed along the marshes of the river. She died a week later. Two years afterward, Jimmie remarried.[69]

In the fall of 1886, Lillie learned that the old suit against her uncle, Thomas Devereux, for a portion of her grandmother's estate had been decided three years previously and $30,000 had been paid to her and her sister's attorney, but he had absconded with the money. She traveled to Raleigh to see if anything could be recouped, but the lawyer had lost the entire amount and was in dire poverty: "He went on spree after spree in New York City until broken in health, as well as purse, he staggered home. He has lived ever since in abject poverty, slowly dying of disease and is an object of charity. So by mismanagement, by neglect and by fraud, the money is gone, and what would have been independence for me is lost beyond recall!"[70] Lillie was furious with Grinfill, who was supposed to oversee the suit. They had "a stormy talk. . . . It is his fault that the money is lost more than any one else's. . . . I was sick and sad over the disappointment. The half of this sum would have made me independent, but now the weary struggle must go on. Perhaps, however, I should have neglected my public work had I received the money. Evidently it was destiny."[71] In this characteristic way, she reframed, in order to find meaning in, the fiasco.

In the beginning of 1887, however, Lillie made a peculiar diary entry: "I got rather worried because there is nothing definite to look forward to."[72] Her days, as they had been for seventeen years, were filled with the business of women's rights—writing letters, hiring halls, lobbying congressmen, writing speeches and essays, holding meetings, going to conventions. She had achieved fame as a powerful leader in the suffrage movement, she was president of both the New York State and the City suffrage organizations, and she was about to have grandchildren. She had seen the movement grow from a ridiculed, unrespectable organization to a legitimate cause for women of all classes, and she could take much credit for the change. But personal losses had mounted, and there was a permanency to them now. Clearly Grinfill would never recover his health, and, with the loss of her grandmother's estate, her last chance for financial ease was gone. There was no longer any hope that her fortunes would be reversed.

However, to get "rather worried because there is nothing definite to look forward to" speaks of a certain kind of fear. Life seemed somehow hollowed out, and Lillie seemed unsure that she could cope without a goal to strive for or a change to look forward to. She had always responded to her losses by throwing herself into some activity, whether writing, studying, or reform. The suicide of her first husband, the initial loss of her fortune, the death of her mother, the debilitating illness of her husband, his loss of income, and the most recent loss of her only chance for financial security all became occasions for work. All of Blake's considerable suffrage and legislative work for women, her grueling speaking tours, her skirmishes in the movement, along with her social and cultural life were carried on despite a backgrounded context of illness, financial hardship, and family tragedy. Her hard work not only accomplished much in the woman's movement, but also served as a kind of drug which blunted pain.

Her expression of despair was repeated in a more alarming way after a November 1887 speaking tour through Michigan. Blake returned home "and behold a blow was struck at my heart by a most dear hand. A dark cloud of sorrow overwhelmed me, so black, so hopeless, that all effort on my part was paralyzed and I seemed to live only to suffer."[73] That "most dear hand" may have been that of Dr. English, her brother-in-law, if, indeed, he was the doctor who gave her a prescription containing addictive doses of morphine. Or it may well have been Dr. Clemence Lozier, Lillie's dearest friend with whom she collaborated on the city's suffrage campaigns. Dr. Lozier was the doctor she turned to in 1881, when she thought she was dying of brain fever. In the midst of Blake's ordeal with morphine, on April 26, 1888, Dr. Lozier died of heart failure at the age of seventy-six. On April 29 Lillie notes in her diary that "I went to the funeral of our dear and venerated Dr. Clemence S. Lozier. She was a wonderful woman and a loyal friend." Neither Blake nor her daughter ever mentions the name of the doctor from whose "most dear hand" Lillie was given morphine. If it was Dr. Lozier, then we can conclude that Blake, too, was a most loyal friend. In a note attached to Blake's diary for 1888, her daughter writes that "all though this year and a large part of the year before my mother was very miserable. Unknown to her and to us, the doctor we had called had given her a prescription to take that contained morphine, so that when we discovered what had been done, she was already unable to get along at all without it. I think that she could never have broken this habit if she had not had a strong will. Even so, it was years before she was completely cured. It destroyed for a long time her ability to work with the brilliancy and vim that had hitherto characterized her."[74]

"This year was one of the saddest of my life," Blake wrote. "The dark shadows which gathered about the close of 1887 deepened to despairing gloom during the winter of 1888, and so wretched are all my memories of those cruel days, that in review it is hard to dwell long on any events, for all are tinged with the melancholy shades of a hopeless and irrevocable sorrow."[75] And still she worked on. In 1888 the first International Council of Women was held. As president of the New York State WSA, she organized a three-day conference for foreign delegates capped by a reception at her home. She accompanied the delegates to Washington, D.C. for the Council. That summer she traveled to San Francisco and spoke in twenty-five different venues in nine states, arriving home in late September.[76] She also continued writing fiction. In her last book, a collection of stories and an essay called *A Daring Experiment*, which was published after delays in 1892, Blake deals with the social and marital implications of democracy, the difficulties of dismantling class divisions, the inequities of wealth, and the unfairness to women of the laws on guardianship of children.[77]

IV

In 1889, Blake played a pivotal role in the union of the National and the American Woman Suffrage Associations. Since her first connection with the suffrage movement, when she worked with Theodore Tilton on the issue of unification in 1870, Blake had pressed for unity. She often attended both the National and the American annual conferences, she engaged speakers, like Julia Ward Howe and Jennie Collins, from the Boston contingent, and she wrote a regular column for the Bostonian *Woman's Journal*. In fact, Lillie Devereux Blake cannot be easily pigeonholed in suffrage politics. Her residence in New York brought her to the NWSA. However, her stance on the Fourteenth and Fifteenth Amendments and her views on marriage and sexual issues placed her more in the milieu of the Boston branch of the woman's movement. So too did her strategy of working toward gradual legislative changes, rather than only a national suffrage amendment. Her ideas concerning the common nature of men and women and her persistent attempts to widen the movement's agenda beyond the sole issue of a national suffrage amendment identified her with a radical minority of post–Civil War suffragists, including Elizabeth Cady Stanton. Blake's lifelong liberalism manifested itself in extra-suffrage activities, speaking on peace during the Spanish-American War, on justice for working women, and on equality in the workplace. Her boldness in pushing forward with the causes to which she was committed, no matter the politics of those around her, would lead to many years of important social reform and, finally, to clashes with Susan B. Anthony.

Anthony's uneasiness with Blake had begun at least as early as 1882, when Blake was directing the movement's energies toward a broad spectrum of legislative initiatives. She had been lukewarm, in 1880, to Blake's strategy of forgoing petitioning in favor of campaigning for politicians favorable to woman's rights. Anthony had begun to believe that it was important to curry favor with politicians on both sides of the aisle, and, most vital, she felt strongly that energies diverted from a suffrage amendment weakened the cause. She wrote to Blake on December 9, 1882, that "it seems to me far wiser to present and push only fair and fully established methods and measures. Then having so many different plans presented must detract from all it seems to me. I very much wish you . . . would concentrate on the one measure of a 16th Amendment."[78] In November 1885, Anthony asked Blake to go to Washington and outlined an ambitious plan of work she wanted undertaken during the opening of Congress: securing sympathetic men on the select committee on suffrage in the Senate, working for the appointment of a similar committee in the House, and obtaining a hearing for the NWSA with Congress, the president, the cabinet and the Supreme Court present: "I looked over the whole country for the woman—last night before sleep would come—and could see none other but Mrs. Blake who could be even hoped for to do this work."[79] Anthony's was an attempt to harness Blake's strengths for the single goal of suffrage.

Shortly after her Nebraska trip, undertaken at Anthony's request, Blake recorded in her diary that at the 1883 NWSA convention in Washington, "Miss Anthony much changed and very irritable. Tried to prevent me from speaking this evening and I was kept in a constant state of excitement until the last moment."[80] Katherine Blake dated Anthony's hostility to the success of *Woman's Place To-Day:* "I feel sure that this brilliant success and its widespread recognition had much to do with Miss Anthony's changed attitude, which had hitherto been not unfriendly. As I look back I can see that her opposition showed itself more or less openly after this period. I have been told that Miss Anthony feared for her own dominance."[81] There may be some truth in Katherine Blake's analysis of Anthony's motivation, but the 1883 convention and Anthony's hostility predated the Dix/Blake Lenten Lectures.

Despite instances of irritation between the two women, throughout the 1880s Anthony closed her letters to Blake with such phrases as "Lovingly yours," "Love and Christmas to the '*reporter*' and the darling daughters. I am proud of the dear girls everywhere and especially those two in New York." "Love to all," "With love and admiration," "Lovingly," "give my love to the dear girls too."[82] In fact, Anthony's systematic exclusion of Blake from significant roles within the movement did not take place until after Anthony's January 1889 push for the controversial unification of the National and the American Associations. Blake was crucial to Anthony's victory during the battle for unification. Then, it seems, her usefulness was over.

Anthony, who set up the willing Blake to make the motion that resulted in unification, organized private meetings to vote on the measure and excluded those known to be in opposition. Matilda Joslyn Gage was adamantly opposed, but, as chair of the NWSA Executive Committee, she should have been notified that unification would come up for a vote. She was not. Instead, Anthony presided in her absence.[83] Gage reacted by leaving the NWSA and forming her own Women's National Liberation Association. Blake reports in her autobiography that "I threw all my influence in favor of Union and, being seconded by Helen M. Gougar [of Indiana] and others, we carried the day, after a long fight. On the last day we were in Executive Session from 10 a.m. to 12 p.m., with recesses for meals, and at last passed the resolution for union by a vote of 32 ayes to 11 noes."[84] A motion was made to bring the issue to a vote of the whole association, but, probably fearing strong opposition, Anthony supported an immediate vote by members of the committee. The motion was pushed through.

Two years earlier, Anthony had written to Rachel Avery that if the associations united, it should be under the NWSA name, "*the name since* the war and now!!"[85] Anthony's remarks reveal her sense that in the merging of the two associations, the American was to be subsumed under the banner of the National. However, Blake moved that the new association be named the National American Woman Suffrage Association, and her motion carried. The anger over the merger, the opposition to it, and the difficulties involved in pushing through the vote go unmentioned in the official account in *The History of Woman Suffrage,* which Anthony controlled. In fact, reflecting Anthony's notion that the newly formed NAWSA was a continuation of the NWSA, the first convention of the NAWSA was called the twenty-second annual. The *History* read as if there had been a seamless history of woman suffrage rather than a serious, sometimes bitter, twenty-year rupture between the Bostonians and the New Yorkers.

Blake had always thought that a united front for the woman's movement would counter the image of quarreling women in which the male opposition took such delight. She never understood the gravity of the implications of unification for her own feminist philosophy. Unification helped Anthony to consolidate the prevailing conservatism of the woman's movement at the end of the century. Radical voices were marginalized as the new association presented a façade of harmony. The National American Woman Suffrage Association became, Ellen Carol DuBois writes, "a suffrage organization that could not tolerate serious political dissent and forced it outside. Throughout its history, the NAWSA was plagued by a series of organizational secessions, beginning with the Women's National Liberation Association, formed by Matilda Gage in 1890, and culminating in the Congressional Union, which broke away from the NAWSA in 1913."[86] Lillie Blake's own National Legislative League, formed in 1900, could be listed among such groups.

In addition, instead of working on a comprehensive spectrum of women's issues to which Stanton, Blake, and Gage, as well as many in the AWSA were devoted, the NAWSA focused solely on a national woman suffrage amendment, and, moreover, it institutionalized a nonpartisan approach to suffrage issues, promoted by Susan B. Anthony, which was in direct opposition to Blake's highly effective partisan politics.[87] Although Blake had been crucial to Susan B. Anthony's push for unification in the face of substantial opposition, the marginalization and erasure of radical voices, the "narrow platform"[88] that excluded a comprehensive view of women's rights, and Anthony's nonpartisan strategy would all serve to obstruct, and ultimately obliterate, the work of Lillie Blake.

The irony deepened when Blake was excluded from the first annual convention, in 1890, of the organization whose name she had suggested: "I am not down for a speech. Susan B. Anthony dislikes me and prevents me from being on the programme when she can; cannot be crushed by her!!!"[89] In 1893, Anthony agreed to let Blake organize a campaign to lobby the New York Constitutional Convention for woman suffrage, and then prevented her from doing so. "Now she writes repudiating the whole thing. She intends to play me some nasty trick, I must work hard to escape," wrote a distressed Blake.[90] Although Blake had long since, in 1879, rejected petitioning as a strategy for gaining political influence, in the fall of 1893, Anthony pressed her to work for a million names on a petition. "I think it arrant nonsense," Blake wrote. "We have had many talks."[91] The next month, Anthony excluded Blake from the platform at the annual convention in Washington. "She is a selfish and treacherous woman," Blake noted in her diary.[92] The next evening, the Executive Committee met at Blake's home. Anthony came with Anna Howard Shaw and Rachel Foster Avery, two of her "little cabinet of girls," as Elizabeth Cady Stanton called the younger women surrounding Anthony. "We had a stormy meeting," Blake wrote in her diary, "which ended in her [Anthony] saying that she would do nothing for this city."[93]

Anthony and her conservative "cabinet" were probably reacting to Blake's dogged struggle (waged along with Elizabeth Cady Stanton, Matilda Joslyn Gage, and others) to widen the agenda of the woman's movement as well as her persistent refusal to be nonpartisan in her legislative lobbying. In addition, and perhaps more to the immediate point, Blake had been involved earlier in the year with Gage's radical treatise *Woman, Church and State*, in which Gage exposed the complicity of the church in the subordination of women.[94] Gage's 1893 book affronted the conservative majority in the association, as did Elizabeth Cady Stanton's *Woman's Bible* three years later. With an eye to demonstrating the religious underpinnings of women's subjugation, *The Woman's Bible* contextualized biblical stories with non-Christian cultural myths and may well have found its source of inspiration in Blake's 1883 *Woman's Place To-Day*, in which she gives feminist readings of biblical texts.

At the NAWSA convention in January 1896, some in Susan's "cabinet," led by Rachel Foster Avery, introduced a resolution that repudiated *The Woman's Bible*. Blake's diary notes "fighting over the Woman's Bible until 6 o'clock."[95]

The liberals—Blake, Charlotte Perkins Gilman, and Clara Colby, who edited *The Woman's Tribune,* a suffrage paper—fought the resolution, but lost to the conservatives 53–41. Stanton wanted to resign from the association, and she wanted Anthony to resign also. Neither did.[96] But Blake and Colby, as the historian Kathi Kern writes, "were essentially disempowered in the wake of the controversy. Blake was replaced by [Carrie Chapman] Catt herself as the NAWSA organizer in Delaware. . . . Colby was turned down as an organizer in California in a political shuffle."[97] The fight over *The Woman's Bible* coalesced the conservative majority in the NAWSA. According to Kern, "The leadership who triumphed in the Bible debate and the ideology they asserted dominated the movement into the twentieth century. . . . the Bible debate would actually cement [the] unlikely alliance of non-religious but politically pragmatic figures like Catt and Alice Stone Blackwell with more conservative evangelical women."[98]

V

On March 10, 1896, shortly after the battle over *The Woman's Bible,* and after thirty years of marriage, Grinfill Blake died. In addition to his tuberculosis, he had contracted an inoperable cancer of the jaw. The *New York Times* noted that "his wife, Mrs. Lillie Devereux Blake, is well known as a writer and reformer. He was always deeply interested in his wife's work, and aided her so long as his strength permitted. He was in the 57th year of his age and had been an invalid for many years."[99] Lillie was sixty-two when Grinfill died and would live without him for seventeen years.

In the aftermath of her defense of *The Woman's Bible,* and soon after her husband's death, Blake was relieved of her assignment to wage the suffrage campaign in Delaware.[100] Susan B. Anthony had not acknowledged Grinfill's death, and when Lillie wrote to her about the Delaware campaign, the first issue she raised was this lapse: "You know that my poor husband after a long and most distressing illness has passed to his rest. I had thought I should receive some word from you, who still remember him as thinking that he was a reporter when he accompanied me to meetings in the days of his health."[101] In earlier days, Anthony had often sent her love to "the reporter," as she affectionately referred to Grinfill, but now not even the death of Blake's husband had been noticed. It may have seemed to Blake that Anthony was practicing the strategy she had advised against Victoria Woodhull and Tennessee Claflin:

"don't talk—don't seem to see or hear or know of them—absolute *silence* and seeming *indifference* are the only weapons with which to meet them and put them to flight!!"[102] However, she wrote back to Blake on April 9:

> Mrs. Stanton in her last letter had told me of the death of your husband, and I fully intended to have written you by next mail; to have congratulated you in that he had passed out of his sufferings here which have been of so many years' duration. I have felt the deepest sympathy with you through these years, because I have known how your every thought of him and your every visit to him was but an added heartbreak to you. So I cannot mourn, nor bid you mourn, that he has passed to the beyond; and I hope the day will soon come to you when these last tragic years can be overlooked and overleapt, and you can see your dear husband as he was in the prime and vigor of his manhood. Yes, I well remember how he used to laugh and tell me he was "a reporter" whenever I met him at the door of 49 West 23rd St., as he came for you at the close of our meetings at the Woman's Bureau. You always seemed so devoted to him and he to you, that I always admired both of you on that very account.[103]

Still, the following January, the annual suffrage convention was held in Des Moines, Iowa (not in Washington, D.C., a venue for which Blake pushed because of its access to legislators), and Lillie was not invited to speak.[104]

Carrie Chapman Catt had written to Blake four days before Grinfill's death to express her sadness over his illness. Rachel Foster Avery, on the other hand, wrote to Blake eight days after Grinfill's death without a word of sympathy. She had written previously wanting clarification concerning Blake's NAWSA Committee on Legislative Advice and had not yet received it. On March 18, she wrote: "Dear Mrs. Blake, You are more than excusable for any delay in answering my late letter. I saw the notice of Mr. Blake's death in a late copy of the Journal." Then, without any further mention of Grinfill's death, she went on immediately to remind Blake of the information she was to send.[105] Such was the cold animosity directed against one who had opposed her on the resolution against *The Woman's Bible.*

The NAWSA Committee on Legislative Advice, which had been formed in 1895 with Blake as chair, supported women throughout the states in their legislative lobbying. The *Woman's Journal* published Blake's leaflet, "Legislative Advice." Workers in other states who shared her broad view of woman's rights highly valued her advice, but Anthony and the new, young leadership of the NAWSA believed that any work other than that for suffrage was a dissipation of energies. From 1896 on, Avery tried to curtail the efforts of Blake's committee.[106] Anthony, using the rhetoric of separate spheres, confided in Avery that "if there ever was anybody that needed curb and bit and hold-backs to keep her in her proper sphere, it is 'Our Lillie.'"[107] Anthony wrote to Blake clarifying the role of the legislative committee as that "of teaching the delegates from the different State Suffrage Associations, who are to be in Washington, the *modus operandi* of calling upon their Congressional delegations . . . to influence their representatives to speak and vote for . . . a Sixteenth amendment prohibiting the disfranchisement of their citizens on account of sex."[108] Blake's idea of legislative work was far broader than this single issue.

When Blake went to the 1899 annual NAWSA convention in Grand Rapids to deliver her report on the work of the Committee on Legislative Advice, Rachel Foster Avery allotted her only fifteen minutes. Within that timeframe, Blake was unable to report on all the activities of the states that had participated in legislative work, but she impressed upon the state suffrage association presidents "the importance of having some one to represent the interests of women constantly at the Capitol during the Legislative sessions, not only to secure favorable legislation, but to prevent legislation inimical to the interests of women."[109] She delivered her report on May 1; the next day, she and her committee members were ousted: The committee itself was not destroyed, but it continued in name only with a new chair and no members.[110]

This action was a terrible blow to Blake. While she loved the attention she received as a public figure, her legislative work was far more important to her than that; it harnessed her organizational, social, and rhetorical skills for work which she fervently believed advanced the cause of women in the long run and alleviated much suffering in the present. Whether fighting the death penalty for women (on the grounds that in terms of rights they were classed with children and idiots) or lobbying for legislation which guaranteed that saleswomen have seats available, so that they need not stand all day long, Blake strove to fight inequality and provide legislation for the basic needs of women.

Blake immediately wrote letters of protest to Anthony and the leaders of the NAWSA. She met with Carrie Chapman Catt, who revealed that Susan B. Anthony was behind the action.[111] "Miss Anthony's antagonism to Mrs. Blake was never vocal," wrote Blake's daughter:

She dealt in innuendoes, in complete silence in reply to praise for Mrs. Blake, a silence with lifted eyebrows. I have before me a letter from Mrs. Ida Husted Harper, in reply to one from me which I wrote after my mother died, trying to find out why Miss Anthony had been so unjust and so unkind. In it Mrs. Harper says, with frankness:

> "I often tried to modify Miss Anthony's feeling toward your mother. She never gave me the slightest reason for this, but some people said it was because she thought your mother was always wishing to supplant her as National President."[112]

Yet if jealousy and fear of competition played a role in the disintegration of Anthony and Blake's relationship, less personal factors led to the dissolution of Blake's committee. Rachel Foster Avery put it bluntly when she wrote to Blake that the reason for the committee change was "your openly and consistently expressed antagonism to the whole trend of work of the Association, as at present conducted."[113] In other words, Blake refused to give up her extra-suffrage concerns. Blake's protest of the action which led to the destruction of the Committee on Legislation is buried in the minutes of the 1900 NAWSA convention.[114]

Blake had an immediate letter of support from the Bostonian Henry Blackwell, who wrote, "I am surprised and sorry to learn that you were not re-appointed by the business committee on the Committee on Legislation and that the single name of Mrs. Johns has been substituted for the entire Committee. I am the more surprised because your excellent report made at the convention showed much effort on your part to secure correct and complete information and gave great satisfaction to all who heard it, myself included."[115] His daughter, Alice Stone Blackwell, who served as recording secretary of the NAWSA and had been a leader of the American Woman Suffrage Association along with and after her mother, Lucy Stone, wrote suggesting that Blake wait before taking any action on the committee dissolution: "Miss Anthony has announced her intention of resigning then [next year], and if she sticks to her determination (which however is not absolutely certain) there may be a pretty lively game of 'puss in the corner' among the offices, and perhaps there will be something you would like better to be a candidate for than that chairmanship." "This is confidential," Blackwell carefully added.[116]

Mary Seymour Howell, a suffrage worker from New York who had collaborated on *The Woman's Bible*, wrote, "What a shame, an awful outrage the way you were treated at the convention. It touches me deeply, for of all the public women, I love and admire you the most . . . I think a new association should be formed without any more delay."[117] Others wrote: "we are so ring-ridden in the National, that our cause is being injured. . . . I fear the National through its red-tape and bossed rule is drifting on the rocks;" "If Miss Anthony had some of your tact what might she not have accomplished. I long for the time when your hand will be at the helm which guides the National Suffrage ship"[118] "I saw some years ago that a few of the younger women were inclined to manage matters. Susan Anthony is the only one of the older women who is now to the front, except yourself. You have stood by, done an immense amount of work and seemed to get on well with them all. Olympia Brown, Phoebe Couzins, Sara Spencer, Matilda Gage, Belva Lockwood, Helen Gougar, Mrs. Shattuck from Boston and many others were 'frozen out' so to speak, but you 'held the fort' and I am quite surprised that you should be 'sat down upon' at this late day."[119] And Elizabeth Cady Stanton wrote to say that she, too, had met with hostility from the NAWSA, and to confess that she had "outgrown the Suffrage Association," one line of which she had founded:

> Since our last conversation my thoughts have often dwelt on you. . . .
> You have not been treated by our young coadjutors with less considera-
> tion than I have been. They refused to read my letters and resolutions to
> the conventions. They have denounced the Woman's Bible unsparingly;
> not one of them has ever reviewed or expressed the least appreciation of
> *Eight Years and More.* . . . Because of this hostile feeling I renounced the
> presidency and quietly accept the situation, and publish what I have to say
> in the liberal papers. . . . I have outgrown the Suffrage Association.[120]

With support from around the country and with Stanton's endorsement, Blake decided to make a run for the presidency of the NAWSA when Anthony retired in 1900. Anthony had already thrown her support behind Carrie Chapman Catt, although she vehemently denied that she had picked a successor. She responded to allegations that she had instructed delegates to the convention to vote for Catt with fury: ". . . some one has been talking . . . and what I am bound to find out now is who that somebody is. . . . I am simply too vexed with the somebody that I am hunting after. I know it is not Mrs. Catt herself, for she would not do such a thing. . . . I think it will be a great deal better for the cause if the *young women* who *do the work feel* that the responsibility of it rests entirely on themselves [emphasis Anthony's]."[121] Stanton biographer Lois Banner writes that although Stanton and Anthony remained close, "there was continuing tension in their relationship. Many of Cady Stanton's speeches during these [final] years allude to her anger against Anthony, who was often allied with her opponents and who was critical of Cady Stanton's *Woman's Bible* and her autobiography, *Eighty Years and More.* . . . Still they kept their disagreements private. The closest they came to open dispute was when they supported different candidates to succeed Anthony as president of the NAWSA in 1900."[122]

"The canvass for the presidency waxes hot," wrote Blake in her diary on February 4, 1900. But on February 13, after making an address titled "Constitutional Argument" before the House Judiciary Committee, she withdrew her name as candidate "in the interest of harmony." The Washington *Evening Star* reported on February 14, 1900, "Mrs. Lillie Devereux Blake, who was the only formidable candidate against Mrs. Carrie Chapman Catt, but who, being a keen politician saw that things were not coming her way this time, in a neat speech to the convention, withdrew her name, which left the field practically clear to Mrs. Catt."[123] Blake was, indeed, a formidable candidate, and her defeat was a significant event that spelled the defeat of the liberal wing of the woman's movement. However, in the *History of Woman Suffrage,* it is recorded only in passing. As in the histories of Barnard College, Blake's role is erased in the interest of obliterating the opposition and of presenting a linear, progressive history undisturbed by the struggles and controversies among its players. Anthony controlled the grand narrative of the nineteenth-century woman's movement as much as she controlled the movement itself. The contributions of Lucy Stone and the AWSA were minimized and its position on the Fifteenth Amendment was distorted, the radical Matilda Joslyn Gage was lost to its history, the amendment to the Constitution which Elizabeth Cady Stanton wrote became known as the Susan B. Anthony amendment, and Lillie Blake's national legislative work and her leadership in New York—Anthony's home state—are forgotten. In 1900, Ida Harper, who, with Anthony, was editing the fourth volume of the *History of Woman Suffrage,* wrote to Blake that "there is no one in the state [of New York] who has kept such close watch on the legislative work and knows so much about it as yourself. It needs a chapter by itself, and this should be written by you. It will be a pleasure to me to give you a chapter in this *History,* and I think also that you deserve to have it."[124] Blake submitted her chapter, but it did not survive

Anthony's animosity: very little found its way into the official *History of Woman Suffrage*.[125]

VI

Prevented by the conservatism and limited agenda of the NAWSA from proceeding with her legislative work, in March 1900, Lillie Devereux Blake left the organization she had served for over thirty years and formed the National Legislative League, with herself as president and Elizabeth Cady Stanton as honorary president. As Blake explained to Henry Blackwell, "there was nothing for me but either to pass the rest of my life in idleness as far as any active Legislative work was concerned, or to form a Society which would back me in the work, it being plain that the NAWSA would not do this."[126] The League's radical agenda was to promote "better conditions for women by the enactment of laws which shall secure to them their just political and civic rights: the abolition of all statutes which discriminate against women and the establishment of the just rule that merit and not sex shall regulate the pay of the worker."[127] Stanton asked Blake to send a circular on the League to the Reverend Antoinette Brown Blackwell, who "has been treated very disrespectfully by Susan's little cabinet of girls," and she promised to send Blake a mailing list "of all I know who have retired from the movement because of snubs by Rachel Foster Avery *et al.*"[128]

Through the League, Blake, now sixty-seven years old, was able to continue the legislative work for which she was most noted—helping to make laws favorable to women and change laws such as those which cost women their citizenship if they married a foreigner or forbade married women from making wills without their husbands' consent.

In 1900–1901, Blake also became involved in the creation of a Margaret Fuller Memorial on Fire Island, off which Fuller had drowned in 1850. Lillie and her daughter Katherine had built a small cottage at Point of Woods in 1895 after Katherine had became principal of her school in New York City and Lillie had received funding through testimonials in her honor. Lillie loved the cottage. She hosted a salon there, but, even more important, she found time to lie in a hammock and listen to the sounds of the sea. Her cottage, which she named "Roofenuf," faced the bay, and "all day it was a joy to watch the sails and the beautiful water, while we could hear the surf thundering on the ocean from only fifteen hundred feet away."[129]

On August 17, 1900, Blake gave a lecture on Fuller and began to develop funding for a memorial tablet and a pavilion in her honor. The pavilion, which has since washed away, was dedicated on July 19, 1901. Blake gives this account:

A perfect day; crowds came on the steamboat and in sailboats. Many friends and two sisters-in-law of Margaret Fuller, Mrs. Richard and Mrs. Alfred Fuller, and a niece, Mrs. Nichols; many strangers. They were met by a committee of ladies at the boat, then we all went to the hall which was decorated. The elderly ladies were in wheel chairs. I presided, Mr. Hand made the address of welcome, and then Rev. Charles Townsend made a beautiful speech. Souvenirs were sent by Mrs. Howland and distributed. Procession with Mr. Hand and myself at the head, went to the pavilion which is impressive. I unveiled the Tablet, a beautiful thing. They all sang "Battle Hymn of the Republic" and we went back to the hotel for dinner. Capt. Arthur Dominy told how he found the bodies of Margaret Fuller and her husband and with another man who had a sloop took them to New York City. Horace Greeley had promised to look after them, should they be discovered, but he refused to have anything to do with them when they came. . . . they were hastily buried, at Coney Island. This is true. . . . I have thus far kept it from the Press.[130]

Phyllis Cole writes that Blake brought together one time antagonists like Thomas Wentworth Higginson and Julia Ward Howe, that she "honored all aspects of Fuller's career" in her speech, and that Charles Townsend honored Blake by saying, "Margaret Fuller's message is heard again on these shores because another woman's receptive heart has vibrated to that deathless mental electricity."[131]

Lillie Blake's receptive heart transcended the closed world of mid-century mores and brought her into the politics of reform. She had little hope that either her literary work or the significant role she played in the woman's movement would survive the editing of history. Throughout her long career, however, Lillie Blake remained true to a feminist agenda based upon an assumption that sexual difference should not be privileged over other differences among people. At the end of the nineteenth century, this vision moved her to the margins of the woman's movement. But at the beginning of the twenty-first century, it locates her more centrally in the unfolding feminist debate on difference and provides a place for her in an expanded literary canon that no longer excludes the political.

In the last years of her life, Blake continued her lecturing and her legislative work. Funds given to her at a testimonial enabled her, accompanied by Katherine and Bessie's daughter Lillie, to embark on a European tour for two months during the summer of 1907. She went to London, Paris, Brussels, Antwerp, Bruges, Dover, back to London and on to Dublin. Blake, who had always attended New York theater and opera, heard Caruso in *Aida* at Covent Garden and in *Ariadne* at the Grand Opera in Paris. She saw the Elgin marbles ("stolen from the Parthenon by Lord Elgin, are a disgrace to England") and the Mona Lisa ("so evil looking that she haunts me").[132] Upon her return she gave one more speech, on suffrage, delivered on May 12, 1908. She ceased her diary in July 1908, and she died on December 30, 1913, after a fall which broke her hip.

VII

The narrator of Blake's last published story, "Roses and Death," is a woman in her eighties, looking over her life, one of passion and triumphs and hardships.[133] The old woman remembers "a wild dream of love. . . . She thrilled even now as she remembered that moonlight scene—the grassy bank under the oak tree, the passionate eyes that looked into hers, the wild embrace when she surrendered her soul; but it had been for naught; after a few short weeks of alternate ecstasy and despair, it had been over." At points in her life "only her indomitable will enabled her to sustain herself," and now she is about to die. She had always been "one of those smiling unbelievers." She knows only that "she knew nothing of a certainty." And when she dies, she is held to earth "for one imperceptible moment . . . by the strong, sweet scent of the roses she had loved." And so I would think did Lillie Devereux Blake die, as she had lived, passionately attached to the world and to its possibilities for transformation.

Retracing

7. On Being Lost

If recollecting were forgetting,
Then I remember not.
And if forgetting, recollecting,
How near I had forgot.
—Emily Dickinson

IN 1996, JOEL MYERSON AND DANIEL SHEALY recovered the lost manuscript of a novel written by Louisa May Alcott when she was seventeen. The
staff at the Houghton Library of Harvard University, where the manuscript is
housed, wondered aloud how anyone could consider a novel lost when, having duly card-cataloged it, they knew just where it was. The library's literal
take on the lostness of a text speaks to the exclusionary politics of canon
formation. Houghton—that restrictive space within the enclave of Harvard
Yard—might serve as an icon both for the elitist literary canon from which
Alcott was excluded and for the attitude which disingenuously denies that
such exclusion takes place. In support of its contention that the novel was not
lost, Houghton's staff stated that, over the last several decades, five people had
consulted it. I was reminded of Virginia Woolf's description, in *A Room of
One's Own,* of the library (even more exclusive than the Houghton) to which
she was denied access because she was a woman: "Venerable and calm with
all its treasures safe locked," she wrote, ". . . it sleeps complacently."[1]

Lostness has little to do with being "safe locked" and everything to do with
the construction of our collective cultural memory, a memory that is as dependent upon forgetting as it is upon remembering. Memory, always selec-
tive, takes what it values and dispenses with the rest. When books go out of
print, or never find their way into print, when they are devalued by exclusionary critical practices, when they are ignored by those who do not notice
their own treasures, then they are lost—to us and to the unfolding literary
tradition in which they might have played a part. Certainly the memory of

nineteenth-century American fiction as written in large measure by women was long, and purposely, forgotten.

Toward the end of the nineteenth century, when there was a concerted move to construct a distinctly American literary history, its framers, whether professors or critics, essayists or editors, explicitly distanced themselves from the tradition of women's writing.[2] William Dean Howells's pronouncements on realism were drawn against the sentimentality of domestic fiction, which, while certainly not written only by women, was associated with them and their issues.[3] Domestic fiction articulated, within a Christian rhetoric, a value system of forbearance and submission on the part of women. The religious rhetoric, not the value system, was a major distinction between much domestic fiction and realistic prose. Although domestic novels have been dismissed as unrealistic, they are filled with the realism of everyday rituals and quotidian toil—but they are women's rituals and the everyday stuff of women's lives. Like realistic fiction, domestic novels depict the lives of the working class as well as of the rich; but these are working women, housekeepers, and mothers. They depict suffering, but the sufferers are women. They depict middle-class values of marriage and family, but the emphasis is on the difficult path of women forced not only to give up themselves, but to desire to give up themselves. In the masculinized rhetoric of realism, these concerns were dismissed as insignificant.[4]

However trivialized, the feminine was also a threat to male hegemony. Howells's silent agenda in his manifestos on realism concerned making literary work real men's work rather than a sissy, womanish activity.[5] The underside of the gendered assumptions of realism are reflected in a representative theme in canonized American fiction—the escape from woman. In prototypical tales from "Rip Van Winkle" to *Huckleberry Finn* and beyond, males are the good-hearted bad boys of a social order dominated by female forces that aggressively seek to domesticate them. Their escape into adventure is a flight from women who seek to keep them, too, forever at home. Both canonized plots and the critical rhetoric which removed women from a central position in American fiction reflect this flight from the female.[6] American literature was to be rugged, individualistic, realistic. It would focus on male activities and the wide world, the cruel and unpleasant world of commerce and industry. "There was no place for a woman author in this scheme," writes Nina Baym. "Her roles in the drama of creation are those allotted to her in a male melodrama: Either she is to be silent, like nature, or she is the creator of conventional works, the spokesperson of society."[7]

In fact, however, only in retrospect does much of women's literature appear to be a token of the status quo. There was not one type of literature written only by women. Men as well as women wrote sentimental and domestic fiction, while women as well as men wrote lurid, sensational literature.[8] Moreover, while cast in opposition to the reformist novels of realism and often seen today as the most conventional of the century's genres, the sentimental novel was the site of radical initiatives.[9] As Philip Fisher argues, only because the sentimental novel succeeded so well in imagining the unimaginable and rendering it obvious, did the genre itself, with hindsight, come to seem obvious or trite. For instance, Harriet Beecher Stowe's success in redesigning the cultural boundary between person and thing so that a black man could be emotionally apprehended as a person has been so profound and so pervasive in American culture that the difficulty of her accomplishment is easy to forget. In fact, part of the cultural work of novels like *Uncle Tom's Cabin*, which insert new realities into our cultural vector, is to induce us to forget the radical nature of those enterprises in order to secure the new reality as an item of unquestionable common sense.

The very development of the American novel was connected, in implicitly gendered terms, with the lowering of its pitch. Frederick Pattee expressed the misogyny of the critical process in his "Feminine Fifties," which characterized the 1850s with ten words—"fervid, fevered, furious, fatuous, fertile, feeling, florid, furbeloved, fighting, and funny" and the "single adjective which combines them all"—feminine.[10] The most denigrated form of literature, nineteenth-century women's fiction, went unread by the twentieth-century educated elite who were taught to ignore it as (to get outside the confines of Pattee's f-word list) didactic. However, American literature has a tradition of didacticism going back to its Puritan roots, shifting over time from sermons and poetic prescripts into novels, which proved to be perfect vehicles for conveying social values. In the nineteenth century, critics reviled Poe for neglecting to conclude his stories with pithy moral tags, while Longfellow was canonized for his didactic verse. Although rhetorical changes favoring the antididactic can be detected as nineteenth-century America transformed itself into a secular society,[11] it was twentieth-century criticism, dominated until the 1970s by the New Critics, which placed aesthetic value above all other and had no place in its dicta for others' didacticism. The modernist "make it new" came to be seen as a universal aesthetic, but it is part of an ideology quite particular to its post-Darwinian moment, in which time is seen as always evolutionary and the new as always a move to a progressively higher plane. Thus the novel "rises" and American literature "develops" as it casts off the inferiority of its immature and feminine past, lowers its pitch and becomes more manly. As Alexander Cowie put it: "Befrilled locutions are out; diction has gone into denim."[12]

By and large, in the critical re-presentation of the works of the past in a mode compatible with current attitudes, the texts that survive are those that reflect and reinforce established ideology. Their didacticism, because it is a didacticism of the status quo, is rendered invisible. In an allegory on gender issues, "A Divided Republic," delivered as a lecture in 1886 and published in *A Daring Experiment* (1892), Lillie Devereux Blake makes visible the didacticism of Howells and Henry James. A total migration of women to uncharted Western territories takes place in Blake's allegory, much to the initial delight of the men left behind:

> There was much rejoicing among the writers also. Mr. Howells remarked that now he could describe New England girls just as he pleased and no one would find fault with him; and Mr. Henry James was certain that the men would all buy the "Bostonians," which proved so conclusively that no matter how much of a stick a man might be, it was far better for a woman to marry him than to follow even the most brilliant career.[13]

Blake, a political writer herself, understood that because their sexual politics reflected the temper of the times, the work of these writers invited aesthetic over political comment.

Fortunately for the legacy of a woman like Blake, memory is always subject to revision; the highlights of an age spotlighted by one generation may be soft-focused by another; what has been forgotten may be remembered again as a more compelling vision of the past is constructed. Nineteenth-century women's fiction, when its relics are safely locked away in hundreds of repositories like the Houghton Library, could pose little threat to a cultural memory built upon its absence. But no canon is inevitable. There is only that which fits the common dogma of a particular moment. As G. R. Thompson and Eric Carl Link put it, we "need to be aware that our construction of tradition around a canon of major works depends upon sets of assumptions, not some self-evident reality."[14] Those assumptions have been questioned by literary critics intent not just on expanding a canon to make room for women, but on rethinking the thematic, cultural, and chronological bases upon which we build our canon.[15]

Finding, like losing, is a tangled process, circumvented by the very course of losing. Before tackling the problems involved in trying to find works that have been lost to our cultural heritage, how do we even know to look when not only the life work but the entire life itself has been lost? To keep treasures so safely locked away that we forget that we have them militates against our ever finding them again. And although literary scholarship has developed an understanding of the politics of canon formation in the mid-to-late nineteenth and the first half of the twentieth centuries which explains why and how the work of women was ignored or denigrated, the Darwinian-like assumption that there is a universal "best" which will survive amid the mediocre literary production of an age still persists. The assumption contains an unstated conclusion that only the inferior are ever lost. But as we recover more works and enrich the social context that produced them, we can begin to see the ways in which our cultural memory has been anesthetized by the inflexibility of our canonical tradition or the constructed seamlessness of our grand narratives.

The process of recovering lost writers and their lost works is not free from a prevailing ideology that currently places primary value on the voices of working-class women. The female voices Blake spoke for include not only those of the working class, but those of well-to-do married women oppressed by the vacuity of their lives. In *Fettered for Life*, the newly married Flora LeRoy laments, "I have literally nothing on earth to do . . . no way of filling up the endless hours."[16] In "The Social Condition of Woman," Blake foregrounded the repetitive minutia of upper-middle-class domestic life:

> . . . the endless sewing that fills up all the leisure of woman's life is a fearful degenerator. I know of nothing more cramping to the mind than this perpetual setting of minute stitches . . . the utter weariness, the heartsickness of many a poor lady who feels each morning when she wakes the lack of any stimulus in life! and sees existence stretching before her an endless world of petty conventionalities and wearisome repetition.[17]

Many feminist critics, having limited sympathy for "poor ladies" whose only problem seems to be too much time on their hands, may silence them with a dismissive sneer. In recovering the lives of lost women, it is easy to fall prey to an ethos that demands oppression based on economic deprivation as justification for our renewed interest.[18] Lillie Blake's life could be approached by accentuating the traumatic blow she suffered when her young husband killed himself, leaving her almost penniless with two very small children to raise. But if we are pressured to validate only the vulnerable, then we perpetuate the convention of woman as victim. In fact, to do so traps us in the oppression of the nineteenth-century patriarchal script, which reads women as attractive only in proportion to their fragility. Lillie Blake wanted women to be valued because of their strength, their courage, and their ability to take care of themselves. Oftentimes these qualities can be appreciated only when foregrounded against economic and social misfortune, but, any life "condemned to stagnation," as Blake felt her own early life to be, is a life to be protested. Blake's struggle to find her voice as a woman began long before she experienced financial crisis; it was rooted in psychosocial oppressions with peculiarly middle-class formulations. It is the weight of these cultural forces upon the formation of an exemplary woman that I have sought to understand.

It might be asked if the saving of a nineteenth-century Italianate villa in New Haven or all the recoveries of foremothers lock feminist energies into a patriarchal modality which values tradition over revolution. I would suggest that the dichotomy may be specious and, as a dichotomy, may itself reflect the prevalence of masculinist modes of thought. Recovering women who have been erased from our cultural landscape and dismissed from our traditions is a disruption of purposeful losing, a revolt against a memory based on suppression. To safely lock away the work of Louisa May Alcott as the Houghton Library has done, to lock out countless women like Virginia Woolf as Oxford University did, or to destroy the home and distort the reputation of Lillie Devereux Blake as Yale University did is to control the construction of our remembrance and of our forgetting. In *Fettered for Life* the burning of a woman's manuscripts by her husband is a trope for the suppression of women's literary tradition. Blake's lost novel, erased from our tradition, is itself about lostness, about lost voices and erased stories. Blake wrote what she called "cunningly-devised fictions" in hopes that her stories might be heard and that her books, dangerous to a remembrance predicated upon forgetting, might not be simply (or perhaps not so simply) safely locked away.

8. Literary Detection: A Postscript on Process

A small iron safe was discovered. . . . It was open, with the key still in the door. It had no contents beyond a few old letters, and other papers of little consequence.
—Edgar Allan Poe, "Murders in the Rue Morgue"

I

LATE IN THE DAY, WHILE I searched the archives of the Wisconsin Historical Society in Madison for traces of publications by Lillie Devereux Blake, an article titled "Novel Reading and Insanity" in the July 25, 1863, issue of Frank Leslie's *Illustrated Newspaper* caught my eye. An insatiable reader of novels hunting for a woman whose name provoked only "Who?" from colleagues, I wondered if that old nineteenth-century prejudice against women novelists and women readers just might contain a grain of truth. I was provided with only partial reassurance:

> Dr. Anstruther, one of London's most eminent physicians, has lately published the result of 40 years' medical experience. Among the noticeable points is novel reading. He says that while novel reading weakens the mind and distorts its perceptions, it diminishes that peculiar earnestness which leads to insanity, adding: "I never knew a person, more especially a woman, addicted to novel reading, who became deranged. Insanity generally springs from brooding over some one idea or grievance—hence frivolous people never go mad."

Safe from insanity on the score of novel reading, or perhaps, as Dr. Anstruther implied, because of frivolous femaleness itself, but still in danger because of a peculiar earnestness, I gravely continued my obsessive search for an unknown author's uncollected work. Weakness of mind and distorted perceptions aside, my elation, whenever Blake's name, a pseudonym, or a familiar title flashed past my eyes, was enough to sustain me during years when no one else seemed terribly interested in my strange pursuit. My solitary scanning and careful shifting of newsprint hour after hour, day after day, in the American Antiquarian Society in Worcester, Massachusetts, did once attract the attention of a man who gave me a card listing his profession as Literary Detective. Victor Berch, retired reference librarian at Williams College, who haunts the archives, offering help to only the most resolute of researchers, has aided scholars in the recovery of many of Louisa May Alcott's periodical pieces. It was he who introduced me to Street and Smith's series of dime novels, the nineteenth-century equivalent of daytime soaps.

Literary detection can sometimes be quite simple. For instance, *Fettered for Life*, like the books of many other lost women writers, could have been easily found by anyone—if one knew to look. I found my first copy simply by asking for it through the interlibrary loan system. Finding Blake's work which had not been collected in book form was a different challenge altogether. The process first involved creating a "finding list," as Joel Myerson, who explained the methodology to me in a hallway during an American Literature Association conference, called it. Initially it was necessary for me to become knowledgeable about nineteenth-century newspapers and periodicals in order to compose a list of sources likely to contain works by Blake. Then by reading her diaries and letters in the Missouri Historical Society, I was able to find references to titles of periodicals, which were added to my finding list. These sources also yielded pseudonyms and titles of stories that would serve to identify her work.

After establishing my finding list, I had to locate the periodicals likely to contain her stories. Blake's publications can be found from Minnesota to Texas, from Washington to Boston. To search any one periodical took trips to several archives, each usually having a scattered number of issues. Subtle changes in masthead titles, new series of established publications, and overlaps in titles from one publication to another often complicated the process of locating a periodical. Sometimes a library's purported holdings of items had been sold; sometimes, although still listed in the catalog, items just could not be found on the shelves or in the warehouses; oftentimes locating papers not called for in decades took hours, even days, of searching on the part of very dedicated reference librarians. Some are irrevocably lost.

The case of the *New York Weekly Mercury* can illustrate the typical search process. In her journal, Blake mentioned that in 1865 the "Mercury" asked for as many stories as she could send them and, in addition, that she published two serialized novels there in 1866. My research revealed the "Mercury" to be the *New York Weekly Mercury; a Journal of American Literature,* published between 1838 and 1870 and advertised as "The Peerless New York Mercury," "Grand Mirror of American Genius," "Great National Banner of Intellect!" Because it is easily and often confused in catalogs and holdings lists with the *New York Mercury,* a mercantile paper first published in the early 1700s and revived between 1839 and 1870, tracking down "Blake's" *Weekly Mercury,* was not at all a straightforward task. For instance, reading through the online OCLC's 1,333 listings for the *New York Weekly Mercury,* I found only six referring to Blake's periodical. The OCLC lists the University of Minnesota as having the *Mercury* for 1866–67, the years Blake serialized her novels, but my trip to Minneapolis left me empty-handed; the volumes could not be found. At the Sterling Library at Yale, I located a partial collection of the *Mercury* in bound volumes, one of which showed signs of having been rescued from a fire. Another volume yielded the first half of "In Prison," an 1865 story by Essex, one of Blake's favorite pseudonyms during the Civil War, but the conclusion of the story in the next number had been entirely cut out, and I have never been able to find another copy. The American Antiquarian Society, which can boast some of the most knowledgeable and helpful reference librarians around—Dennis Laurie and the late Joyce Tracy among them—yielded two of Blake's *Mercury* stories, but did not have a complete run of the paper and owned only one number from 1866.

My last hope was the Library of Congress, which reportedly had an almost complete run of the *Mercury* on microfilm. But I have learned that at the largest repositories, where technicians often replace reference librarians, the task of locating rare items can be a frustrating experience. Repeated dead ends finally brought me to a Library of Congress reference librarian who, over a period of several weeks, traced the history of the master microfilm copy of the *Mercury.* Our thought was that even if the shelf copies of the microfilm had been lost, the master would exist, and that even if the master microfilms had been lost, there might be the possibility of locating the original source. Oftentimes original items are destroyed in the filming process, but in some cases items are borrowed from archives around the country, filmed, and returned. It was the hope of reference librarian Elizabeth Jenkins Joffe that if the master microfilms could not be located, the original source might be available.

It seems, however, that a vast library may not know what it does *not* have.

Although the technicians of the Library of Congress repeatedly advised me that the issues of the *Mercury* I wanted were temporarily off the shelf, the disappointing results of Joffe's research concluded that the extensive holdings listed in the library's catalog had never been part of the collection, and the Library of Congress had never had the complete set on microfilm. It had but three volumes, each of which I had previously located elsewhere. The conclusion to "In Prison," Blake's serialized novels, and many other stories are probably lost for good, but at least I am not endlessly returning to the Library of Congress looking for what I was too frequently told was not, at that moment, on the shelf.

When I did find the periodicals and newspapers for which I was looking, they usually were not indexed and often lacked a table of contents. And, in the nineteenth century, most essays and stories lacked any identification as to author; only with cross-references to titles or pseudonyms found in letters, diaries, or journals was there a chance of identifying Blake's work, and without such clues, many of her stories will remain lost to her particular canon.

Once a periodical or newspaper was located, it had to be examined painstakingly, page by page. Thus, before publishing a word on Blake, I spent years as a literary detective, sifting through newsprint to recover her work and reading scraps of handwritten letters and diaries to recover her life. Sometimes the smallest bit of information would explode into significance. In the New Haven Colony Historical Society, I looked in census books for references to Lillie's childhood addresses. The dates of her address on Church Street put her, during a nine-month period, within a block and a half of the *Amistad* Africans. Her house on Trumbull Street, scheduled for demolition within a matter of days, was the site of my introduction to a two hundred-year-old New Haven culture which encourages intellectual excellence on one hand while reining in female independence with the other. Only because my arrival in New Haven was timed, accidentally, to coincide with her home's scheduled demolition, was I led to solve the biggest mystery of Lillie Blake's personality— how a radical thinker came to be tightly controlled by social prescriptions.

Most of Blake's personal papers are located in the Missouri Historical Society in St. Louis, where I first worked in cramped, dusty quarters on the second floor of an old building in the Park and then in St. Louis's beautifully restored synagogue.[1] After hours in a brownish reading room in the Park, I became fluent in reading Blake's difficult handwriting and in the process, holding the pages she had held, I sometimes came too close. When I began my research, I was, like Lillie, a mother alone with two very young children. I remember the wave of nausea which almost overwhelmed me when I read her description of her young husband's suicide. There is an emotional immediacy in handwritten manuscripts or even personally typed pages which computer printouts cannot match. I went with Blake through her struggles and her triumphs and then, later in her life, faced her disappointments and despair. It quite wrung me out and left me feeling anxious and depressed: were there never any happy endings? How about just a sustained period of peace?

Paul Rosenblatt writes of his physical and emotional exhaustion, "too drained to do anything but sleep," after his archival visits, "breathing the inevitable dust."[2] He made a point of visiting archives near friends, with whom he stayed and by whom he was sustained. Luckily, I had tagged along on my first trip to St. Louis with my friend the T. S. Eliot scholar Lois Cuddy, who was in town for the annual Eliot conference. She and I and Emily Miller, reference librarian at the Historical Society who was extremely helpful to me, talked it all out at the Corner Wine Bar over plates of paté. Emily writes that the Corner Wine Bar has closed now, and the young husband whom she married after our evening there talking of Lillie's husband, has died, too. How eerily the circle of life knots tightly around one theme.

I read other people's diaries, as well as Blake's, especially those of students who were at Yale in 1854. Reading people's diaries is an intrusive act, fascinating for insatiable novel readers and useful for those who want to feel what it was like to live in another time, but guilt-laden for those who have been trained in the value of privacy and circumspection. One diary entitled "DIARY of a SCHOOL BOY NAMED L. E. Baldwin Esq. WRITTEN BY FITZ HOPPS AND CANDLE LIGHT Written for the most PART with a pen and not with a quill," which I read in the Whitney Library of the New Haven Colony Historical Society, reminded me of my offense: "DWIGHT FOSTER acted a dishonourable part in READING this book—and so do YOU."

While my initial affective connection with Blake was of enormous benefit in helping to sustain my prolonged research, concomitant study into the nature of autobiography taught me to be wary of losing my distance or of assuming the literal truth of any autobiographical account. Even a diary is a text that shapes and omits in order to create a persona. Besides Blake's handwritten diary, which she began when she was thirteen and continued for most of her life, she left an unpublished autobiography which she typed on the recently invented typewriter that her daughter Katherine gave to her in 1897. Katherine also made typescripts of some of the diaries in preparation for her own biography of her mother.

Blake's first diary in the Missouri Historical Society collection runs from February 22, 1847, to May 31, 1847, followed by a six-year gap. A diary dated August 12, 1853–August 12, 1854, is followed by a five-and-a-half-year gap until 1860. The other handwritten papers from the pre-1860 period include a collection of Blake's first fictions, dated 1850–51 and titled "Sealed Pages A Strictly private Collection of MY OWN WRITINGS, Part 1st." Handwritten diaries continue from 1860 through May 1870 and from 1900 through September 1903.

It is possible to establish that other diaries had been kept by comparing references to the diaries in the three other sources. For instance, in both Blake's unpublished autobiography and Katherine's biography of her mother, references are made to diary entries dated 1848. Katherine's typescripts of the diaries run from 1859 through 1907. Apparently many of the handwritten diaries were discarded after the typescript was made. This is particularly unfortunate in at least two instances. First, the 1859 diary contained material about the death of Blake's husband and the months immediately afterward. Although Katherine began typing this material, she found it too upsetting to continue. Thus we have neither a typescript nor the handwritten diary to trace Blake's grief and the process of transformation which stemmed from it, although Blake herself quotes from these diaries in her unpublished autobiography. Second, we no longer have the handwritten diaries during a major portion of Blake's suffrage period, from 1870 to 1900. If they still existed, her handwritten accounts of her increasing estrangement from Susan B. Anthony and her unsuccessful bid for president of the National American Woman Suffrage Association in 1900 could be compared to the more public document of the typescript and the edited versions of the biography and the autobiography.

Katherine was not alone in her revisions and deletions of her mother's diaries. Lillie spent time in December 1859 in rereading the journals from before her marriage and "destroying those parts which seemed least worthy of presentation" (December 14, 1859 typescript of Diary). Oftentimes, I had at least four versions of events, each with its own subtle editing. These I compared with external evidence from such sources as land records or letters in the archives of other women with whom Blake worked—among them Susan B. Anthony, Elizabeth Cady Stanton, Matilda Joslyn Gage, and Lucy Blackwell.

Detecting the differences among all these sources helped lead me to my own version of the truth.

Only after my course of literary detection uncovered much of Blake's work and life could the more difficult process of establishing her within the context of American culture begin. Many scholars in American and Women's Studies opened the way for my work by questioning every aspect of received traditions that excluded women from serious scholarly consideration. My work builds upon the reconceptualization of aesthetic assumptions and historical processes which has taken place over the last generation.

Lillie Devereux Blake has been my constant companion for a decade now. Strong-headed, strong-hearted, a fighter against injustice, flirtatious, overly concerned with her looks, naïve about the insidious power of envy, determined in work and determined in love, she etched upon the world a life of good purpose. Whether sailing out to the Statue of Liberty on a cattle barge or traversing the Nebraskan wilderness by stagecoach, whether amusing herself by stealing other women's beaux or falling profoundly in love with a handsome stranger in a boardinghouse, whether collaborating with Elizabeth Cady Stanton and defending Matilda Joslyn Gage or holding a door shut so that Dr. Mary Walker couldn't get in, whether holding her head high as she walked the streets of provincial New Haven or waiting out Victoria Woodhull's threats of blackmail, Lillie Devereux Blake displayed courage and spunk her whole life long. She not only fought for the rights of women and the dispossessed, she fought poverty, depression, morphine addiction, *and* Susan B. Anthony. Hers was a life that should never have been lost. Yet no matter how effective the powers of erasure, the etching of her life left enough of an imprint that its substance could be retraced.

II

Like Paul Rosenblatt, along the route of my own literary detection, I was sustained by old friends and new landladies, who were alike in their graciousness and their unending willingness to express delight in my work. Ruth Colson, my landlady for a month in Madison, Wisconsin, before she resigned from driving a bus to become a Dean's list scholar, left me to tend her house and water her plants when she was on the road. In Cambridge, my landlady was Ruth Medalia, the granddaughter of the father of Phenomenology, Edmund Husserl, and herself the "Angel of Cambridge" who connects the town's soup kitchen with its restaurants and bakeries. I treasure our morning talks and the private art tour that she provided me amid bags of bread for the soup kitchen. For work in New Haven and Stratford, Ruth and Roy Fine and Ruth and Bernie Green have frequently provided me, and often my children too, with wonderful conversation, delicious meals, and bed. My sister, Cathy Farrell Sheahan, often bunked me in a tree house room just off her artist's studio, so that I could work at the Library of Congress all day and come home to sympathy, sometimes combined with a double kayak cruise along Annapolis's Spa Creek. For an archival researcher with children, challenges are many, but fortune has given me friends and my kids' godparents, Claire and Bob McCorry, who uncomplainingly took my children in so that I could daily travel the archival circuit on the East Coast. My former student and nanny, master chef Neda Mroueh, spent many a day on the beach with Matthew and Elizabeth so that I could persevere in my mad pursuit. Every literary detective should be blessed with sidekicks like mine.

I wish to thank archivists, editors, and colleagues for their help and encouragement, especially: Clark Dougan, whom I met on the MLA shuttle bus a decade ago and who has patiently awaited this book ever since; editors Kay Scheuer and Carol Betsch; Joyce Bradbury of the Stratford Historical Society; Emily Miller of the Missouri Historical Society; John Tedeschi and Yvonne Schofer of the Cairns Collection; Anstress Farwell of the Friends of Hillhouse Avenue; David Prout for his fine index; Butler University's English Department; G. R. Thompson, Terence J. Martin, the late Elaine Hedges, Susan Gubar, Carolyn Karcher, Rosalind Rosenberg, Jane Tompkins, Alan Noulin, Alfred Bendixen, David S. Reynolds, and my late mentor at Brown University, David H. Hirsch, who encouraged me always.

I am indebted to the National Endowment for the Humanities for both a summer research grant and a year-long fellowship, without which this book could not have been written; to the Friends of the Library of the University of Wisconsin for a summer grant-in-aid; to Butler University and President Geoffrey Bannister for Academic Grants and generous subsidy of my NEH Fellowship; and to the Feminist Press, the pioneer press in the recovery of lost women's writing, which reintroduced Blake to the American canon when it reissued *Fettered for Life*. I am grateful to the directors of that press, Florence Howe and Jean Casella. I have "tried out" portions of this book on my wonderful students at Butler University who make teaching a joy and whose enthusiasm, questions, and challenges have directly inspired this work.

I thank Dr. David Price and Dr. Mary Lou Mayer and my friends who lovingly cared for me when I needed it most: Ann and Chris Stack; Lois Cuddy; Susan Jensen; my sister, Cathy Farrell Sheahan; Claire and Bob McCorry; Patricia Cox; Marge Bernardo; Heidi Schaub; my cousins Jayne Regan Harris, Jeannie Farrell Robinson, and Beth Regan Cogswell; Jim Jensen; Bill Durfee; the late Jon Barwise; Ruth and Werner Beyer; Jim Watt and Lee Verner; Elizabeth and Dick Thompson; George and Esther Gaber; Deborah and Bill Landers; Evans Woollen; Malcolm Woollen; Susan Neville; Shirley Daniell; Peter and Julia Bondanella; Joanne Audretch; Helle Barnstone; David and Rachel Hertz; and my late, loving godmother, Ruth McLaughlin.

And of course, and always, my most profound gratitude is to my family: my children, Matthew and Elizabeth, my step-daughter, Lisa, and my husband, Giancarlo Maiorino.

Since graduate school, Lois Cuddy and I have analyzed together both literature and life; we have critiqued each other's manuscripts and given hard advice on each other's lives. When I had to begin chemotherapy on the opening day of the trial against Yale University in its attempt to demolish Lillie Blake's childhood home, Lois, professor of English and Women's Studies at the University of Rhode Island, stepped in as the expert witness. Later that year, when I was bedridden, she came from Rhode Island to Indiana to make me soups and apple sauce, to take my daughter shopping for a prom dress, to do my laundry. She returned home on a Friday, gave a Phi Beta Kappa lecture on Saturday, and decided she needed to do more for me, so she flew back on Monday to make more soups, do more laundry, and sit with me and talk. I wonder how Lillie Blake coped without a friend like Lois. I dedicate this book to her.

Notes

Chapter 1

1   Wallace Stevens, *Collected Poetry and Prose* (New York: Library of America, 1997): 415. All subsequent quotations from "An Ordinary Evening in New Haven" are from this source.

2   I draw on William Howard Wilcox, *History of Stratford, Connecticut 1639–1939* (Stratford: Stratford Tercentenary Commission, 1939): 614–615. When Lillie visited Stratford in 1897 after years of absence, she found it "Oh, so changed! Trolly cars, little shops, the beautiful trees dead!" (Diary, June 12, 1897). All Blake writings cited in these notes are listed, with complete bibliographical information, following the Notes.

3   Blake's maternal grandmother was the daughter of Judge Pierrepont Edwards of New Haven, the son of Jonathan Edwards. Pierrepont's sister, Eunice, while visiting the relatives of Pierrepont's wife in New Jersey, met and married the visiting Thomas Pollok, a wealthy landowner and descendant of the first governor of North Carolina. Their daughter married Blake's paternal grandfather, John Devereux, whose life was the stuff of a popular novel: a seafaring Irish rover who had been well educated in France but had refused to enter the church and was thereafter ostracized by his family, he went to sea, serving as a midshipman on a British ship, dueled with and killed his superior officer (he referred to the incident as an "unfortunate accident"), and quickly sailed for New York, but was shipwrecked off the coast of North Carolina where he met and charmed into marriage Frances Pollok, an extremely wealthy heiress.

Blake's maternal grandfather was Judge Samuel William Johnson, the son of the Honorable William Samuel Johnson, Connecticut's representative to the first Continental Congress, a framer of the Constitution, Connecticut's first United States senator, and president of Columbia College from 1787 to 1800.

4   Stevens, v, 9.

5   Ibid., xx, 1–10.

6   Lillie Devereux Umsted, *Southwold* (New York: Rudd and Carleton: 1859): 34.

7   Elm Cottage is mentioned in both Blake's unpublished autobiography and her daughter's biography, but the Stratford Historical Society had no record of an "elm cottage." Joyce Bradbury, however, found land records confirming that Mrs. Sarah Devereux owned property across the street from the Episcopal church. There is now more than one house across from

the church, but oral history has it that in the house now known as the Golden Rooster Consignment Shop (previously called Christ Church House after the Episcopal church which bought it) a deed with Eli Whitney's name on it was found tucked away in the back of a closet. Land records show that in 1861, Eli Whitney, Jr., gave Mrs. Devereux a mortgage on property across from the church. Joyce Bradbury obtained a copy of the deed from the church records. Mrs. Devereux sold Elm Cottage to Mary and William Strong of Stratford on March 14, 1862. An 1867 map indicates the Strong house in the position of the Golden Rooster. From these two pieces of evidence supplied by Joyce Bradbury, it seems clear that the Golden Rooster is Elm Cottage.

8   Stevens, xviii, 1–2.

9   Litchfield was the site of the first law school in the United States, founded in 1784 by an abolitionist and early advocate of women's rights. The Litchfield Historical Society maintains an ongoing exhibit in the Tapping Reeve House.

10   Autobiography, 3:23.

11   *Patten's New Haven Directory* (New Haven: James M. Patten, 1839, 1840): alphabetical listing.

12   I follow here the New Haven Colony Historical Society *Amisted* exhibition and Edward D. Atwater, ed., *History of the City of New Haven* (New York, W. W. Munsell, 1887): 239. During the revolt, the Africans killed the ship's captain and cook, and forced the crew to sail for Africa. At night the crew would change course, so that the *Amistad* made a circuitous route northward, finally anchoring off Long Island on August 26, 1839, two months after leaving Cuba. The ship was captured by the U.S.S. *Washington* and towed to New London, Connecticut, where a hearing was held and the prisoners were bound over for trial.

13   While it was not unusual at this time to depict Native Americans in classical contexts, sitting on Roman stools, for instance, I assume that the issues of slavery in general and the *Amistad* case in particular inflamed the racist attitudes that erupted in the Artist Fund Society incident.

14   Henry T. Blake, *Chronicles of New Haven Green from 1638 to 1862* (New Haven: Tuttle, Morehouse, & Taylor, 1898): 174. See also Lydia Maria Child's "Letter from New-York, Number 12," first published in the *National Anti-Slavery Standard*, December 2, 1841: 103, and reprinted in Carolyn Karcher, ed., *A Lydia Maria Child Reader* (Durham: Duke University Press, 1997): 209–215.

15   H. T. Blake, *Chronicles of New Haven Green*, 75.

16   Ibid., 71.

17   Ibid., 73.

18   George Beckwith, Diary (manuscript housed in the New Haven Colony Historical Society): July 31 and August 1, 1854. Quoted with permission.

19   Nineteenth-Century Student Disciplinary Cases (uncataloged box of index cards), Manuscripts and Archives, Yale University Library. Quoted with permission.

20   Autobiography, 6:1.

21   Narrative of riots follows H. T. Blake, *Chronicles of New Haven Green*, 238–239. Diarist is L. E. Baldwin (manuscript housed in the New Haven Colony Historical Society): March 21, 1854.

22   *Patten's New Haven Directory*, 1840, 1841, 1842, 1843, alphabetical listing. Blake's grandmother's sister Henrietta married Eli Whitney, the inventor of the cotton gin. In the 1840s

their son, Eli Whitney, Jr., who was first cousin to Lillie's mother, helped Mrs. Devereux to settle in New Haven and in 1861 aided her with a mortgage taken out on her property in Stratford.

23 A. J. Davis, *Rural Residences* (New York: The Architect, 1837).

24 Quotation follows Eric Robert Papenfuse and Catherine Ann Lawrence, "An Open Letter to Richard C. Levin," *Yale Daily News,* November 4, 1998. Professor Vincent Scully has described Maple Cottage as a "nobly-massed building" (*Yale Herald News,* November 13, 1998, 3).

25 Papenfuse and Laurence, "An Open Letter."

26 Autobiography, 5:34.

27 She was thus spared, noted her granddaughter, the ridicule he afforded many of his hosts in *American Notes:* Katherine Devereux Blake and Margaret Louise Wallace, *Champion of Women: The Life of Lillie Devereux Blake* (New York, Fleming H. Revell, 1943): 19.

28 Maria Trumbull Dana, "Hillhouse Avenue: A Brief Sketch" (manuscript housed in the New Haven Colony Historical Society, dated 1954): 17.

29 Diary, February 6, 1847.

30 Dana, "Hillhouse Avenue: A Brief Sketch," 37. The letter from Aaron Skinner to Sarah Prichard is erroneously dated 1860. Aaron Skinner died in 1858, and Mrs. Devereux had sold Maple Cottage by 1856, so the party Skinner describes had to have taken place prior to 1856. My thanks to Anstress Farwell for bringing not only Skinner's letters but much of the social history of the Hillhouse/Trumbull neighborhood to my attention.

31 Friends of Hillhouse Avenue, *Maple Cottage News,* Newsletter dated November 1998, 2.

32 Dana, "Hillhouse Avenue: A Brief Sketch," 36.

33 Friends of Hillhouse Avenue, *Maple Cottage News,* December 1998, 2.

34 Dana, "Hillhouse Avenue: A Brief Sketch," 38. This letter is also erroneously dated 1860. Because Skinner died in 1858 and Ingersoll is now the owner of Maple Cottage, the occasion described must have taken place sometime between 1856 and 1858. It cannot be, as Dana states, the same letter and same date as that cited above.

35 Henrietta Silliman Dana, *Hillhouse Avenue from 1809 to 1900* (New Haven: Tuttle, Morehouse, & Taylor, 1907): 8.

36 In *Fettered for Life* (New York: Sheldon, 1874, 1885; rpt., with Afterword by Grace Farrell, New York: Feminist Press, 1996), when Blake's protagonist works as a bookseller offering a collection of poetry illustrated with pictures of the poets' homes, the single author she names is Sigourney, whose house in Hartford is pictured. My thanks to Anstress Farwell for reminding me of Blake's reference to Sigourney and for informing me of Sigourney's place in the Hillhouse/Trumbull neighborhood.

37 L. H. Sigourney, *Letters to Young Ladies* (New York: Harper & Brothers, 1849): 11, 245, 253.

38 Theodore Dwight Woolsey "Women in Modern Civilization," June 28, 1855: 52–53. *Woolsey Family Papers,* Manuscripts and Archives, Yale University Library. Quoted with permission. The Woolsey-Devereux family Connection was through Jonathan Edwards.

39 Autobiography, 5:37.

40 My gratitude to the Barnard historian Rosalind Rosenberg for contacting me upon her discovery of Blake's portrait.

41 *Dana Collection,* Whitney Library of the New Haven Colony Historical Society, vol. 107: 86.

42 *New Haven Register,* November 9, 1999: 1.

43 According to information provided to me by the Whitney Library of the New Haven Colony Historical Society, Mrs. F. B. Dexter was born Theodosia Mary Wheeler probably in 1848 and died in 1941 at the age of ninety-three. Fifteen years younger than Lillie Devereux, she came to live in New Haven in 1852, and thus was six during "the scandal." Clearly her knowledge of it was secondhand and overheard. In 1880 she married Franklin Bowditch Dexter, who tutored math and Greek in Yale's Sheffield Scientific School. They were married for forty years and had one daughter, Dorothea Mary, who married a Harvard professor. Mrs. F. B. Dexter, a Colonial Dame, served (as a volunteer) as director of the Home Missionary Society at Center Church, the Congregational church on New Haven Green. (Anstress Farwell, New Haven architectural historian, tells of a long history of competition in New Haven between the Congregationalists and the Episcopalians, whose church is also on the Green. The Devereuxs were Episcopalian.)

44 Autobiography, 6:11.

45 Atwater, ed., *History of the City of New Haven,* 366.

46 Diary, August 12, 1853–August 12, 1854. The following entries read:
   Nov. 6. Returned home.
   Nov. 25th Thanksgiving day.
   Dec. 18 [unreadable, probably the title of a lecture she attended].
   Dec. 22nd College closed.
   Dec. 25th Christmas at Stratford.
   —1854—
   Jan. 1st Received calls.
   Jan. 4th College came together.
   Jan. 6th My fiancée arrived.

47 The diary continues: "I wanted to see him for I [unreadable word] the first meeting and necessary [unreadable word] last [unreadable word] still."

48 Autobiography, 6:3.

49 YRG 41-M: 8-page petition, December 13, 1854, by William H. L. Barnes, Manuscripts and Archives, Yale University. Quoted with permission. All quotations from Barnes are from this unpaginated source.

50 YRG 9 (Vol. 1850–1862): Faculty record, December 14, 1854, regarding Barnes, Manuscripts and Archives, Yale University Library. Quoted with permission.

51 Ibid.

52 Autobiography, 6:9.

53 Theodore Winthrop's mother was President Woolsey's sister.

54 Autobiography, 12:7.

55 T. Winthrop to T. D. Woolsey, December 22, 1854, Correspondence, 1854, Woolsey Family Papers, Manuscripts and Archives, Yale University Library. Quoted with permission.

56 Ibid.

57 Autobiography, 1:7.

58 H. T. Blake, *Chronicles of New Haven Green,* 173. "The statute prescribing the penalty was repealed in 1830" (178).

59 Brother C. Edward, "Eli Whitney: Embattled Inventor," *American History Illustrated* 8 (February 1974): 47.

60 Atwater, ed., *History of the City of New Haven,* 366.

61 Memorandum to Members of the Connecticut Historical Commission from Friends of Hillhouse Avenue regarding "New information on Maple Cottage," November 1, 1998. Reported in the *New Haven Register,* November 3, 1998, A2.

62 *Friends of Hill House v. Yale University,* No. CV 98-PJR 0419300S (Connecticut Superior Court Judicial District of New Haven, January 15, 1999): 1–102. Yale's consultant testified: "I did have a researcher working with me. We had many many conferences on what was found. I frankly did a great deal. We were the first to uncover Lily [*sic*] Devereux Blake long before any information was provided to us by the Friends of Hillhouse Avenue" (48). When challenged by plaintiff's attorney, Yale's consultant stated: ". . . when that letter [from Grace Farrell to Yale President Richard Levin of October 28, 1998] was given to . . . my researcher, I made a comment by saying I have never heard frankly of Lillie Devereux Blake. And I said to my researcher, here is a letter about Lillie Devereux Blake. My researcher replied, yes, I read all about her at the library, and I have all sorts of notes on Lillie Devereux Blake. Based on that I merely told you that we as a team knew about Lillie Devereux Blake, with very little effort, before that letter was given to us, I believe by the Friends if I'm not mistaken for our perusal and our consideration in the preparation of our report. And we were happy to consider it and peruse it, and it is, in fact, summarized a little later on in our report." The Friends attorney: "In fact, when you say summarized, a large portion of your report about Lillie Devereux Blake comes right out of this letter" (54–55).

   Friends of Hill House Avenue Post-Trial Brief No. CV-98–419300-S (Connecticut Superior Court Judicial District of New Haven, April 14, 1999) states that Yale's consultant "testified that he and his assistant were the first to uncover Lillie Devereux Blake. But, the only information about the significance of Lillie Devereux Blake in his report comes in quotations from her biographer" (22).

63 *Friends of Hill House v. Yale University,* 48.

64 "But unfortunately with respect to Mrs. Blake, what we know about her while she lived at the subject property was that a scandal came to light with regard to one of the Yale students who was expelled. And we know the family had to leave town as a result of the scandal. We note for instance from the Dana Archives that she was a great belle. That's the exact word used. If you wish I'll read you the quote. She was a great belle to all Yale students who all chased after her, and eventually this great scandal erupted." Ibid., 47.

65 *Autobiography,* 6:3.

66 Interview with the *Yale Daily News,* (September 16, 1999, 3, 7). My thanks to Anstress Farwell for bringing this interview to my attention.

67 Elizabeth Mills Brown, *New Haven: A Guide to Architecture and Urban Design* (New Haven: Yale University Press, 1976): 121.

68 George Steiner, *After Babel* (London: Oxford University Press, 1975): 466.

69 Brown, *New Haven: A Guide,* 121.

70 Steiner writes, "The new, even at its most scandalous, has been set against an informing background and framework of tradition. . . . the 'makers of the new'—have been neo-

classics, often as observant of canonic precedent as their seventeenth-century forebears" (*After Babel*, 466).

71   Ibid., 466.

72   Joy S. Kasson, *Marble Queens and Captives: Women in Nineteenth-Century American Sculpture* (New Haven: Yale University Press, 1990): 48.

73   Ibid., 50.

74   In *Women and Sisters: The Antislavery Feminists in American Culture* (New Haven: Yale University Press, 1989), Jean Fagan Yellin writes, "instead of signifying that woman should engage in public action to end her oppression . . . the icon of an enchained female signifies that the appropriate womanly response to tyranny is resignation" (99–100).

75   Ibid., 124.

76   "Among time's images," Stevens sets windy nights against marble statues; on the Sound the sea shivers; into the streets, we descend "and inhale a health of air" (viii, 2).

77   Susan Stanford Friedman writes, "Not recognizing themselves in the reflections of cultural representation, women develop a dual consciousness—the self as culturally defined and the self as different from cultural prescription": "Women's Autobiographical Selves: Theory and Practice," in Shari Benstock, ed., *The Private Self: Theory and Practice of Women's Autobiographical Writings* (Chapel Hill: University of North Carolina Pennsylvania, 1988): 39.

78   "Spring Fling goes home to Cross Campus" and "The News' View: Yale has the right to demolish Maple Cottage," *Yale Daily News*, November 6, 1998.

Chapter Two

1   Fanny Fern, "Hints to Young Wives," *Olive Branch*, February 14, 1853.

2   Theodore Dwight Woolsey, "Women in Modern Civilization," June 28, 1855, 15. *Woolsey Family Papers*, Manuscripts and Archives, Yale University Library. Quoted with permission.

3   Ibid., 48.

4   John Gregory, *A Father's Legacy to his Daughters* (London: J. D. Dewick, 1801): 36, 37. First published in 1775, *A Father's Legacy* was frequently reissued through the middle of the nineteenth century. In 1883, Lillie Devereux Blake wrote that "Lady Mary Wortley Montagu . . . advised that her granddaughter should be educated, but that the fact should be concealed that it should not interfere with her marriage!": *Woman's Place To-Day* (New York: J. W. Lovell, 1883), 25–26.

5   Edward H. Clarke, *Sex in Education; or A Fair Chance for Girls* (1872; Boston: James R. Osgood, 1875): 37.

6   Gerda Lerner, "The Lady and the Mill Girl: Changes in the Status of Women in the Age of Jackson," *Mid-Continent American Studies Journal* 10 (1969): 7.

7   Susan Warner, *The Wide, Wide World*, with an Afterword by Jane Tompkins (New York: Feminist Press, 1987): 9.

8   Diane Long Hoeveler, *Gothic Feminism: The Professionalization of Gender from Charlotte Smith to the Brontës* (University Park: Pennsylvania State University Press, 1998): xi.

9   The Feminist Press provides the final chapter, which was omitted from the 1850 publication.

10   David S. Reynolds, *Beneath the American Renaissance* (Cambridge: Harvard University Press, 1989): 182–183.

11   Mary Putnam Jacobi, "Women in Medicine," in Annie Nathan Meyer, ed., *Woman's Work in America* (New York: Henry Holt, 1891): 195–196.

12   See, for example, Anita Levy, *Other Women: The Writing of Class, Race, and Gender, 1832–1898* (Princeton: Princeton University Press, 1991). Levy cites sociological studies as early as the 1830s which isolate not the abysmal living conditions caused by industrialization, but the slatternly behavior of lower-class females as a causative factor in diseases of the poor (36).

13   *Autobiography*, 6:2.

14   "By no fault of mine, and certainly without any effort on my part, this gentleman became fascinated by one whom he had looked upon only as a 'strong minded woman' and who was old enough literally to be his mother.

       "After leaving the place where we met, I did not see him for several months, although he wrote to me, but having met him again, the spell was so far renewed that he quitted his college, and followed me to New York.

       "As might have been expected, his engagement was presently broken, but although I had at first been distressed at his taking so decided a step as this of changing his whole career in life on my account, I had the satisfaction of seeing him succeed admirably in journalism which he had chosen as a career, while his devoted friendship was a very pleasant thing to me during many years" (Ibid., 31:20).

15   Ibid., 6:2. Both Blake in her autobiography and Katherine Devereux Blake in her biography quote this passage from a diary that no longer exists.

16   Ibid., 3, 2.

17   Diary, February 22, 1847–May 31, 1847, passim.

18   *Autobiography*, 5:38.

19   Ibid.

20   Sister Katie is Catharine Beecher, headmistress of the Hartford Female Seminary. From James Parton, ed., *Fanny Fern: A Memorial Volume* (New York: Carleton, 1873): 36–37.

21   Joyce Warren, *Fanny Fern: An Independent Woman* (New Brunswick, NY: Rutgers University Press, 1992): 94.

22   I agree with Lauren Berlant, "The Female Woman: Fanny Fern and the Form of Sentiment," in Shirley Samuels, ed., *The Culture of Sentiment: Race, Gender, and Sentimentality in Nineteenth-Century America* (New York: Oxford University Press, 1992), who writes: "There are many texts spread throughout her career that validate sentimental ideality in a non-ironic sense. . . . In texts like 'A Word to Mothers,' which argues that 'a mother's reward is in secret and in silence,' she invokes maternal martyrdom as an unfailing index of moral and practical virtue. In texts like 'Bogus Intellect' and 'Two Kinds of Women,' she repeatedly asserts that married women's submission to a domestic regimen must precede any incursions into the public sphere. . . . Non-coherent about the value of domestic ideology and women's rights agitation, Fern has no single position on the woman question—except that she consistently stages the baptism of woman's lot in her continual confrontation with the stereotype to which she must submit, either under duress or spurred on by desire. . . . Fern's reading of domestic sentimentality acts as an apology and a consolation for the anguish of living under patriarchy, but this critical pose does not align Fern solidly with feminism—or at least authorize her female audience to rupture relations with domestic fantasy" (274).

23   *Autobiography*, 6:2.

24 Ibid., 9. Jonathan Knight (1789–1864) was a highly esteemed surgeon on the faculty of the Yale Medical School and twice president of the American Medical Association. In 1863 the army hospital of New Haven was named Knight Hospital in his honor: Edward D. Atwater, ed., *History of the City of New Haven* New York: W. W. Munsell, 1887: 276, 72.

25 James Fordyce, D. D., *Sermons to Young Women* (1765; Philadelphia: Thomas Dobson, 1787). 3d ed.

26 Sandra Gilbert and Susan Gubar, *The Madwoman in the Attic* (New Haven: Yale University Press, 1979): 25.

27 Autobiography, 7:6. It was actually one year before her marriage, and in May rather than the June she notes. Her handwritten diary of August 1853–August 1854 notes on May 19, while she was in Raleigh: "Burned myself while dressing for a party."

28 Anonymous, "My Last Conquest," *Harpers Weekly,* November 14, 1857, 734.

29 This is also the theme of "The Dead Letter," published under the pseudonym Essex in the *New York Weekly Mercury,* November 11, 1865, 3.

30 Gilbert and Gubar write in *No Man's Land,* vol. 1 (New Haven: Yale University Press, 1988), that "Edwardian suffrage polemics, like much female-authored fiction of the period, employed military imagery, often couched in a rhetoric of sacrifice, in order to glimpse the possibility of female victory in the battle of the sexes" (67).

31 "My Last Conquest," 734.

32 I follow here Karen Halttunen, *Confidence Men and Painted Women: A Study of Middle-Class Culture in America, 1830–1870* (New Haven: Yale University Press, 1982).

33 Jane Tompkins, Afterword to Warner, *The Wide, Wide World,* 600.

34 Augusta Jane Evans, *St. Elmo* (1867; New York: G. W. Dillingham, 1896): 562.

35 Autobiography, 6:6.

36 Ibid., 11:6.

37 L.D.U., "Shot Through the Heart. A Tragedy of Fredericksburgh," *Knickerbocker Monthly* (May 1863): 413–421.

38 Autobiography, 14:8–9. Transcription of Diary, Wednesday, December 24, 1862.

39 My thanks to Joyce Bradbury of the Stratford Historical Society for locating the *Record of Confirmations* from Christ Church, Stratford.

40 Autobiography, 8:5.

41 Women who separated from their husbands found that any wages they earned could be seized. Fanny Fern, for instance, left her brutal second husband, who responded by trying— though unsuccessfully—to undermine her every attempt at earning her own living.

42 Autobiography, 6:4.

43 Ibid., 8.

44 Ibid., 4.

45 Andrea Moore Kerr, *Lucy Stone: Speaking Out for Equality* (New Brunswick: Rutgers University Press, 1992): 8.

46 Elizabeth Cady Stanton to Susan B. Anthony, January 24, 1856, Susan B. Anthony Collection, Library of Congress.

47 Autobiography, 6:6–7.

48 While Blake reports that her visits to Mammoth Cave provided the background for several stories, to date I have found only "A Tragedy of the Mammoth Cave."

49 I am indebted to Park Ranger Joy Medley Lyons at Mammoth Cave National Park for information concerning Mat Bransford and for her gracious permission to use the park archives in her office, which provided me with other details noted in the text.

50 *Autobiography*, 6:3.

51 *Selected Writings of Emerson*, ed. Donald McQuade (New York: Modern Library, 1981): 742. The Mammoth Cave was also setting and inspiration for sensational literature of the time. For example one nineteenth-century title in the park archives ran *Startling disclosures! Mysteries solved! or the history of Esther Livingstone, and dark career of Henry Baldwin: this narrative not only pictures the singular career of Esther Livingstone, and the crimes of Henry Baldwin, but the scenes in which they were actors in the Mammoth Cave, are related by the wretched Baldwin in a bold, truthful, but absorbing style. And the murder of Miss Annie Harnley in Charleston on the night of her marriage, is in these pages terribly explained.*

52 Charles Dickens, "A Tour of Mammoth Cave," *All The Year Round*, January 19, 1861: 343–344.

53 By a New Contributor, *Knickerbocker Monthly* (February 1858): 111–121.

54 Nathaniel Hawthorne, *The Blithedale Romance* (1852; New York: W. W. Norton, 1978): 207.

55 Anonymous, *Knickerbocker Monthly* (May 1858): 449.

56 I follow here Nina Auerbach, who writes of those who "purge women of violence and desire," when they might instead laugh at the "pernicious fantasy of female purity so many realists embrace" and celebrate "heroines who express hungers they are told not to feel, look at what they are forbidden to see": *Romantic Imprisonment: Women and Other Glorified Outcasts* (New York: Columbia University Press, 1985): xxi.

57 Gilbert and Gubar, *No Mans Land*, 1:67.

58 *Autobiography*, 6:6.

59 Ibid., 9.

60 Lydia Sigourney, *Letters to Young Ladies* (New York: Harper and Brothers, 1849): 179.

61 *Champion of Women*, 33.

62 *Autobiography*, 6:8.

63 Ibid., 11; *Champion of Women*, 34.

64 *Autobiography*, 6:4.

65 Ibid., 11.

66 *Champion of Women*, 45.

67 Louisa May Alcott, *Moods* (1864; New Brunswick: Rutgers University Press, 1991, with an Introduction by Sarah Elbert): 67.

68 "A Word to Mothers," in Parton, ed., *Fanny Fern, A Memorial Volume*, 170.

69 See Isabelle Lehuu's discussion, "Sentimental Figures: Reading *Godey's Lady's Book* in Antebellum America," in Samuels, ed., *The Culture of Sentiment*: "In particular, the female gentility embodied in the imagery of Mother and Child revealed both the feminization of American religion and a softening of American Protestantism" (84).

70 Morgan Dix, *Lectures on the Calling of a Christian Woman and her Training to Fulfil It* (New York: D. Appleton, 1883).

71 George B. Forgie, *Patricide in the House Divided: A Psychological Interpretation of Lincoln and His Age* (New York: W. W. Norton, 1979): 178–179. Forgie cites G. F. Simmons, "Prospects of Art in this Country," *Christian Examiner* (November/December 1839): 311–312, and Charles Eliot Norton, "The Advantages of Defeat," *Atlantic Monthly* (September 1861): 364.

72 Kasson, *Marble Queens and Captives*, 223.

73 Ibid., 237.

74 Blake, *Woman's Place To-Day* (New York: John W. Lovell Co, 1883): 7.

75 Autobiography, 6:11.

Chapter Three

1 Joy S. Kasson *Marble Queens and Captives: Women in Nineteenth-Century American Sculpture* (New Haven: Yale University Press, 1990): 60. An exception to this generalization was Lucy Stone's response to Powers's statue. She saw it in Boston where she was giving anti-slavery lectures: "There it stood in the silence, with fettered hands and half-averted face—so emblematic of women. I remember how the hot tears came to my eyes at the thought of the millions of women who must be freed." Stone was inspired that night to begin her long career as a woman's rights lecturer (Andrea Moore Kerr, *Lucy Stone: Speaking Out for Equality* [New Brunswick: Rutgers University Press, 1992]: 51–52). In 1850, Elizabeth Barrett Browning, who knew Hiram Powers when they both lived in Florence, wrote a sonnet on *The Greek Slave*, which pitches ideal beauty against the social corruption epitomized by slavery.

2 *Fettered for Life*, 195.

3 David S. Reynolds describes the *tableaux vivants* or *poses plastiques* in *Beneath the American Renaissance* (Cambridge: Harvard University Press, 1989): 214–215. In a far less erotic context, Blake tells of tableaux given and charades acted in the New Haven homes where the Revolver Club held its open houses (Autobiography, 6:9).

4 Reynolds, *Beneath the American Renaissance*, 108.

5 See also William Ware's 1838 novel *Zenobia*, and Poe's 1838 short story "The Psyche Zenobia," later retitled "How to Write a Blackwood Article."

6 Nathaniel Hawthorne, *The Blithedale Romance* (1852; New York: W. W. Norton, 1978): 221.

7 Ibid., 206.

8 Lydia Sigourney, *Letters to Young Ladies* (New York: Harper and Brothers, 1849): 253.

9 Reynolds, *Beneath the American Renaissance*, 373.

10 The *French and Italian Notebooks*, vol. 14. of *The Centenary Edition of the Works of Nathaniel Hawthorne*, ed. Thomas Woodson (Columbus: Ohio State University Press, 1980): 156–157. In Hawthorne's entry for April 8, 1843, he reacts with boredom and sarcasm to Emerson's praise of Fuller: "Mr. Emerson came, with a sunbeam in his face; and we had as good a talk as I ever remember experiencing with him. My little wife, I know, will demand to know every word that was spoken; but she knows me too well to anticipate anything of the kind. He seemed fullest of Margaret Fuller, who, he says, has risen perceptibly into a higher state since their last meeting. He apotheosized her as the greatest woman, I believe, of ancient or modern times, and the one figure in the world worth considering. (There rings the supper-bell)." Note the patronizing reference to his wife and the pun on Fuller and fullest.

11 Kasson, *Marble Queens and Captives*, 161.

12 Thomas Woody, *Women's Education in the United States*, 2 vols. (New York: Science Press, 1929): 1:105.

13 Eleanor Flexner, *Century of Struggle: The Woman's Rights Movement in the United States* (1959; Cambridge: Harvard University Press, 1975): 134.

14 Woody, *Women's Education in the United States*, 1:106.

15 In *Beneath the American Renaissance*, David Reynolds writes that 57 percent of the volumes published between 1774 and 1860 were of the "highly wrought, adventurous" type (338).

16 E.D.E.N. Southworth, *The Hidden Hand or Capitola the Madcap*, ed. Joanne Dobson (New Brunswick: Rutgers University Press, 1988): 156, 111, 193.

17 Ibid., introduction, xxix.

18 Issues of class have generally been omitted from the important debate concerning the nature of nineteenth-century womanhood. Early scholarship tended to define the condition of all nineteenth-century women from a model that described only the situation of middle-class white women.

19 Southworth, *The Hidden Hand*, 376.

20 Ibid., 174–175.

21 Ibid., 456.

22 Ibid., 109, 173.

23 Anonymous, "The Social Condition of Woman," *Knickerbocker Monthly* (May 1863): 385.

24 Southworth, *The Hidden Hand*, 174.

25 *Southwold*, 117.

26 Ibid., 81.

27 Ibid., 148, 142, 191, 7, 118, 172–173.

28 Theodore Dwight Woolsey, "Women in Modern Civilization," June 28, 1855: 35, 37, 44, *Woolsey Family Papers*, Manuscripts and Archives, Yale University Library. Quoted with permission.

29 Elizabeth Cady Stanton, Susan B. Anthony, and Matilda Joslyn Gage; eds., *History of Woman Suffrage, 1848–1861*, vol. 1 (Rochester, N.Y.: Susan B. Anthony, 1881): 850–851.

30 *Woman's Place To-Day*, 14.

31 Stanton, "Has Christianity Benefited Woman?", *North American Review* (May 1885): 390.

32 Blake served on Stanton's Revision Committee, contributing nine of the twenty-two selections not written by Stanton. A number of other woman wrote the remaining thirteen selections.

33 *Southwold*, 18.

34 Not unlike the worldwide economic decline which occurred in 1857, just before Blake began to write her novel.

35 For an extensive discussion of this issue, see Anita Levy, *Other Women: The Writing of Class, Race, and Gender* (Princeton: Princeton University Press, 1991).

36 Kate Ferguson Ellis writes that the Gothic novel "can be distinguished by the presence of houses in which people are locked in and locked out": *The Contested Castle: Gothic Novels and the Subversion of Domestic Ideology* (Urbana: University of Illinois Press, 1989): 3.

37 *Southwold*, 105.

38 Ibid., 194.

39 Ibid., 198.

40 My reference, of course, is to Sandra Gilbert and Susan Gubar's landmark study, *The Madwoman in the Attic* (New Haven: Yale University Press, 1979).

41 *Southwold*, 227–228.

42 Ibid., 22. Four years later, Louisa May Alcott would use similar language to introduce her heroine in "Pauline's Passion and Punishment," a story in the sensational genre published in *Frank Leslie's Illustrated Newspaper* in January 1863. "To and fro, like a wild creature in its cage, paced that handsome woman, with bent head, locked hands, and restless steps," begins the story. Alcott creates a woman, also jilted by a man in need of money, who enacts a revenge devised with malicious cunning. Her story ends with not one but two victims plunging headlong over a cliff. Reprinted in *The Feminist Alcott: Stories of a Woman's Power,* ed. Madeleine B. Stern (Boston: Northeastern University Press, 1996).

43 Blake, "The Social Condition of Woman," *Knickerbocker, Monthly* (May 1863): 383.

44 See Nina Auerbach, *Romantic Imprisonment: Women and Other Glorified Outcasts* (New York: Columbia University Press, 1985): xxi.

45 Autobiography, 7:3.

46 Ibid., 5.

47 Ibid.

48 Sigourney, *Letters to Young Ladies*, 183.

49 As David Reynolds says of *Southwold*, "the skeptical intellect of the restless, frustrated heroine is a projection of Blake's own attempt to venture ambitiously into the realm of dark philosophizing and complex artistry" (*Beneath the American Renaissance*, 402).

50 Autobiography, 7:8.

51 Transcript of Diary, January 18, 1859.

52 Transcript of Diary.

53 Autobiography, 8:3.

54 Transcript of Diary, 1859, 7.

55 *Champion of Women*, 39.

56 Diary June 6, 1859, transcribed in Autobiography, 9:3.

57 Autobiography, 9:3.

58 Ibid., 8:6.

59 Ibid., 9:1.

60 *Champion of Women*, 35–36.

Chapter Four

1 My thanks to Joyce Bradbury of the Stratford Historical Society for identifying Lillie's pond. The Sterlings were the same family that built and endowed a maintenance fund for, among other buildings, the Sterling Quadrangle at the Yale Divinity School.

2 Autobiography, 10:3.

3 "The Social Condition of Woman," 23.

4 Lillie Devereux Umstead to Sarah Devereux, December 22, 1861, Blake Archives, Missouri Historical Society.

5 Blake writes, almost twenty years later: "Marriage would of course have relieved me from many of the embarrassments of my situation, but I never thought of it as a resource or even as a thing to be desired. I had resolved on the contrary that I would make for myself if pos-

sible an independent place and I wished to owe my position to my own exertion, and not to any man's protection" (Autobiography, 11:3).

6 Land Records are in the collection of the Stratford Historical Society. Deeds are in the collection of the Historian's Office, Christ Episcopal Church, Stratford.

7 These facts are reconstructed from scattered information in Blake's Autobiography, especially 3:29 and 9:4, and in *Champion of Women.*

8 Autobiography, 9:4. Transcript of Diary, July 1, 1859.

9 Autobiography, 9:5.

10 Transcript of Diary, February 12, 1860.

11 "To me there is something intensely repugnant in this arrogating a knowledge of the actions and thoughts of the Deity and narrowing his inconceivably sublime system down to the comprehension and wants of this contracted world" (ibid.). She continued to read fiction. Harriet Beecher Stowe's "The Minister's Wooing" she found not at the level of Stowe's other work, and the very popular novel *Beulah* by the secessionist Augusta Evans she described as "extremely disagreeable and unnatural, without talent enough to redeem it" (Autobiography, 10:4). Perhaps she was reacting negatively to the reduction of the ambitious, successful Beulah to a submissive child-woman who gives up her independence for marriage.

12 Transcript of Diary, December 11, 1859.

13 *Saturday Evening Post,* October 21, 1871, 1; October 28, 1871, 1.

14 Transcript of Diary, May 10, 1860.

15 Ibid., May 10, 1861. Thirty-six years later, when Lillie visited the grave "the moss was thick on his monument." Diary, June 12, 1897.

16 *Rockford* (New York: Carleton, 1863): 6.

17 Anonymous to Lillie Devereux Umsted, July 3, 1863, Blake Archives, Missouri Historical Society.

18 Harriet Beecher Stowe, "The True Story of Lady Byron's Life," *Atlantic Monthly* (September 1869): 295–313; reprinted in Joan D. Hedrick, ed., *The Oxford Harriet Beecher Stowe Reader* (New York: Oxford University Press, 1999): 542; Hedrick, Introduction, 16.

19 *Rockford,* 204.

20 "A Lonely House," *Atlantic Monthly* (January 1861): 41.

21 James Russell Lowell to Lillie Devereux Umsted, April 3, 1860, transcribed in Autobiography, 10:2.

22 As Paula Bennett, in *My Life a Loaded Gun: Female Creativity and Feminist Poetics* (Boston: Beacon Press, 1986), writes: "However legion the stories of women's anger and destructive power, these are not qualities that women in our society have been encouraged to own. On the contrary, such stories have traditionally been used to help socialize women out of their feelings of rage. The appearance in women of anger, like darkness, mess, and even the erotic, is the source of tremendous anxiety—in both women and men—and it has been condemned . . . as ugly and unfeminine" (250–251).

23 "A Lonely House," 42.

24 In 1860, "the great question of the day," divided many a house throughout the country. Lillie would have listened to political debates when, with her children, she visited Frank's

family in Philadelphia and again in New Haven where she spent a week visiting John DeForest and his wife, who was a special friend of Lillie's. DeForest, even then a well-known writer, would become more so with the publication in 1867 of his Civil War novel, *Miss Ravenel's Conversion.*

25 Autobiography, 11:4.

26 Transcript of Diary, November 11, 1860.

27 Autobiography, 11:5.

28 "As former slave holders and residents of North Carolina we have always felt a deep sympathy with the South and while fully realizing how horrible the institution was, understanding it perhaps better than anyone who had not seen the actual working of the 'peculiar institution,' we yet felt that the course which the North had pursued on the subject had been such as to aggravate and inflame the people of the South rather than to lead them to any careful consideration of the wisest measure which could be adopted to remove a curse for whose origin both sections were responsible" (ibid., 3–4). Abolitionists like Lydia Maria Child would have had little tolerance for such cautious stances: "Slavery and Freedom are antagonistic elements. One must inevitably destroy the other. Which do you choose?" She wrote in *The Patriarchal Institution, as Described by Members of Its Own Family* (New York: American Anti-Slavery Society, 1860): 53.

29 Autobiography, 12:1, 4.

30 Ibid., 1.

31 Joel Myerson, Daniel Shealy, and Madeleine B. Stern, eds., *The Journals of Louisa May Alcott* (Boston: Little, Brown, 1989): 105. While George Rable enumerates many variations of "If only I were a man," Drew Gilpin Faust cites "useless" as the term women used to describe themselves in Civil War letters and diaries: Rable, "'Missing in Action': Women of the Confederacy" (136), and Faust, "Altars of Sacrifice: Confederate Women and Narratives of War" (176), both in Catherine Clinton and Nina Silber, eds., *Divided Houses: Gender and the Civil War* (New York: Oxford University Press, 1992).

32 Autobiography, 12:2–5. Transcriptions from Diary, April–May 1861.

33 Autobiography, 11:1. "No doubt I might have made a success of lecturing if I had at that time undertaken it, but my mother was intensely opposed to any appearance in public and I had to be contented with the smaller returns of desultory literary work" (2).

34 Maurine Hoffman Beasley, "Pens and Petticoats: The Story of the First Washington Women Correspondents" (diss., George Washington University, 1974): 109.

35 Confederate privates made $11 a month, while Union soldiers made $13: Jean Pfaelzer, ed., *A Rebecca Harding Davis Reader* (Pittsburgh: University of Pittsburgh Press, 1995): 471 n. 7. An inquiry made to Arthur W. Henrick confirmed Pfaelzer's information and provided additional data from *The Revised U.S. Army Regulations* (Washington: Government Printing Office, 1863), which may be viewed at <http://www.hometown.aol.com/webmasacwa/index.html>. Henrick notes that "the Pay for Union soldiers was raised in August, 1864 from $13 to $16, but inflation in the north doubled prices so the raise was a weak one. CSA troops (Privates) were stuck at $11 a month, so their pay, from 1861 to 1864 dropped by 90%" (e-mail message from A. W. Henrick to G. Farrell, May 18, 2001). The data posted on Henrick's website, show Union officers earning upwards of $103 a month.

36 Autobiography, 13:2, 4.

37 It was published in the *Atlantic Monthly* in February 1862. Julia Ward Howe, *Reminiscences* (Boston: Houghton Mifflin, 1899): 270–274.

38 Autobiography, 13:2–3.

39 I follow here Maurine Hoffman Beasley, *A Documentary History of Women and Journalism* (Washington, D.C.: American University Press, 1993), *The First Women Washington Correspondents* (Washington, D.C.: George Washington University Press, 1976), and "Pens and Petticoats"; and Ishbel Ross, *Ladies of the Press* (New York: Arno Press, 1974).

40 For example, Beasley writes: "Samuel Wilkeson, chief of *New York Tribune's* Washington bureau, rushed into print to defend Simon Cameron, Lincoln's first Secretary of War, accused of war profiteering in the purchase of shoddy goods for the Army. Wilkeson's reward was to obtain copies of War Department documents before the *Tribune's* competitors" ("Pens and Petticoats," 90).

41 Autobiography, 13:1. These letters provide further evidence in Lillie's favor against New Haven's 1854 rumors.

42 Transcript of Diary, December 2, 1861.

43 Ibid., December 29, 1861.

44 Umsted to Sarah Devereux, December 30, 1861, Blake Archives, Missouri Historical Society.

45 Umsted to Sarah Devereux, January 26, 1862, Blake Archives, Missouri Historical Society.

46 Umsted to Sarah Devereux, January 19, 1862, reprinted in *Champion of Women*, 55.

47 A Peaceable Man, "Chiefly About War Matter," *Atlantic Monthly* (July 1862): 46.

48 Autobiography, 14:4.

49 Transcript of Diary, December 15, 1861.

50 Autobiography, 14:8. Erastus Corning was president of the New York Central Railroad; in 1869, William Wilson Corcoran founded Washington's Corcoran Museum of Art.

51 Umsted to Sarah Devereux, January 3, 1862, Blake Archives, Missouri Historical Society.

52 Autobiography, 13:7–8.

53 Blake's allusion here is to the result of master-slave rape, a topic not fully aired until the publication of Harriet Jacobs's *Incidents in the Life of a Slave Girl* (1861).

54 Umsted to Sarah Devereux, January 19, 1862, reprinted in *Champion of Women*, 55; typescript by Katherine Devereux Blake of her mother's newspaper articles from 1861–62, Blake Archives, Missouri Historical Society.

55 Autobiography, 13:3; *Champion of Women*, 48.

56 Autobiography, 13:9.

57 Typescript by Katherine Devereux Blake of her mother's newspaper articles from 1861–62, Blake Archives, Missouri Historical Society. During the presidential campaign of 1864, Anna Dickinson, known as the "Joan of Arc" of the abolitionist movement, told the following joke: "A little old lady summarized McClellan's generalship appropriately when she said, 'Why, my dear, what are these people attacking poor little General McClellan for? I am sure that he never attacked anybody'": Wendy Hamand Venet, *Neither Ballots nor Bullets: Women Abolitionists and the Civil War* (Charlottesville: University Press of Virginia, 1991): 144.

58 *Atlantic Monthly* (July 1862): 46, 47. Hawthorne arrived in Washington on the very day that the Army of the Potomac marched out. Although they shared the acquaintance of the artist

Carl Leutze (who was busy frescoing the interior of the Capitol), there is no evidence that Blake and Hawthorne met each other.

59   Carolyn L. Karcher, ed., *A Lydia Maria Child Reader* (Durham: Duke University Press, 1997), 378.

60   Venet, *Neither Ballots nor Bullets,* 123–124.

61   Umsted to Sarah Devereux, transcript, March 2, 1862, Blake Archives, Missouri Historical Society.

62   Umsted to Sarah Devereux, transcripts, March 10, 14, 16, 1862, Blake Archives, Missouri Historical Society.

63   I follow here Kathleen L. Endres, "The Women's Press in the Civil War: A Portrait of Patriotism, Propaganda, and Prodding," *Civil War History* 30 (March 1984): 31–53.

64   Playing on Lillie's name—Elizabeth Devereux—"Essex" may allude to Robert Devereux, earl of Essex, who was put to death by his purported lover, Elizabeth I, in 1601.

65   Endres, "The Women's Press," 36. Wendy Hamand Venet reports that abolitionist Lydia Maria Child "huffed 'So *this* is what the people are taxed for!'" after reading about Mrs. Lincoln's expenditures (*Neither Ballots nor Bullets,* 123).

66   "A Wild Night Ride. A Story of the War," *Forney's War Press* March 1, 1862, 1.

67   Autobiography, 14:10.

68   Ibid., 10–11.

69   Jean Pfaelzer, in *Parlor Radical: Rebecca Harding Davis and the Origins of American Social Realism* (Pittsburgh: University of Pittsburgh Press, 1996), writes, "Despite the informative rhetorics of abolition tales and slave narratives, most popular literature—domestic fiction as well as plantation fiction—still pictured the African American as the contented slave, the comic minstrel, the fulsome mammy, or the wretched freedman" (81).

70   Sharon M. Harris, *Rebecca Harding Davis and American Realism* (Philadelphia: University of Pennsylvania Press, 1991).

71   Rebecca Harding Davis, "Blind Tom," *Atlantic Monthly* (November 1862): 581.

72   Rebecca Harding Davis, "John Lamar," *Atlantic Monthly* (April 1862): 417, 421, 418.

73   "Free Labor in the British West Indies," *Atlantic Monthly* (March 1862): 274.

74   "Fremont's Hundred Days in Missouri," *Atlantic Monthly* (March 1862): 377.

75   Abolitionist, feminist, and former slave Sojourner Truth asked "And Ain't I A Woman?" in her 1851 speech before a women's rights convention in Akron, Ohio. For a detailed analysis of the iconography and ideology of this question, see Jean Fagan Yellin, *Women and Sisters: The Antislavery Feminists in American Culture,* (New Haven: Yale University Press, 1989).

76   A dialogue between a slaveholder and a Union colonel from "Freemont's Hundred Days in Missouri" *Atlantic Monthly* (March 1862), illustrates:

> "Colonel, I am told you have got my boy Ben, who has run away from me."
>
> "'Your boy?'" exclaimed the Colonel; "I do not know that I have any boy of yours."
>
> "Yes, there he is," insisted the master, pointing to a negro who was approaching. "I want you to deliver him to me: you have no right to him; he is my slave."
>
> "Your slave?" shouted Colonel Lovejoy, springing to his feet. "That man is my servant. By his own consent he is in my service, and I pay him for his labor, which is his right to sell and mine to buy." (377)

77 *Atlantic Monthly* (November 1862): 581.

78 What we have here is a mixture of late eighteenth-century paternalism and the inherited tradition of looking at the poor, whatever their skin color, as objects of charity. The racial culture of American abolitionists can be seen as a variation on the European tradition that, since the Renaissance, had produced a body of treatises on the poor that promulgated their heavenly rewards as an unfailing compensation for their earthly indigence. This is the inherited context of Harriet Beecher Stowe's *Uncle Tom's Cabin; or, Life among the Lowly.*

79 Thomas Wentworth Higginson, "Gabriel's Defeat," *Atlantic Monthly* (September 1862): 337–345, and *Army Life in a Black Regiment* (Boston: Fields, Osgood, 1870).

80 Endres writes, "The slavery issue, when mentioned [in the mainstream women's publications], was pictured in terms that a mother could identify with, such as the loss of a child by sale" ("The Women's Press," 44).

81 Umsted to Sarah Devereux, undated, Blake Archives, Missouri Historical Society.

82 Autobiography, 15:2.

83 Ibid., 14:7. Transcription of Diary, December 20, 1862.

84 Autobiography, 14:8. Transcription of Diary, December 22, 1862.

85 Autobiography, 15:1.

Chapter Five

1 I follow Wendy Hamand Venet, *Neither Ballots nor Bullets: Women Abolitionists and the Civil War* (Charlottesville: University Press of Virginia, 1991): 49, and Blake, Autobiography, 15:2.

2 As Venet writes: "Although prewar female activists such as the Grimké sisters, Abby Kelley Foster, and Elizabeth Cady Stanton were gifted orators, they often had been dismissed as shrill and unladylike. Dickinson, with her sumptuous clothes and dramatic lecture style, was seen by many as patriotic, theatrical, and feminine; in short, a true woman" (*Neither Ballots nor Bullets,* 54).

3 Autobiography, 15:2.

4 Ibid., 33:7–8. Transcript of Diary, June 2, 1878. Blake spoke on the closing of a working women's hotel.

5 "Throughout the war Anna Dickinson lectured on woman's rights. Her standard speech on the subject, usually titled 'Rights and Wrongs of Women' or 'A Plea for Woman,' had helped to thrust her into the national limelight in 1860." After May 1864, Dickinson "ceased to speak on the presidential question, lecturing instead on 'the condition of women,' a favorite topic and a speech which [William Lloyd] Garrison described as 'the best and most eloquent I have ever heard from her lips'" (Venet, *Neither Ballots nor Bullets,* 142).

6 Frank Luther Mott, *History of American Magazines 1850–1865,* 5 vols. (Cambridge: Harvard University Press, 1930–68; vol. 2, 1938): 2:49.

7 Lori D. Ginzberg, *Women and the Work of Benevolence: Morality, Politics, and Class in the nineteenth-Century United States* (New Haven: Yale University Press, 1990): 213.

8 See Ellen Carol DuBois, *Feminism and Suffrage: The Emergence of an Independent Woman's Movement, 1848–1869* (Ithaca: Cornell University Press, 1978).

9 Angelina Grimké Letters on the Equality of The Sexes, and the Condition of Woman (Boston: Isaac Knapp, 1838): 18.

10 Henry Wright, *The Empire of the Mother over the Character and Destiny of the Race* (Boston: B. Marsh, 1870): 4.

11 As Nancy F. Cott notes, "For women who previously held no particular avenue of power of their own—no unique defense of their integrity and dignity—this [social power based on women's special female qualities] represented an advance": *The Bonds of Womanhood* (New Haven: Yale, University Press, 1977): 200.

12 "In basic ways, the women's organizations of the 1870's and 1880's continued the prewar tradition of women's benevolent and moral reform activity. Their leaders tended to stress women's unique virtues and special responsibility to the community, rather than the identity of men's and women's public roles, which had been the distinguishing argument of women's rights": Ellen Carol DuBois, Introduction, in DuBois, ed., *Elizabeth Cady Stanton/ Susan B. Anthony: Correspondence, Writings, Speeches* (New York: Schocken, 1981): 172.

13 E.C.S., "Miss Becker on the Difference in Sex," *The Revolution*, September 24, 1868, 184–185. The debate goes on. See Naomi Schor, "Reading Double: Sand's Difference," in Nancy K. Miller, ed., *The Poetics of Gender* (New York: Columbia University Press, 1986): 248–269, for a discussion of the biologically and historically based assumptions underlying the notion of radical difference between the sexes; and Elizabeth L. Berg, "Iconoclastic Moments: Reading the *Sonnets for Helene,* Writing the *Portuguese Letters,*" in the same volume, 208–221. Berg writes: "it is important to insist on the partial nature of sexual identity, to remind oneself that gender is not the only difference among people, nor even the essential difference, that the move to privilege gender as the primary defining characteristic of people participates in the same logic of oppression as the masculine philosophy one criticizes, for by that gesture one subsumes what is different from oneself (a different color, a different class, a different sexual orientation, a different belief) into a universal that denies that other even as it pretends to represent it. Feminism, if it is to escape the phallocentric, or egocentric, appropriation of all representation, must be partial; more than that, it must be a continual reminder that there is nothing impartial" (220).

14 Blake wrote that if all women were allowed employment, then no woman would "ever be reduced to the degrading necessity of marrying for a support—that is, selling herself because she sees with despair that, as society is at present constituted, and from the defects of her education, there is no hope of earning an honest livelihood" ("Social Condition," 382– 383, 387).

15 Stanton, "Speech to the McFarland-Richardson Protest Meeting," May 1869, reprinted in DuBois, ed., *Stanton/Anthony,* 129.

16 DuBois, *Stanton/Anthony,* 97.

17 Venet, *Neither Ballots nor Bullets,* 148. She continues: "The league marked an organizational transition as well. Whereas prewar women had formed regional antislavery, woman's rights, benevolent, and temperance societies, the league was a national feminist-abolitionist movement.

"The league's tactics also marked a transition. Women reformers in the early decades of the nineteenth century had emphasized moral suasion. By the time of the Civil War, some abolitionists had already broken with Garrison's approach, to advocate a political solution to the slavery question. The Woman's National Loyal League with its emphasis on political petitioning and its leaders' involvement in the philosophical issues of the 1864 presidential campaign demonstrated the continuing shift from the moral suasion of antebellum reform to the electoral and constitutional issues that would dominate the Reconstruction era" (148). In addition, "while encouraging male participation, the League was organized and directed by women. Its creation, therefore, was a development of tremendous significance in the history of the woman's rights movement" (136).

18 Edwin G. Burrows and Mike Wallace, *Gotham: A History of New York City to 1898* (New York: Oxford University Press, 1999): 970.

19 *Autobiography*, 15:3–4.

20 I follow here Iver Bernstein, *The New York City Draft Riots: Their Significance for American Society and Politics in the Age of the Civil War* (New York: Oxford University Press, 1990).

21 My thanks to Karen Dandurand for this information.

22 Richard Wightman Fox, *Trials of Intimacy: Love and Loss in the Beecher-Tilton Scandal* (Chicago: University of Chicago Press, 1999): 180.

23 *Frank Leslie's Illustrated Newspaper,* August 1, 1863: 293, 300–301.

24 All published in *Frank Leslie's Illustrated Newspaper:* Louisa May Alcott, "Pauline's Passion and Punishment," January 3 and 10, 1863; Julia Ward Howe, "The Darkened House," March 21, 1863, 407; Mrs. Lillie Devereux Umsted, "The Tenant of the Stone House," August 1, 1863, 297–298, and August 8, 1863, 313–314; L. Devereux Umsted, "The Gloved Lady," August 22, 1863, 345–346, and August 29, 1863, 361–362; Louisa May Alcott, "Enigmas," May 14, 1864, 117–119; Lillie Devereux Umsted, "A Visit to a Fortuneteller," July 2, 1864.

25 "The Gloved Lady," 346.

26 *Autobiography*, 15:5. For another account of such harassment, see Fannie Fern, *Ruth Hall and Other Writings,* ed. Joyce W. Warren (New Brunswick: Rutgers University Press, 1986).

27 Blake, *Zoe: or, True and False* (New York: American News Company, 1866): 15.

28 Ibid., 73.

29 "The Gloved Lady," 361.

30 *Autobiography*, 16:1.

31 Ibid., 2.

32 Ibid. Shelley's lines from "The Fugitives" read:

> One boat-cloak did cover
> The loved and the lover—
> Their blood beats one measure,
> They murmur proud pleasure
> Soft and low;—

33 "Visit to a Fortuneteller," 229.

34 *Autobiography*, 16:3.

35 Ibid., 5.

36 Ibid., 17:2.

37 Ibid., 3.

38 Ibid., 6.

39　Blake writes that she sold *Josephine Peyton* for $250 (Ibid., 18:1). Her daughter notes that *Josephine Peyton* and *Blanche Grafton* were sold for $200 each (*Champion of Women,* 62).

40　*Champion of Women,* 62.

41　Lillie Devereux Umsted Blake, *Forced Vows; or A Revengeful Woman's Fate* (New York: Beadle and Adams, 1870): 16.

42　Ibid., 14, 24.

43　Ibid., 16–17.

44　Autobiography, 17:6.

45　Transcription of Diary, May 9, 1866. In her autobiography, Blake dates her marriage as May 10, 1866 (18:1); although she dates her tenth anniversary as May 9. Katherine Devereux Blake uses the May 9 date in *Champion of Women,* 66. May 10 was the date that Frank Umsted died, and so, perhaps, would have been avoided as a wedding date. Grinfill Blake was twenty-six, the age at which Frank Umsted had died.

46　Autobiography, 18:2.

47　Transcript of Diary, May 13, 1866.

48　Autobiography, 18:2.

49　Ibid., 19:2.

50　Transcript of Diary, March 17, 1867.

51　Autobiography, 19:5–6.

52　Transcript of Diary, August 12, 1867.

53　Summary of Diary by Katherine Devereux Blake, fall 1867.

54　Autobiography, 20:3.

55　*Champion of Women,* 189.

56　Ibid., 72.

57　Burrows and Wallace, *Gotham,* 821, 971.

58　Ibid., 960.

59　*Champion of Women,* 71, 72.

60　Max O' Rell and Jack Allyn, *Jonathan and His Continent,* trans. Mrs. Paul Blouët (New York: Cassell, 1889): 84–85.

61　Autobiography, 21:1; *Champion of Women,* 73.

62　"Mrs. Elizabeth B. Phelps, a wealthy and practical philanthropist of New York City, in 1869 had purchased a large house at 49 East 23rd Street, near the National Academy of Design, which she dedicated to the 'Woman's Bureau.' She proposed to rent the rooms solely for the use of women's clubs and societies, and enterprises conducted by women" (*Champion of Women,* 75).

63　Ibid., 80. Grinfill was mischievously "incorrigible" on the topic of Susan B. Anthony. Katherine Devereux Blake writes that "one of my vivid memories is seeing [my mother] stop on the threshold of our door as they were leaving for a suffrage meeting. She put her hand gently on his arm, looking up at him pleadingly as she said, 'Now, Grinfill, promise me that you will be good tonight.' I can still see my gentle stepfather's smile as he looked down into her face and said, 'All right, Lillie dear, I'll promise, if you'll promise to keep that cantankerous, cross-eyed old maid's elbows out of my sides.'"

64　L.D.B., "'Women Do Not Want to Vote,'" *Revolution,* July 29, 1869, 51–52. "The *Revolution* gained in literary reputation; its contributors were among the best-known women writers of the day—Alice and Phoebe Cary, Anna Dickinson, Laura C. Bullard, Lillie Devereux Black, Paulina Wright Davis, Eleanor Kirk, Olive Logan, Mary Clemmer, and Matilda Joslyn Gage": Alma Lutz, *Created Equal: A Biography of Elizabeth Cady Stanton* (New York: John Day, 1940): 165.

65   Autobiography, 21:2–3.

66   Ibid., 4.

67   *Champion of Women*, 78.

68   Andrea Moore Kerr, *Lucy Stone: Speaking Out for Equality.* (New Brunswick: Rutgers University Press, 1992): 54.

69   Glenna Matthews, *The Rise of Public Woman: Woman's Power and Woman's Place in the United States, 1630–1970* (New York: Oxford University Press, 1992): 113. For a discussion of the social forces that mitigated against women finding their voices, see Barbara Bardes and Suzanne Gossett, *Declarations of Independence: Women and Political Power in Nineteenth Century American Fiction* (New Brunswick: Rutgers University Press, 1990): 38–69.

70   Autobiography, 21:8.

71   Ibid., 7.

72   It was not until the passage of the Fourteenth Amendment, which gave the vote to male former slaves, that the Constitution inserted the word "male" to specify the gender of the enfranchised. As historian Eleanor Flexner puts it in her standard account of the nineteenth-century women's rights movement, suffrage leaders were "appalled at the appearance, for the first time, of the word 'male' in the Constitution. Its three-fold use in the proposed Fourteenth Amendment, always in connection with the term 'citizen,' raised the issue of whether women were actually citizens of the United States": *Century of Struggle: The Woman's Rights Movement in the United States* (1959; Cambridge, Harvard University Press, 1975): 146.

73   My thanks to Carolyn L. Karcher for encouraging me to push this position further than I had. See her introductory material in *A Lydia Maria Child Reader* (Durham: Duke University Press, 1997): 342, and her *The First Woman in the Republic: A Cultural Biography of Lydia Maria Child* (Durham: Duke University Press, 1994).

74   Quoted by Eric Foner in *Reconstruction: America's Unfinished Revolution* (New York: Harper and Row, 1988): 313, in the course of his discussion of Train's affiliation with Stanton and Anthony.

75   Transcript of Diary, February 17, 1875.

76   Autobiography, 21:9; *Champion of Women*, 79.

77   Autobiography, 22:2.

78   Ibid., 3.

79   Transcript of Diary, October 2, 1880. She could not support the Democrats in 1872: "Horace Greeley!" she blurted out with disgust in her diary. "The man who had openly declared himself opposed to giving women any political equality! Whose paper had persistently misrepresented our movement and assailed our leaders, doing more than any other journal in America to discredit our cause. Horace Greeley for President!" (*Champion of Women*, 96). But, "while regretting his bigoted opposition to our reform," Blake did admire Greeley "for his remarkable talents and his kindly benevolence of character" (Autobiography, 6; Transcript of Diary, June 29, 1872).

80   Autobiography, 33:6.

81 Ibid. The *New Haven Register* wrote that "the change of heart is a welcome shift from the bulldozer tactics at Maple Cottage. There, Yale unleashed its police force on preservationists who tried to save the Trumbull Street house built in 1837 [*sic*]" (editorial, September 26, 1999).

82 Transcript of Diary, March 25, 1870.

83 *Autobiography*, 23:2. Kathleen Barry in *Susan B. Anthony: A Biography of a Singular Feminist* (New York: New York University Press, 1988) writes: "While Anthony and Stanton were campaigning in the West in the spring of 1870, several reformers met in New York City with Blackwell, Stone, and other American leaders to try to bring about a unification of the two organizations. Seventy-seven-year-old Lucretia Mott, who rarely left home anymore, traveled to New York hoping to resolve the problems" (210).

84 DuBois, *Feminism and Suffrage*, 164.

85 Autobiography, 23:7; Diary, October 23, 1870.

86 For biographical details on Woodhull and Claflin, I follow Emanie Sachs, *"The Terrible Siren," Victoria Woodhull* (New York: G. P. Putnam, 1928); Johanna Johnston, *Mrs. Satan: The Incredible Saga of Victoria C. Woodhull* (New York: G. P. Putnam, 1967); Mary Gabriel, *Notorious Victoria* (Chapel Hill: Algonquin Books, 1998); and Barbara Goldsmith, *Other Powers: The Age of Suffrage, Spiritualism, and the Scandalous Victoria Woodhull* (New York: Knopf, 1998). The latter two distort Woodhull's importance in the suffrage movement. See my review in *Resources for American Literary Study* 25, 2 (1999): 265–268.

87 Woodhull wrote an autobiography which achieved its goal of convincing her husband that she had been the leader of the American woman's rights movement, but it can be refuted on so many factual points that it should convince no one else. Even her husband, when on an 1892 visit to the United States hoping to find proof to refute the gossip that had followed his wife to England, encountered puzzling inconsistencies and little support for Woodhull's version of her life. He took her back to England.

88 *Champion of Women*, 88.

89 Harriet Beecher Stowe, *My Wife and I* (New York: Sully and Kleinteich, 1899): 8:268; reprint of 1871 edition, New York: J. B. Ford.

90 Autobiography, 33:1: During the winter of 1869–70, Blake spoke on "The Jury Question," "Woman's Sphere," "The Heroines of History" and on the Fourteenth and Fifteenth Amendments, in which she "carefully reviewed the argument afterwards advanced by others, that woman could claim the vote under these two amendments, and declared that [she] did not believe in the logic of any such claim." In *Champion of Women*, Katherine misstates her mother's position: "She reviewed in detail the arguments, and declared that under the two Amendments that gave suffrage to the Negro, woman also should claim the right to vote" (82).

91 Suzanne M. Marilley, *Woman Suffrage and the Origins of Liberal Feminism in the United States, 1820–1920* (Cambridge: Harvard University Press, 1996): 68. See also Rogers M. Smith, "'One United People': Second-Class Female Citizenship and the American Quest for Community," *Yale Journal of Law and the Humanities* 1 (1989): 229–293. Senator William Blair of New Hampshire sent Blake, with his compliments, the following clipping from a newspaper: "Lillie Deveraux [*sic*] Blake is weary of the argument that women should not be allowed to vote because they are not fitted for military service. They do not need to go to war

she points out; they can be represented by substitutes. And she adds that 'the male voters of the country thought enough of men who sent substitutes to the Civil War to elect one of them President not long ago, and to re-elect him, too.' It must be admitted that the point is well taken" (Senator Blair to LDB, November 23, 1895. Missouri Historical Society).

92   Autobiography, 24:5.

93   Transcript of Diary, May 13, 1871.

94   Ibid., May 24, 1877; Autobiography, 32:4–5.

95   Transcript of Diary, May 25, 1871.

96   Venet, *Neither Ballots nor Bullets*, 158.

97   *Champion of Women*, 93–94.

98   Transcript of Diary, January 25, 1872.

99   Ibid., April 18, 1872. *Champion of Women* (90) mistakenly dates this as spring of 1871. See below for discussion of the relationship between Theodore Tilton and Victoria Woodhull, which Tilton ended when she told him that she planned to "fabricate embarrassing stories about leaders of the women's movement whom Tilton admired." Theodore Tilton testified to this effect at the civil trial against Henry Ward Beecher as cited in Altima L. Waller, *Reverend Beecher and Mrs. Tilton: Sex and Class in Victorian America* (Amherst: University of Massachusetts Press, 1982): 136.

100   *Champion of Women*, 90–91.

101   Ibid., 91; Lutz, *Created Equal*, 221; Kerr, *Lucy Stone*, 171.

102   Kerr, *Lucy Stone*, 275 n. 50.

103   Transcript of Diary, May 8, 1872.

104   See Elisabeth Griffith, *In Her Own Right The Life of Elizabeth Cady Stanton* (New York: Oxford University Press, 1984): 151ff. Katherine Devereux Blake conflates details of the May 1871 and 1872 conventions, citing them as all taking place in 1871.

105   Transcript of Diary, May 9, 1872.

106   Lutz, *Created Equal*, 220.

107   See Barry, *Susan B. Anthony*, 242–245; Griffith, *In Her Own Right*, 151–152; Autobiography, 25:8.

108   Transcript of Diary, May 16, 1872.

109   Autobiography, 25:8.

110   Transcript of Diary, October 31, 1872.

111   Lutz, *Created Equal*, 221. In addition to the sources concerning Woodhull listed above, for the Beecher-Tilton scandal, I have relied on Waller's *Reverend Beecher and Mrs. Tilton* and Fox's *Trials of Intimacy*.

112   Theodore Tilton, "Victoria C. Woodhull: A Biographical Sketch," *Golden Age Tract No. 3* (New York, 1871).

113   Autobiography, 30:4. Blake's statement is perhaps truer than she knew. Altima Waller's thesis (*Reverend Beecher and Mrs. Tilton*) paints Congregationalism and Beecher's ideas concerning "affinity" and the "Gospel of Love" on the backdrop of the affair.

114   Transcript of Diary, February 26, 1872.

115   Susan B. Anthony. "Daybook" entry for April 5, 1874, Susan B. Anthony Collection, Library of Congress.

116 *Home Journal*, May 6, 1874; *New York World*, April 13, 1874. Virginia Blain et al., *The Feminist Companion to Literature in English* (New Haven: Yale University Press, 1990): 103; David Reynolds, *Beneath the American Renaissance* (Cambridge: Harvard University Press, 1989): 401.

117 Transcript of Diary, March 28 and April 26, 1874.

118 For work on this subject see especially Jean Fagan Yellin, *Women and Sisters: The Antislavery Feminists in American Culture* (New Haven: Yale University Press, 1989), and Karen Sánchez-Eppler, "Bodily Bonds: The Intersecting Rhetorics of Feminism and Abolition," in Shirley Samuels, ed., *The Culture of Sentiment: Race, Gender, and Sentimentality in Nineteenth-Century America.* (New York: Oxford University Press, 1992). While the connection between women and slavery was useful rhetorically for the middle-class white women in the suffrage movement, it should be pointed out that it gave a distorted view of the realities of slavery, and its use belies the troubled relationship between white woman-suffrage leaders and blacks. In this regard, see Angela Davis, *Women, Race, and Class* (London, 1982).

119 Autobiography, 40:6.

120 Ibid., 3.

121 Ibid., 4.

122 Ibid., 7; Transcript of Diary, May 18, 1882, and January 29, 1883.

123 *Champion of Women*, 173–176.

124 Lisa Duggan, "'Sexual Secrets Revealed!': Sex, Scandal, and Tragedy in the Popular Press, 1890–1900," paper read at the Organization of American Historians Annual Meeting. New York City, April 1986. As quoted by Matthews, *The Rise of Public Woman*, 3.

125 Marjit Stange, "Personal Property: Exchange Value and the Female Self in *The Awakening.*" *Genders* 5 (Summer 1989): 107.

126 As noted earlier, in her journals, Blake relates similar forms of harassment when she entered editorial offices to pick up her paychecks. For another account by a woman bookseller, see Anonymous, *Facts, by a Woman* (Oakland, Calif.: Pacific Press, 1881).

127 As Susan Gubar writes, "cross-dressing becomes a way of addressing and re-dressing the inequities of culturally-defined categories of masculinity and femininity." Susan Gubar, "Blessings in Disguise: Cross-Dressing as Re-Dressing for Female Modernists," *The Pushcart Prize* 7 (New York: Avon, 1982–1983): 479. In her novel, Blake could deal in a most effective way with the issue of cross-dressing, even if, in real life, she treated Dr. Mary Walker, who always wore male clothes, with intolerance.

128 The caged bird became an increasingly popular image in late nineteenth-century writing; for examples see Kate Chopin, *The Awakening*, Frank Norris's *McTeague*, and Mary Wilkins Freeman's "A New England Nun." For a brief history of the imagery of the caged bird, moving from French Rococo erotic painting, in which the cage signified secure possession (from the male's perspective) through eighteenth-century political ideology, in which the uncaged bird signified freedom, see Lorenz Eitner, "Cages, Prisons, and Captives in Eighteenth-Century Art," in Karl Kroeber and William Walling, eds., *Images of Romanticism: Verbal and Visual Affinities* (New Haven: Yale University Press, 1978): 13–38. See also Victor Brombert, "The Happy Prison: A Recurring Romantic Metaphor," in David Thorburn and Geoffrey Hartman, eds., *Romanticism: Vistas, Instances, Continuities* (Ithaca: Cornell University Press, 1973): 62–79, for a discussion of the cage as a nostalgic place of se-

curity and a metaphor of interiority, and Sharon M. Harris. *Rebecca Harding Davis and American Realism* (Philadelphia: University of Pennsylvania Press, 1991).

129 In their critique of patriarchal authority, contemporary feminists often center on the gaze, claiming that "woman's place in culture is constructed by man's view of her, by a look that emanating from his position of self-identity seeks to circumscribe hers." Mary Ann Doane, "Woman's Stake: Filming the Female Body," *October* (Summer 1981): 34. For other discussions of gazing see E. Ann Kaplan. "Is the Gaze Male?" in Marilyn Pearsall, ed., *Women and Values: Readings in Recent Feminist Philosophy* (Belmont, Calif.: Wadsworth, 1986): 231; John Berger, *Ways of Seeing* (London: Penguin, 1972); Nancy K. Miller, *Subject to Change: Reading Feminist Writing* (New York: Columbia University Press, 1988), especially chapter 7, "Performances of the Gaze"; and Mary Devereaux, "Oppressive Texts, Resisting Readers and the Gendered Spectator: The *New* Aesthetics," *Journal of Aesthetics and Art Criticism* 48 (Fall 1990): 337–347.

130 *Home Journal,* May 6, 1874.

131 DuBois, *Stanton/Anthony,* 193.

132 James Parton, ed., *Fanny Fern, A Memorial Volume* (New York: Carleton, 1873): 408–409.

133 Gilman, in fact, knew Blake. There is evidence that she was entertained at Blake's home on at least one occasion (Transcript of Diary, December 11, 1896: "Mrs. Charlotte Perkins Stetson was here"); she collaborated with Blake on the defense of Elizabeth Cady Stanton's *Woman's Bible* against an NAWSA resolution denouncing it (see Chapter 6); and Blake and Gilman shared billing for a two-part article entitled "The Successful Home." Side by side on the page, Blake wrote on "The Office of the Father," while Gilman wrote on "The Office of the Mother": *Success 7,* 127 (December 1904): 802.

Chapter Six

1 Quoted by Thomas Woody, *A History of Women's Education in the United States,* (New York: Science Press, 1929): 1:88–89. Original source: James Orton: *Liberal Education of Women* (New York: A. S. Barnes, 1873): 321.

2 Charles W. Eliot, "Woman's Work and Woman's Wages," *North American Review* (August 1882): 14.

3 Edward H. Clarke, *Sex in Education; or A Fair Chance for Girls* (1873; Boston: James R. Osgood, 1875): 37, 39, 87.

4 Quoted in ibid., 106.

5 Ibid., 112–113, 91–93.

6 S. Weir Mitchell, *Wear and Tear or Hints for the Overworked* (1872; 8th ed., Philadelphia: J.B. Lippincott, 1897): 56.

7 Clarke, *Sex in Education,* 157.

8 From their inceptions, both institutions also admitted blacks. Oberlin was founded in 1834, Butler in 1855.

9 Morgan Dix, S.T.D., *Lectures on the Calling of a Christian Woman and Her Training to Fulfil It* (New York: D. Appleton, 1883): 72, 78.

10 Marian Churchill White, *A History of Barnard College* (New York: Columbia University

Press, 1954): 12. Women are referred to as "girls" throughout this book, although male students are "men."

11   Annie Nathan Meyer, *Woman's Work in America* (New York: H. Holt, 1891): 42.

12   Annie Nathan Meyer, "Beginnings of Barnard," *Columbia University Quarterly* (September 1935): 296–320.

13   Alice Duer Miller and Susan Myers, *Barnard College: The First Fifty Years* (New York: Columbia University Press, 1939): 8.

14   Blake was never an official member of Sorosis, although she worked and socialized with many of its members and invariably attended its events as a guest. Although she never explains her lack of membership, it was most likely a result of Charlotte Wilbour's hostility. Wilbour was the founder of the club and served as its president for many years.

15   White, *A History of Barnard College*, 10.

16   [No author], *A History of Barnard College* (New York: Barnard College, 1964).

17   Meyer, *Woman's Work in America*, 44.

18   Meyer, "Beginnings of Barnard," 307.

19   *Woman's Place To-Day*, 6.

20   Elizabeth Cady Stanton, Susan B. Anthony, and Matilda Joslyn Gage, eds., *History of Woman Suffrage, 1876–1885* (Rochester, N.Y.: Susan B. Anthony, 1886): 3:436.

21   Transcript of Diary, April 7, 1883.

22   *Champion of Women*, 154.

23   Elinore Hughes Partridge, ed., *American Prose and Criticism, 1820–1900* (Detroit: Gale, 1983): 192–193.

24   Transcript of Diary, March 4, 1883.

25   Meyer, "Beginnings of Barnard," 309.

26   Ibid.

27   Meyer, *Woman's Work in America*, 44. She quotes from herself here, with a note "See article by Annie Nathan Meyer in *University*, February 22, 1888."

28   Meyer, *Woman's Work in America*, 42.

29   *Woman's Journal*, December 1, 1888, 383. Blake's granddaughter, Lillie Devereux Robinson, entered Barnard in the fall of 1905.

30   Transcript of Diary, October 17, 1873.

31   Ibid., May 26, 1881: "Went to the convention to make a report for delegates. It was cut out by pressure. Miss Anthony announced me, Mrs. Hooker stepped in front of her and announced Mrs. Lockwood; Mrs. Snell, Mrs. Lozier, Mrs. Saxon and I held indignation meeting over the matter."

32   Autobiography, 30:1–2.

33   Blake includes this speech in ibid., 26:4–5.

34   Transcript of Diary, October 7, 1872.

35   Autobiography, 26:6.

36   Ibid., 6–7.

37   Transcript of Diary, November 14, 1872: "Mrs. Wilbour was there before me and with her a regular ring who, by ballot, put her in as president, Mrs. Hull, chairman of the Executive Committee, and made me corresponding secretary. I am glad enough to be rid of responsibility, but was rather provoked at the way in which the thing was done."

38 Ibid., February 13, 1873.

39 *Albany Express,* February 19, 1873. Reprinted in full, in *Champion of Women,* 101–105, and in Autobiography, 27:2–7.

40 *Champion of Women,* 103.

41 Transcript of Diary, February 19, 1873.

42 Quoted in *Champion of Women,* 106.

43 Transcript of Diary, January 25, 1874.

44 Autobiography, 27:5–6.

45 Transcript of Diary, October 16, 1879; Autobiography, 34:6.

46 Autobiography, 40:2.

47 Transcript of Diary, January 19, 1882.

48 Ibid., December 22, 1886.

49 Autobiography, 35:2.

50 Autobiography, 37:8.

51 Ibid., 38:2.

52 Transcript of Diary, November 3, 1880.

53 *Proceedings of the Thirty-Second Annual Convention of the National American Woman Suffrage Association Held at Washington, D.C., February 1900,* ed. Rachel Foster Avery (Philadelphia, n.d.): 28.

54 Transcript of Diary, October 10, 1886.

55 Ibid., October 28, 1886.

56 Ibid., October 24, 1882.

57 Ibid., October 3, 1882.

58 Ibid., November 13, 1875.

59 Ibid., October 6, 21, and 22, 1882.

60 Ibid., October 26 and November 2, 1882; Autobiography, 40:19.

61 Lillie Devereux Blake, "Lost in a Blizzard." Located in scrapbook dated 1893, edited in text, Blake Archives, Missouri Historical Society.

62 Transcript of Diary, March 20, 1881. See also Autobiography, 39:2–7.

63 Autobiography, 30:5.

64 Ibid., 31:8.

65 *Champion of Women,* 120, 126.

66 Autobiography, 34:1.

67 Ibid., 41:1.

68 Ibid., 44:2.

69 Transcript of Diary, June 9 and 10 and August 11, 1889; June 17, 1897; June 21 and 29, 1899.

70 Transcript of Diary, November 26 and December 21, 1886. The amount is corrected in hand to $80,000 (Autobiography, 44:4).

71 Transcript of Diary, December 22, 1886.

72 Ibid., January 2, 1887.

73 Autobiography, 45:6.

74 Transcript of Diary, appended after December 30, 1888, entry.

75 Autobiography, 46:1.

76 *Champion of Women,* 170.

77   LDB, *A Daring Experiment* (New York: Lovell, Coryell, 1892).

78   Susan B. Anthony to Lillie Devereux Blake, December 9, 1882, Missouri Historical Society.

79   Anthony to Blake, November 18, 1885, Missouri Historical Society.

80   Transcript of Diary, January 23, 1883.

81   *Champion of Women*, 154.

82   Anthony to Blake, June 28 and December 19, 1882; July 7, 1884; March 16, 1886; No date, 1889; all at Missouri Historical Society.

83   I follow here Harriet Robinson Shattuck, "Notebook re: union of National and American Woman Suffrage Associations by HRS," January 1889, Harriet Hanson Robinson/Harriet Robinson Shattuck Collection, Schlesinger Library, Radcliffe College.

84   Autobiography, 47:1.

85   Susan B. Anthony to Rachel Foster Avery, November 11, 1887, Anthony-Avery Papers, University of Rochester Archives.

86   Ellen DuBois, *Elizabeth Cady Stanton/Susan B. Anthony: Correspondence, Writings, Speeches* (New York: Schocken, 1981): 181.

87   "The 'nonpartisan' posture that Anthony helped to shape remained the official strategy of the NAWSA for the next thirty years, and was carried over, after the vote was won, into the NAWSA's successor, the League of Women Voters" (ibid., 181).

88   Elizabeth Cady Stanton to Lillie Devereux Blake, undated, 1900, Missouri Historical Society.

89   Transcript of Diary, February 18, 1890.

90   Ibid., June 11, 1893.

91   Ibid., November 17, 1893.

92   Ibid., December 21, 1893.

93   Ibid., December 22, 1893.

94   Sally Roesch Wagner writes, "One of the few women who stood beside Gage when she took on her unpopular battle against the Church was Lillie Devereux Blake, one of the major figures in the NWSA" ("Matilda Joslyn Gage: Forgotten Feminist," Internet essay, SWagner711 @aol.com).

95   Transcript of Diary, January 24–27, 1896.

96   Lois W. Banner writes that "the new generation of suffragists rejected anticlerical action as politically inexpedient. But in their overwhelming quest for suffrage, they temporized on religious as well as on other issues, making feminism the conservative and largely ineffective force it would become once suffrage was achieved after the First World War": Lois W. Banner, *Elizabeth Cady Stanton A Radical for Woman's Rights* (Boston: Little, Brown, 1980): 165.

97   Kathi L. Kern. "Rereading Eve: Elizabeth Cady Stanton and *The Woman's Bible*, 1885–1896," *Women's Studies* 19 (1991): 382.

98   Ibid., 378.

99   *New York Times* Obituary, March 11, 1896.

100 Transcript of Diary, April 19, 1896: "Recently Mrs. Catt asked me if I would go to Delaware to speak in May. Miss Anthony asked me last fall if I would take charge of the campaign there, and I said yes. Now I have a letter from Mrs. Catt saying that she is going in my place! I am troubled about this as I would rather be friends with her than have a quarrel. I have

written to Miss Anthony." In a letter to Blake dated April 16, 1896, Catt insists that Blake's omission from the Delaware campaign was the result of a misunderstanding. Missouri Historical Society.

101 Blake to Anthony, April 2, 1896, Missouri Historical Society.

102 Typescript of letter from Anthony to Blake, February 27, 1888, Missouri Historical Society. The date on the typescript is probably incorrect. Contents of the letter place it sometime between 1873 and 1875.

103 Anthony to Blake, April 9, 1896, Missouri Historical Society.

104 Transcript of Diary, January 5, 1897: "The Annual Convention of the National Suffrage Association was [*sic*] held this year at Des Moines, Iowa. I have not been invited to speak and do not intend to go. It is very sad that jealousy should so control my colleagues that they will not do me justice."

105 Rachel Foster Avery to Lillie Devereux Blake, March 18, 1896, Missouri Historical Society.

106 See Avery to Blake, February 20 and 28, and March 18, 1896, Missouri Historical Society.

107 Anthony to Avery, March 3, 1897, Anthony-Avery Papers, University of Rochester Archives.

108 Anthony to Blake, January 13, 1898, Missouri Historical Society.

109 Minutes of the Suffrage Convention, April 27–May 4, 1899. *Proceedings of the Thirty-First Annual Convention of the National American Woman Suffrage Association, Grand Rapids, Michigan, April 27 to May 3, 1899,* ed. Rachel Foster Avery (Warren, Ohio, n.d.): 46.

110 Transcript of Diary, May 21, 1899: "I have just received an insult from the Business Committee of the NAWSA. The day after I read my fine report at Grand Rapids they destroyed my committee!!!"

111 Ibid., May 24, 1899: "I have written letters of protest to Miss Anthony and other leading officers, and this morning had an interview with Mrs. Catt. She says the destruction of the committee was Miss Anthony's doing. I am so indignant."
   May 25, 1899: "Alas, alas!"
   June 2, 1899: "I am continuously indignant about the insult at Grand Rapids. Mrs. Catt says S.B.A. did it. She sailed for Europe yesterday. I had intended to give her a sendoff, but not now!"

112 *Champion of Women,* 197.

113 Avery to Blake, June 5, 1899, Missouri Historical Society.

114 *Proceedings of the Thirty-Second Annual Convention of the National American Woman Suffrage Association Held at Washington, D.C. February 1990,* ed. Rachel Foster Avery (Philadelphia, n.d.). The minutes for February 7, 1900, read:
   The recording Secretary read a letter received in regard to the vote of the Business Committee after the last National Convention, by which they elected Laura M. Johns as Committee on Legislation, in place of Lillie Devereux Blake and the other former members of that Committee. In this letter, Mrs. Blake claimed that this action on the part of the Business Committee had been unconstitutional.
   The Corresponding Secretary, Rachel Foster Avery, read from the published minutes the record of the formation of the Committee on Legislation, showing that this Committee was originally created by the Executive Committee, not by the Convention, and that after the last National Convention, the Executive Committee elected no Committee

on Legislation, but, before adjournment, voted to refer all unfinished business to the Business Committee.

Mrs. Blake, after hearing the record, acquiesced in the constitutionality of the action. (14)

115 Henry B. Blackwell to Lillie Devereux Blake, May 19, 1899, Missouri Historical Society.

116 Alice Stone Blackwell to Lillie Devereux Blake, July 27, 1899, Missouri Historical Society.

117 Mary Seymour Howell to Lillie Devereux Blake, June 18, 1899, Missouri Historical Society.

118 Josephine K. Henry to Lillie Devereux Blake, May 25, 1899, and Martha R. Almy to Lillie Devereux Blake, May 3, 1899, Missouri Historical Society.

119 Marilla M. Picker to Lillie Devereux Blake, May 31, 1899, Missouri Historical Society.

120 Stanton to Blake, June 14, 1899, Missouri Historical Society.

121 Susan B. Anthony to Clara Colby, January 10, 1900. Clara Colby Collection.

122 Banner, *Elizabeth Cady Stanton,* 171–172.

123 Washington *Evening Star,* February 14, 1900. Patricia G. Holland and Ann D. Gordon, eds., *The Papers of Elizabeth Cady Stanton and Susan B. Anthony* (Wilmington, Del.: Scholarly Resources, Inc., 1992).

124 Quoted in *Champion of Women,* 210.

125 As Blake wrote: "I have been hard at work on a history of what I have done during the years from '84 to 1900, for Mrs. Harper who is getting up the fourth volume of Women Suffrage. As Miss Anthony is directing its writing, I shall probably have small recognition" (Transcript of Diary, June 28, 1900).

126 Lillie Devereux Blake to Henry Blackwell, June 13, 1900, Missouri Historical Society. ". . . and after the election of the new President not the slightest request was made to me to give any aid in any direction of active work. For this I do not in the least blame Mrs. Catt, for whom I have only the kindest feelings; it is a question of radical difference of views as to policy between us. Both she and Miss Anthony openly declare that they do not believe in trying to modify existing laws for the benefit of women."

127 "The New York Legislative League Auxiliary to the National Legislative League," Flyer, n.d., Missouri Historical Society.

128 Stanton to Blake, shortly before March 27, 1900, Missouri Historical Society.

129 Autobiography, fifth page of the unpaginated and unnumbered volume of 1895.

130 Transcript of Diary: August 17, 1900; July 19, 1901; October 1, 1901.

131 Phyllis Cole, "The Nineteenth-Century Women's Rights Movement and the Canonization of Margaret Fuller," *ESO: A Journal of the American Renaissance* 44 (1998): 27.

132 Transcript of Diary, July 27 and August 8, 1907.

133 LDB, "Roses and Death," *Short Stories* 29, 1 (January 1898): 98–101.

Chapter Seven

1 Virginia Woolf, *A Room of One's Own* (1929; New York: Harcourt Brace Jovanovich, 1957): 8. Daniel Shealy in conversation related the Houghton staff's statement.

2 As Sandra Gilbert and Susan Gubar put it in *No Man's Land,* vol. 1 (New Haven: Yale University Press, 1988): "the emergence of modern male literary discourse . . . can be seen as an attempt to construct *his* story of a literary history in which women play no part" (154). See

also Nina Baym, "Melodramas of Beset Manhood: How Theories of American Fiction Exclude Women," *American Quarterly* 33 (1981): 123–139, rpt. Baym, *Feminism and American Literary History: Essays* (New Brunswick: Rutgers University Press, 1992): 3–18; Paul Lauter, "Race and Gender in the Shaping of the American Literary Canon: A Case Study from the Twenties," *Feminist Studies* 9, 3 (1983): 435–463, and his *Canons and Contexts* (New York: Oxford University Press, 1991): 22–47; Jane Tompkins, *Sensational Designs: The Cultural Work of American Fiction 1790–1860* (New York: Oxford University Press, 1985); Amy Kaplan, *The Social Construction of American Literary Realism* (Chicago: University of Chicago Press, 1988); and Joanne Dobson, "The American Renaissance Reenvisioned," in Joyce W. Warren, ed., *The (Other) American Traditions* (New Brunswick: Rutgers University Press, 1993): 164–182. Charlene Avallone, in "What American Renaissance? The Gendered Genealogy of a Critical Discourse," *PMLA* 112 (October 1997): 1102–1120, traces the "encoding of gender discrimination in renaissance aesthetics" (1104) from Charles Richardson's *American Literature, 1607–1885* (1886, 1888) to F. O. Matthiessen's *American Renaissance* (1941). Michael Davitt Bell, in "Gender and American Realism in *The Country of the Pointed Firs*," in June Howard, ed., *New Essays on "The Country of the Pointed Firs"* (Cambridge: Cambridge University Press, 1994): 61–80, discusses "the heavily gendered assumptions at the heart of American realist thinking" (66); June Howard in her introduction traces the development of an elite New England literary culture in the 1850s under the commercial aegis of the publisher James T. Fields (later editor of the *Atlantic Monthly*), the masculinized American tradition after the Civil War, the process of canonization by academic critics of the 1920s, and the reconsiderations of the canon which began in the 1960s. Joyce W. Warren and Margaret Dickie's collection, *Challenging Boundaries: Gender and Periodization* (Athens: University of Georgia Press, 2000), explores how the structure of periodization tends to eliminate woman from the canon.

3   In "The American Renaissance Reenvisioned" (p. 169), Joanne Dobson writes: "*Sentimental* is perhaps the most overworked, imprecise, misapplied, emotionally loaded, inadequately understood term in American literary classification. Yet in actuality it denotes a major imaginative mode of nineteenth-century American literary expression. Not exclusively a woman's expressive mode, in American literature in particular it has been so defined. As Judith Fetterley says about conventional critical thinking, 'One might well ask whether "sentimental" is not in fact a code word for female subject and woman's point of view and particularly for the expression of women's feelings' [*Provisions: A Reader from 19th-Century American Women* (Bloomington: Indiana University Press, 1985): 25]. If this is indeed so, and I think it clearly is, then the consistently pejorative treatment of the word in conventional critical usage indicates a reaction linked to what Susan Harris defines as a fundamental 'revulsion from the feminine' in modern criticism [*19th-Century American Women's Novels: Interpretive Strategies* (New York: Cambridge University Press, 1990): 2–8]. A bias toward masculine experience, as Nina Baym convincingly documented, has served to structure our literary priorities and preferences ["Melodramas of Beset Manhood"]. In addition, a gendered anxiety equating 'emotional' with 'feminine' and nervously rejecting both has also operated as a primary shaping factor in the construction of the American literary canon."

4   Listen to the rhetoric of Alfred Habegger's account in *Gender, Fantasy, and Realism in American Literature* (New York: Columbia University Press, 1982): Realism "bore in art an adver-

sary or corrective relation to a major type of novel, women's fiction. Women's fiction was characterized by an idealized heroine, a strong appeal to the reader's fantasies or daydreams, a great deal of 'domestic' social and psychological detail, and a plot based on love interest that led up to a decisive speech—'I love you.' . . . Realism was an analysis of quiet desperation. Attempting to break out, and to help their readers break out, of a suffocated, half-conscious state, Howells and James had to be circumstantial. . . . But why would James and Howells be so concerned to oppose popular women's fiction? Why would a high mimetic art go to the trouble to be so aware of, so responsive to, an often cheap fantasy art? . . . Full of sober and comprehensive assessments, Howells and James were very different from the euphoric women's novels that preceded them. These earlier books were full of extreme highs and lows, a passionate brooding over the problem of being female. The male realists tried to deal with this and other problems more dispassionately" (106–107).

5   Habegger writes: "*Sissy! Baby! Crybaby!* These taunting insults, so inadmissable in civilized life, are the key to many aspects of masculine American male culture" (ibid., 57).

6   Josephine Donovan writes that we have "a cultural identity and a canon that have been narrowly defined according to the chauvinistic thematics of male culture. It is one that privileges (in the case of American literature) hybristic juvenile fantasies of escape and redemption through violence, notions that still pervade popular culture. Reconceiving American literature, and indeed Western culture, to include women's masterpieces might help to establish new bases for that culture's identity, away from one characterized by dominance, escapist violence, competition, and exploitation toward one governed by a sense of humility, humanity, and compassion, born of the realization that . . . the deaths and resurrections of everyday life, the wresting of story from infirmity, are the stuff of great literature" ("Women's Masterpieces," in Warren and Dickie, eds., *Challenging Boundaries*, 36).

7   Baym, "Melodramas of Beset Manhood," *Feminism and American Literary History*, 16–17. For readings of women's fiction as upholding the status quo, see especially Alexander Cowie, "The Vogue of the Domestic Novel, 1850–1870," *South Atlantic Quarterly* 41 (October 1942); Henry Nash Smith, "The Scribbling Woman and the Cosmic Success Story," *Critical Inquiry* 1 (September 1974): 47–70; and Barbara Welter, "The Cult of True Womanhood: 1820–1860," *American Quarterly* 18 (Summer 1966): 151–174.

8   See David S. Reynolds, *Beneath the American Renaissance* (Cambridge: Harvard University Press, 1989): 338.

9   See Philip Fisher, *Hard Facts: Setting and Form in the American Novel* (New York: Oxford University Press, 1987). Other critics who argue that nineteenth-century women's fiction was not simply reflecting and upholding the status quo include: Helen Waite Papashvily, *All the Happy Endings: A Study of the Domestic Novel in America, the Women Who Wrote It, the Women Who Read It, in the Nineteenth Century* (New York: Harper & Brothers, 1956), who contends that the domestic novelists strenuously rejected the status quo; Ann Douglas Wood, "The Scribbling Women and Fanny Fern: Why Women Wrote," *American Quarterly* 23 (Spring 1971): 3–24; Dee Garrison, "Immoral Fiction in the Late Victorian Library," *American Quarterly* 28 (Spring 1976): 71–89; and Janice Radway, "The Utopian Impulse in Popular Literature: Gothic Romances and 'Feminist' Protest," *American Quarterly* 33 (1981): 140–162. Mary Kelley, "The Sentimentalists: Promise and Betrayal in the Home," *Signs* 4 (Spring 1979):

434–446, differs with Papashvily, Wood, and Garrison, arguing that the sentimentalists upheld the concept of an ideal domestic life, but portrayed its loss, and, thus, the genre is "expressive of a dark vision of nineteenth-century America" (446), while Joanne Dobson, "The Hidden Hand: Subversion of Cultural Ideology in Three Mid-Nineteenth-Century American Women's Novels," *American Quarterly* 38 (1986): 223–242, calls this fiction a "conflicted literature" which sincerely affirms the domestic ideology of the time even as it is "shot through with indications of dissatisfaction and dissent" (226).

10 Fred Lewis Pattee, *The Feminine Fifties* (New York: D. Appleton-Century, 1940): 3–4.

11 See Reynolds's discussion of the antididactic tendency of the "dark-temperance mode" of nineteenth-century reform writing as well as the general "divestment of didacticism" in the nineteenth-century's move toward secularism (*Beneath the American Renaissance*, 54–91).

12 Alexander Cowie, *The Rise of the American Novel* (New York: American Publishing, 1951): "The voice of our prose has lowered its pitch and become more husky. The sentence is now shorter, with a lower centre of gravity. Understatement and deliberate de-emphasis have become habitual with many writers. Befrilled locutions are out; diction has gone into denim" (754).

13 LDB, *A Daring Experiment and Other Stories* (New York: Lovell, Coryell, 1892): 352.

14 G. R. Thompson and Eric Carl Link, *Neutral Ground: New Traditionalism and the American Romance Controversy* (Baton Rouge: Louisiana State University Press, 1999): 174.

15 See Joan Kelly, "Did Women Have a Renaissance?" *Women, History, and Theory* (Chicago: University of Chicago Press, 1984): 19–50; Annette Kolodny, "The Integrity of Memory: Creating a New Literary History of the United States," *American Literature* 57 (1985): 291–307; Elaine Hedges, "Introduction: Repositionings: Multiculturalism, American Literary History, and the Curriculum," *American Literature* 66 (1994); and Joyce W. Warren, "The Challenge of Women's Periods," in Warren and Dickie, eds., *Challenging Boundaries,* ix–xxiv.

16 (New York: Sheldon, 1872): 264.

17 *Knickerbocker Monthly* (May 1863): 385.

18 As Carolyn G. Heilbrun comments: "To transform the private ambition to the public record is always difficult for women; if one can speak on behalf of an oppressed or despised group, one is more easily encouraged by that fact to take up the pen of self-revelation. To say this is not to try to anoint the woman of 'privilege' with the stigma of suffering. Rather it is to suggest that the very fact of 'privilege' has prevented the women who supposedly 'enjoy' it from acknowledging or recording their own profound dissatisfaction": "Non-Autobiographies of 'Privileged' Women: England and America," in Bella Brodzki and Celeste Schenck, eds., *Life/Lines: Theorizing Women's Autobiography* (Ithaca: Cornell University Press, 1988): 75–76).

Chapter Eight

1 Lillie's daughter Bessie and her husband John Beverly Robinson resided in St. Louis during the years that he was professor of architecture at Washington University. Her granddaughter gave Blake's papers to the Historical Society.

2 Paul Rosenblatt, *Bitter, Bitter Tears: Nineteenth-Century Diarists and Twentieth-Century Grief Theories* (Minneapolis: University of Minnesota Press, 1983): vii–viii.

A Blake Bibliography

Diaries and Biographies

Diary: Blake's handwritten diaries were begun when she was thirteen and continued for most of her life. Those extant include the first, which runs from February 22, 1847, to May 31, 1847, followed by a six-year gap; another dated August 12, 1853–August 12, 1854, is followed by a five-and-a-half-year gap until 1860; 1860 through May 1870, followed by a gap of three decades; and from 1900 through September 1903. The diaries are housed in the Missouri Historical Society and are quoted with permission.

Transcripts of Diary: In preparation for her biography of her mother, Blake's daughter Katherine Devereux Blake made typescripts of some of her mother's diaries. The typescripts run from 1859 through 1907. Unfortunately, it appears that many of the handwritten diaries were discarded after the typescripts were made. The diary transcripts are housed in the Missouri Historical Society and are quoted with permission.

Autobiography: Blake's Autobiography is an unfinished, unpublished typescript begun in 1873. There are forty-eight numbered chapters, one subsequent unnumbered chapter, and fragments of additional unfinished chapters. It includes excerpts from her diaries, both those which are extant and those no longer existing. It is housed in the Missouri Historical Society and is quoted with permission.

Champion of Women Katherine Devereux Blake and Margaret Louise Wallace, (New York: Fleming H. Revell, 1943). The biography includes excerpts from LDB's diaries, both extant and no longer existing.

Books

A Daring Experiment. New York: Lovell, Coryell, 1892.

Fettered for Life. New York: Sheldon, 1874, 1885; rpt. New York: Feminist Press, 1996.

Forced Vows. New York: Beadle and Adams, 1870.

Ireton Standish, Weekly Mercury, 1866–1867.

Rockford. New York: Carleton, 1863.

Southwold. New York: Rudd and Carleton, 1859.

Woman's Place To-Day. New York: J. W. Lovell, 1883.

Zoe. American News Company, 1866.

Pamphlet

The Fables. New York: Oliver J. Blaber, 1879.

Periodical Publications

FICTION

"Brothers by Birth—Foes in the Field." *Forney's War Press,* March 21, 1863, 1.

"Carrying False Colors." *Forney's War Press,* May 3, 1862, 1, 8.

"A Clap of Thunder." *New York Ledger,* January 27, 1866, 3.

"The Dead Letter." *New York Weekly Mercury,* November 11, 1865, 3.

"Found Drowned." *New York Weekly Mercury,* October 5, 1867, 4.

"In Prison." *New York Weekly Mercury,* May 27, 1865, 6–7; June 3, 1865, 5–6.

"John Owen's Appeal." *Harpers New Monthly Magazine* (December 1860): 72–81.

"Life on the Mountains." *Forney's War Press,* October 24, 1862, 1; November 1, 1862, 1; November 8, 1862, 1, 8.

"A Lonely House." *Atlantic Monthly* (January 1861): 40–51.

"Lost in a Blizzard." *The Press* (1893): clipping in Blake archives, Missouri Historical Society.

"A Midsummer Sail." *Forney's War Press,* September 20, 1862, 1, 8.

"My Cruise in the Dream." *Home Journal,* November 29, 1862, 1; December 6, 1862, 1.

"My Last Conquest." *Harpers Weekly,* November 14, 1857, 734 ff.

"The Rescued Fugitives." *Forney's War Press,* March 22, 1862, 4.

"A Romance of the Battle of Fair Oaks." *Forney's War Press,* July 26, 1862, 1, 8.

"Roses and Death." *Short Stories* (January 1898): 98–101.

"Shot Through the Heart: A Tragedy of Fredericksburgh." *Knickerbocker Monthly* (May 1863): 413–21.

"The Slave's Revenge." *Forney's War Press,* November 15, 1862, 1.

"Ten Years' Devotion." *New York Sunday Times,* August 22, 1875, 1.

"The Tenant of the Stone House." *Frank Leslie's Illustrated Newspaper,* August 1, 1863, 297–298; August 8, 1863, 313–314.

"Tessie's Merry Christmas." *Albany Sunday Press,* December 23, 1883: clipping in Blake archives, Missouri Historical Society.

"A Tragedy of the Mammoth Cave." *Knickerbocker* (February 1858): 112–121.

"The Veteran's Last Parade." *Sunday Press,* December 25, 1882: clipping in Blake archives, Missouri Historical Society.

"A Visit to a Fortuneteller." *Frank Leslie's Illustrated Newspaper,* July 2, 1864, 229–230.

"Who Won the Prize." *Saturday Evening Post,* October 21, 1871, 2.

"A Wild Night Ride." *Forney's War Press,* March 1, 1862, 1.

"Are Women Fairly Paid?" *Forum* (October 1886): 201–211.

"Brutality." *Evening Journal,* November 21, 1899: clipping in Blake archives, Missouri Historical Society.

"The Case of Susan B. Anthony." *New York Times,* May 31, 1873, 5.

"Co-Education." *New York Times,* December 24, 1899, 23.

"Dr. Hammond's Estimate of Woman." *North American Review* (November 1883): 495–501.

"The Duties of the Father." *New York Times,* April 11, 1905, 10.

"Forgotten Belles." *Fashions* (May 1898): 152–153.

"Jailoress Jones." *Era* (March 1876): clipping in Blake archives, Missouri Historical Society.

"Kate Cobb's Fate." *Evening Telegram,* January 25, 1879: clipping in Blake archives, Missouri Historical Society.

"Kate Southern." *Evening Telegram,* May 20, 1878: clipping in Blake archives, Missouri Historical Society.

"Ladies in the White House." *Evening Telegram,* March 7, 1885: clipping in Blake archives, Missouri Historical Society.

"Legislative Advice." *Woman Suffrage Leaflet 7* (May 1895).

"Looking Backward to Two Christmas Days of Long Ago," *New York Times,* December 18, 1904: clipping in Blake archives, Missouri Historical Society.

"Martha Washington and Other Notable Women of the Revolutionary Period." *Business Woman's Journal* 1 (May–June 1889): 1, 74–76.

"Memory of the Civil War." *New York Press,* June 12, 1898: clipping in Blake archives, Missouri Historical Society.

"Needed Reforms: Seats for Shop Girls." *Christian Union,* February 19, 1882: clipping in Blake archives, Missouri Historical Society.

"Notes and Comments." *North American Review* (March 1886): 317.

"Objects to Prizefighting." *New York Times,* September 18, 1899, 6.

"The Office of the Father." *Success* (December 1904): 802.

"Our Indian Policy." *Evening Telegram,* April 18, 1879: clipping in Blake archives, Missouri Historical Society.

"Police Matrons." *Christian Union,* April 1, 1882: clipping in Blake archives, Missouri Historical Society.

"Reminiscences." *New York Times,* February 15, 1899: clipping in Blake archives, Missouri Historical Society.

"Silver Lake." *Evening Telegram,* September 27, 1878: clipping in Blake archives, Missouri Historical Society.

"The Social Condition of Woman." *Knickerbocker Monthly* (May 1863): 381–88.

"A Speaker's Fright." *Era* (1876): clipping in Blake archives, Missouri Historical Society.

"U.S. Grant." *Evening Telegram,* April 17, 1886: clipping in Blake archives, Missouri Historical Society.

"When Women Grow Old." *Home Journal,* July 1, 1974, 1.

"Woman's Conjugal Rights." *Christian Union,* March 28, 1882: clipping in Blake archives, Missouri Historical Society.

"Woman's Plea for Woman: Mrs. Blake on Men's Jokes at Women's Expense." *Evening Telegram,* February 5, 1879: clipping in Blake archives, Missouri Historical Society.

"The Women of Utah." *Evening Telegram,* February 11, 1879: clipping in Blake archives, Missouri Historical Society.

"Work for Lady Orators." *New York Times,* November 3, 1871, 2.

POETRY

"A Coquette's Retrospection." *Knickerbocker* (May 1863): 412.

"Despair." *Knickerbocker* (May 1858): 449.

"Love and Death." *Galaxy* (November 1873): 661.

"Reparation." *Galaxy* (April 1871): 592–593.

"The Sea People." *Galaxy* (December 1875): 789.

Index

Grace Farrell is the Rebecca Clifton Reade Professor
of English at Butler University. She is the author of
numerous essays and chapters on nineteenth- and
twentieth-century fiction. Her books include *From Exile
to Redemption: The Fiction of Isaac Bashevis Singer;
Critical Essays on Isaac Bashevis Singer; Isaac Bashevis Singer:
Conversations;* and an edition of *Fettered for Life*
by Lillie Devereux Blake.